Active Retirement Investing

the process

Whether you:

do your own investing,
want to check on your current adviser,
or are simply looking for help with planning your future.

This book is for you!

D1026180

Especially for advisers, this book will finally give you a step-by-step process to follow, adding value to your client-adviser relationship

by

Hunter William (Bill) Bailey MSFS, CFS, Author
Nashoba (Nash) Ren Bailey CFS, CAS, CIS, CTS, CES, Author

Is your financial clock ticking?
What was right for you a few years ago may be wrong for you today.
Our saying is...
"Isn't your future worth updating your past?"

So...

Whether you:
do your own investing,
want to check on your current adviser,
or are simply looking for advice,
this book is for you!

_____   _____

Especially for advisers, this book will finally give you a step-by-step process to follow adding value to your client-adviser relationships

Aspiring Millionaires' Publishing House
7509 Madison Ave. Suite 107, Citrus Heights, CA 95610
www.HunterWilliamBailey.com
(916) 863-1266 or (800) 603-1393

'Active Retirement Investing--The Process'

by Hunter William Bailey and Nashoba Ren Bailey

Limit of Liability and Disclaimer of Warranty

Publisher's Cataloging-in-Publication

Bailey, Hunter William, 1953 & Bailey, Nashoba Ren, 1997

Active Retirement Investing--'the process' / Hunter William Bailey
& Nashoba Ren Bailey

ISBN 978-0-9618781-1-5

1. Finance, Personal. 2. Investments. 3. Retirement income. 4. Saving and investment. 5. Insurance. 6. Estate Planning. 7. Tax Planning — United States.

Printed in the USA.

Copyright 2020

For additional copies and discounts for this book go to www.HunterWilliamBailey.com or contact:

Aspiring Millionaires' Publishing House
Citrus Heights, California

Aspiring Millionaires' Publishing House
7509 Madison Ave. Suite 107
Citrus Heights, CA 95610
www.HunterWilliamBailey.com
(916) 863-1266 or (800) 603-1393

Previous publications:

Aspiring Millionaire, a basic look and introduction to the Investing and financial-planning process. By Hunter William (Bill) Bailey, Copyright © 1988

Wealth Strategies: Investing for Your Retirement. By Hunter (Bill) William Bailey Copyright © 2009

Take the leap! Control your destiny with self-determination and confidence,
because it's okay to be
occasionally wrong but never in doubt.

Dedication

This book is dedicated to you--the investor, you--the client, or you--the adviser-- interested in learning an investment process designed to follow traditional planning steps with innovative investment techniques. In a world of "at your fingertips" financial data, hype, and advertisements, making the right decision is imperative.

When money and assets can be digitally transferred, leveraged, sold, or stolen, the pressure is on. Who can you trust and where can you turn? With so many scams and schemes being created that change logic into fantasy, numbers into misleading results, basic accounting into false images, you need to research the facts.

For a presentation of bottom-line facts and information, welcome; you have found the right place. We will break down complicated facts and concepts and draw on examples of real-life situations. We'll revisit the same thought throughout the book to make sure it sticks. Like learning a new language, we must learn, speak, and repeat complex thought processes to fully understand them. Don't be discouraged if you don't understand everything; that's why you are reading this book. This process is designed to give you an awareness of the full workload you will be facing if you plan to do your own investing--or what to look out for when hiring an adviser. For practicing advisers, this is a process you can perform for your clients, and it will help ensure you are providing value with integrity.

Consider the paradox of skills: as absolute skill increases, relative skill among competition shrinks. Performance becomes more consistent, and the competition falls behind.

Contents

You will begin your journey of self-assessment and discovery, the goal being to generate and implement your future financial plan.

What happens when you begin "the process"? What are your goals and priorities? Everything must move in the same direction so that the development of a plan becomes apparent.

Phase I Financial-planning process

To reduce and avoid replicating the financial-planning process, we will segment the process, allowing you to save time and effort.

Planning present and future net income cash flow from all sources in preparation for surviving a long duration of life and future inflation concerns.

A review of all the necessary insurance policies that we all generally avoid. A very brief, yet important look at what protection you currently have, or what you might be missing to protect all that you have worked a lifetime to acquire.

A brief yet very necessary evaluation of your estate-planning documents: will, durable power of attorney, living trust, special-needs trust, asset-protection trust, private retirement trust, pre-marital documents, etc.

Taking advantage of the various tax deductions, exemptions, credits, and capital gains through proper investing is imperative to keeping more of what you earn. This section will go over things like tax-free bonds, capital gains tax rates, tax-deductible retirement plans, tax-deferred retirement annuities, tax-deferred real estate exchanges, step-up in basis at death, Roth IRA conversation, etc.

Learn how the experts assess the quality of an investment fund and the corresponding portfolio that holds it. Most investors are completely unaware that various complex "components" create the actual investment--elements such as expenses, historical volatility, the risk versus reward, market risk, credit ratings, diversification, past performance compared with various indexes and categories, yield, etc.

As a follow-up to every diagnostic review, you will learn to create a post-diagnostic follow-up list, a very important and serious "to-do list."

It's at this point in the process that you will begin to ascertain your level of interest in either doing it yourself or hiring an adviser. With your long list of things to follow up on, your future workload becomes apparent. Regular updates to this list are imperative.

By utilizing post-diagnostic reviews, you have a clearer understanding of your present situation and can now plan your future portfolio.

Although you can sell and reposition your older investment funds, you'll want to avoid costly mistakes. Selling even poor-performing "long-held" investments can trigger accumulated capital gains taxes in non-retirement accuonts.

Choosing the right funds through diversification--among fund companies, types of funds, and internal securities--is important, to minimize defaults and bankruptcies.

A method of allocation designed to layer internal investment, utilized as preparation for emergencies, income, and lump-sum distributions.

Portfolio structure designed to obtain maximum diversification and allocation among different fund structures, while minimizing the overall portfolio's internal expense ratios.

The final step in construction uses lateral and vertical integration together. Multiple portfolio parameters and several investment-fund structures bring us to the point where the ultimate portfolio is created. Historical volatility, standard deviation, market risk, yields, combined fund expenses, average bond credit risks, internal funds' historical ratings, and returns are all assessed to determine the best allocation for this new portfolio.

Now that you have created one or more new portfolios, the work has just begun! You'll need to monitor your portfolio and the funds inside of it:

you'll watch for news on interest rates and political events.

you'll track fund alerts on the funds you hold.

you'll shop for new funds that better fit your needs.

you'll analyze currently held funds.

you'll sell certain funds that exceeded their upside performance expectations, posing a risk to rapid declines.

you'll re-evaluate everything

Learning how to properly register accounts, manage required minimum distributions, reallocate your portfolio, plan investment-tax basis, prepare monthly income distributions, update beneficiary and trustee designations, etc.

Test your preparedness with a 25-question quiz and readiness checklist

Preface

Personal financial planning is critical. It assures that what a person worked so hard to acquire during their life is preserved for future years. Accumulating assets is not the only effort required to provide financial security. What's the point of saving, sacrificing, and taking risks during the accumulation stage, only to lose everything because you were not insured properly, not protected by the necessary legal documents, or experienced losses in the market from misallocated funds? Financial planning is the most important financial activity you will ever do, the goal being to maximize investment returns while, at the same time, minimizing risks.

There is a multitude of risks that come with not having the proper financial plan in place. You might be paying unnecessary taxes, which could cost you thousands of dollars by missing important tax deductions that could be advantageous. What if you are uninsured and a loss or lawsuit occurs? You could lose everything--both your home and all your investments!

If your legal documents are not in order, your assets will go to the wrong people. How would you feel if hostile family members inherited all that you have worked a lifetime to accumulate? We often hear about inflation; what do you do when the goods and services you need double in price? If your investments are not evaluated, you might be in highly inappropriate positions, paying too much in expenses and fees and running the risk of the next big market crash substantially reducing or destroying your retirement nest egg. Some investors buy whatever investments are trending upwards, only to see them crash in the next downturn and never recover.

Look, you only have three choices when it comes to your financial situation:

Ignore your financial positions, insurances, estate documents, and taxes. We shouldn't have to tell you why this is a bad idea: You will have no plan in place or knowledge of what to do, should certain emergencies arise. How will you know what losses are covered? How will you know whether you are paying the amount of taxes you should be paying? You could lose *everything you own* if your finances are not in order.

Do your own evaluations, investing, and planning. Will you have all the information and experience necessary to make essential decisions? People frequently make mistakes with their finances because they can't see in the rear-view mirror. This can be done; however it requires extensive research and learning about how one move can affect the other.

Hire an adviser to help you through the process. Although you could do this process yourself, you will need to know every step of the process and how your adviser should proceed. If you hire one, you will need to know what to look for and what to expect. You will need to ensure that you are not given inappropriate advice and that your adviser is acting in your best interests.

Think about the financial-planning process like you might a lengthy worldwide travel vacation. You could plan out every step of your world travel by yourself--airline tickets, transfers, trains, cabs, hotels, hostels, passport, visa, restaurants, medical assistance, customs, money exchanges, languages, laws, etc. Some people have traveled all their life and are happy and comfortable with taking on the challenge of planning and navigating their own way. Others, however, would rather enjoy this new experience with ease by hiring a travel agent. With the travel agent, you have a plan, years of experience, and resources to depend on. All you need to be concerned with is which excursion to take or which meal to choose.

The most important question to ask yourself is whether you want to take on the task of planning, implementing, and monitoring your plan, or instead, outsourcing this task to a financial adviser. This plan should include insurance issues, legal matters, tax concerns, and investment decisions. The goal is to answer the questions regarding what you and your family would do if you were disabled, retired today, or died.

   In this publication, you will acquire the necessary tools and information to make the correct decisions about your financial future, whether that means creating and implementing your financial plan on your own or doing so with the help of a qualified adviser. We call this information "The Process" because it is the same process that the reader should follow when reviewing his or her finances, and we believe this is what other advisers should be doing, as well.

The Process is broken into three phases: First dealing with analyzing what you have done in the past; then consider the necessary actions to take right now; and finally, wrapping up with ongoing maintenance and objectives for the future. Let's look at what each of these phases will cover.

Phase I—Financial planning process: We'll review your financial planning, such as old investments you might still own, cash-flow planning, insurance review, estate planning, and tax planning. We are dealing with the past here. We will review everything you have already established and those areas you have not. Questions, such as whether there are any mistakes in your financial past, need to be asked.

Phase II—New Portfolio Construction Process: "Rules-based investing" using new investment selection and analysis, portfolio allocation, construction, historical backtesting, and parameter alignment. This section will help you construct the most appropriate portfolio, matching your individual cash-flow needs, time frame, and risk tolerance. Here, we will look at your present planning and investment needs.

Phase III—Investment, portfolio, and estate-monitoring process: After the new investments are selected and portfolios created, you'll learn the many steps involved in monitoring your investments and portfolios: updating account registrations, monitoring mandatory distributions, and beneficiary payouts. This section deals with future ongoing planning activities.

No matter what you decide to do with your investments, whether this means doing it yourself or hiring an adviser to take care of it for you, the information in this book is critical to achieving a successful retirement. You might ask, "Why would I need to know all this if I am hiring an adviser to do the work for me?" The reason it is important to understand these concepts is that, when armed with the knowledge in this book, you will be more than able to determine whether your adviser is working in your best interests or if they are in it for themselves.

There are two different ways advisers can be compensated for their work: from fees or commissions. When an adviser is fee-based, they will almost always be serving your best interests, because when your investments do well, they make more money. It's a win-win scenario. However, when an adviser is paid via commissions after selling you investment products, they might only be suggesting a certain investment because it gives them the largest up-front commission. After they've cashed in on that commission, they have no incentive to keep reviewing your investments because they won't make more money by doing so! Now, this isn't to say that all advisers who make money from commissions are out to get you by suggesting wildly inappropriate investments; but it is something to keep in mind when choosing an adviser.

If doing your own investing, it is incredibly important that you do not miss a single piece of your financial plan. Any error can result in fees, unnecessary tax liability, unwanted transfer of assets, and much more. Your ultimate estate value can be developed without unnecessary losses due to liquidations in down markets, uninsured casualty losses, excess taxes, or even lawsuits designed to separate you from your life's efforts. Remember that creating your financial plan is a **job**. There's a reason this is a profession! Financial advisers must be heavily qualified and held accountable, *so you must be too.*

If you aren't sure whether to do it yourself or hire an adviser, this book will help you make that decision. You will learn all the important steps required to establish a successful financial plan, investment plan, and estate plan. If it confuses the heck out of you, fine! Go ahead and hire somebody you trust. At least you understand the basics so you can trust your adviser more since you'll understand what they are doing for you. If you are ambitious and ready to take on the task of being your "own" adviser, fantastic! Get ready to take on the most important project of your life! If you only want advice, hire a CPA and hourly financial planner. They will give you advice, and you will be responsible for acting.

This process of discovery will allow you to make the right decisions on the details that matter the most. Good luck!

Author
Hunter William (Bill) Bailey
MSFS, CFS, CIS, CTS, CET, CAS

Born in 1953, the lifestyle that Hunter William Bailey ("Bill") experienced was very similar to people raised in the "Baby Boomer" generation. Having witnessed his father's PTSD episodes, resulting from military service during WWII, Bill was taught to "duck and cover" during the Cold War days. However, Bill never imagined that he would develop his post-traumatic stress. It is understandable that he did, though. At five years of age, Bill's home caught on fire, requiring a heroic local firefighter to carry Bill in his arms out of a burning home. Everyone survived, thanks to an observant neighbor. This was just the beginning...

Several other challenges in addition to this harrowing experience in Bill's early life helped to build his resilience and resourcefulness, serving him well in his current career as a successful financial-planning adviser. His story is inspiring. Enduring many family troubles at home as a young man, higher education was neither within reach nor an expectation. Yet, due to his perseverance, out of five family members, Bill was the only one to graduate from high school, not to mention college. Impressively, Bill also pursued his talents as a gymnast, during high school. Doing so enabled him to attend a four-year college on a sports scholarship. He achieved the level of Collegiate All-American Gymnast.

Looking back, Bill believes the struggles he conquered ended up being a blessing. He particularly remembers life in high school being difficult, due to a learning deficiency caused by severe dyslexia, hearing loss as a child, and a dysfunctional family environment. As a child, Bill was placed in special-education classes. Bill recalls being told by his mother that his third-grade teacher had suggested that he might be "mildly retarded" --a very offensive term by today's standards. While in special-education classes, however, Bill discovered that he was able to help other students who also had learning deficiencies. He enjoyed teaching others, finding that he was able to break down complex details into more basic concepts. This ability went on to serve Bill well, working as a financial-planning adviser. Bill enjoys being able to give his clients valuable assistance, making complex concepts and strategies more tangible and accessible when navigating the very important issues of finance, taxes, investments, and estate law.

To graduate from high school and rise above the family conflicts was Bill's obsession. To become a member of law enforcement, his first career path, Bill had to distance himself from the criminal offenses two of his family members had been involved in. He worked as a jailer at the same correctional facility where his father served time on weekends for multiple drunk-driving offenses, and also where another family member served time for drug offenses and strong-armed robbery. Unfortunately, Bill's four other family members passed away at an early age from lifestyle issues: drugs, alcohol, smoking, etc.

Inspired by his father's military service, Bill also felt obligated to serve, once out of college. Thus, he entered the local sheriff's department as a reserve deputy sheriff, where he served for over 30 years. Having witnessed the extreme ranges of life and death while on duty, he developed a great appreciation for life's freedom, at the same time remaining aware of the risks we all face. Once, rushing into a situation upon hearing "shots fired," Bill recalls his concern about whether he was prepared: Was he wearing his bulletproof vest? Was his emergency radio working? Was backup on the way? Was his sidearm in good working order? And most importantly, was his training going to serve him? Law enforcement, as well as the military, is all about training and planning--not unlike life and the financial-planning process!

Here's some background on what led Bill to become a financial-planning adviser. Though Bill had originally planned on becoming a full-time deputy sheriff, his experience was that the relatively new concept of affirmative action made it very difficult to gain full-time employment with benefits. As fate would have it, however, with no foreseeable secure job prospects other than working part-time as an on-call reserve deputy sheriff with no benefits, a suggestion was made that he could try selling life insurance and mutual funds. 1980 turned out to be a year of new goals, learning experiences, and commitments.

Not being initially interested in sales, yet needing an alternative income, Bill began the very slow process of getting started in the business and putting into practice the concept of "the client's best interests." Unfortunately, back then, income was made by selling products and earning an up-front commission.

Entering the financial-planning business in late 1980 with no experience at making a living as an adviser, Bill found that life was difficult at first. In Bill's early years in this business, he also worked at the local county jail as a guard to earn income to fund his financial-planning training process. He sat far up in a guard tower with an assault rifle in one hand and his investment study books in the other. Staying awake while watching for escapees and listening to audio financial-planning-training recordings occupied his shift.

Bill had to take the securities exam several times (due to dyslexia and other learning difficulties mentioned above). However, Bill's passion, drive, and fear pushed him forward. In addition to the college degree, Bill had already earned in criminal justice, Bill finally passed the securities exam after several attempts.

Over the years, writing books on the financial industry have helped Bill to gain the confidence he needed to feel worthy and confident to serve others. Only after watching an interview of Charles Schwab, in which Schwab explained that he, too, had severe dyslexia and that this condition was "the greatest gift" he could have been given, did Bill realize that he, too, had an unusual ability to run his own business.

After viewing this interview of Schwab, Bill realized he was not learning-disabled, but very brilliant and special. Though lacking confidence and financial resources in the early years, Bill decided to again return to studies later in life--completing his master's degree in financial services at age 60. A father of a wonderful and independent son, Bill has accomplished everything he set out to achieve for himself in life.

Now, with over 40 years under his belt as a financial adviser witnessing the 1987 crash, 1989 Saving & Loan crisis, Y2K, the 9/11 attack, the 2008 Financial crisis, 2010 flash crash and 2020 global pandemic,--this being his third published book--and armed with his master's degree and various certifications, Bill is inspired and well-positioned to give back to others by sharing his encouragement and wisdom through this publication, various investment workshops, and personal consultations.

Co-Author
Nashoba (Nash) Ren Bailey

Author, financial researcher, and content contributor, Nash acts as consultant and editor. His experience and qualifications give him insight into the needs of investors and financial advisers. Nash has earned several financial designations, listed below. He spent his childhood watching his mother and father run a small, independent financial-planning office where he witnessed ongoing client meetings and the various investment-management processes.

While growing up, Nash learned many skills that contributed to his understanding of not only finance but entrepreneurship, as well. Growing up in the country as a child, Nash's first swimming lesson was in the river that surrounded his homestead. Rattlesnakes were a big danger; on two occasions, he was required to dispatch a "live" and angry rattlesnake, since it was threatening a family member next to the house. Normally, he and his father attempted to catch and release snakes, but these two snakes had acted aggressively toward a passerby.

His first exposure to firearms wasn't until he was ten years old. While enjoying the small river on his property with his very large dog Hailey, she alerted to a male stranger near his property holding a handgun. Nash, his dog Hailey and his Dad Hunter all retreated to the house. This was the first time he witnessed his father arming himself with his former police weapon. Soon after the encounter a Sheriff's helicopter flew in and hovered over the stream area where the armed man was last spotted. As the helicopter searched the creek area for the armed man, Nash's property became overrun with armed local sheriff's deputies carrying rifles and handguns. Things ultimately worked out however, the man with a gun was distraught over a breakup with his girlfriend and considering suicide.

Nash made his first investments in individual stocks at the age of ten, just before the crash of 2008, then reinvested during the downturn; he benefited handsomely in later years. Having witnessed not only the financial crisis in 2008, but he also witnessed the 2010 flash crash (where the DOW dropped over a thousand points within a day with everyone wondering what happened after the market fully recovered within days), market highs in 2019 and the global pandemic and subsequent market crash in 2020. During these periods learning how his parents dealt with fund selections and asset allocation. He assessed and selected his first real estate investment project for his mother at the age of 12. Reviewing the location, square footage, price, interest rates, layout, and expenses, Nash, his father, and his mother all worked together to purchase a property during the bottom of a severe recession in the summer of 2009. With Nash's keen eye on real estate values and his mother Amy's talent for design the property value has since nearly doubled.

Nash believes that with the training he's received and his resources, he is well equipped to understand the needs of his readers, which include investors, advisers, and financial institutions.

Nash's Designations
The certifications listed below have provided Nash with a substantial base of research and information necessary to reach his professional goals. Nash has completed these through the Institute of Business and Finance, located in San Diego, California. Presently, he is enrolled in

additional training courses through The American College of Finance. He plans to continue his research and financial-editing services while progressing through advanced levels of financial planning and investment research.

CFS—Certified Fund Specialist
This is an in-depth study and analysis of the different investment vehicles available to investors. This is one of the areas in which Nash was first exposed to the risk-metrics-and-parameters analysis he refers to in this publication. This and all the courses he's taken required months of dedicated study and analysis to achieve a better understanding of how the most popular investments are constructed.

CIS—Certified Income Specialist
This is an area of study that takes into consideration all sources of income available from investment programs, employer retirement plans, social programs, and insurance-guarantee contracts. Analyzing all the sources of potential income and expense is very important. Something that is also important to analyze is when the income might start, how long the income might last, and whether the income can keep pace with inflation and taxes. This is one of the most important areas, relevant to retirees, that Nash has studied.

CTS—Certified Tax Specialist
This is one of the more complex areas of study since the tax laws and logic for those laws tend to change from one year to another. With this line of study, Nash can write about the pros and cons of the various investment decisions one can make. Moving from one investment to another may trigger regrettable tax consequences if the overall picture is not viewed and planned for. Although moving investments around might improve the overall allocations, one needs to be aware of all the different tax schedules and limitations before acting.

CES—Certified Estate and Trust Specialist
The process of determining necessary documents to assure preservation of a person's assets, income, and the estate is managed for the benefit of a disabled owner and beneficiary. After death, these documents become even more important in assuring the protection and transfer of income, assets, and family heirlooms. This course of

study provides Nash an awareness of the legal process and documents available to protect one's estate from outside creditors and unintended beneficiaries, making Nash a better researcher, writer, and speaker.

CAS—Certified Annuity Specialist
This area of study provides Nash a full understanding of the benefits and controversies associated with annuities. Understanding the complex details of insurance contracts, life expectancy, taxes, and guaranteed income, Nash can assess the internal cost vs. the long-term benefits of annuity investments.

Nash is not a practicing financial adviser at present. He spends his time researching, training, and completing his financial education, all to help his father in future years.

Consulting Editor, Certified Tax Specialist
Certified Estate & Trust Specialist
Amy L. Sunderland

Amy L. Sunderland, Nash's mother, is the Director of Operations for Bill's investment firm, Wealth Strategies. See www.hunterwilliambailey.com for regulatory disclosures and affiliations. Fully licensed with the Series 7 securities license, Amy oversees not only administrative operations but also acts as a primary administrative trader for all portfolios with the firm.

Amy has worked for the firm since 1994, assisting with accounting and client service and investment buy-and-sell orders. Amy holds the designation of Certified Tax Specialist (CTS); and Certified Estate and Trust Specialist (CES), from the Institute of Business & Finance (IBF). These specialties allow Amy to maintain a good understanding of the details she must assist Bill's clients with, regarding investment cost basis, capital gains on sales, and trust account registrations.

With a college degree in general studies, also specializing in architectural design, Amy has been instrumental in advising Bill and Nash in real estate design and planning. Her skills have proved useful in contributing to the renovation of Bill's Citrus Heights office, Grass Valley office, and the Orangevale/Folsom offices.

Disclosure—a must-read

Dear Reader, this book is intended to provide basic information about financial planning, including details of specific investment vehicles, portfolio construction and allocations, the stock and bond markets, and income taxes.

Economic conditions will change; therefore, the ideas presented in this book should be considered general and not taken as specific, individual advice. Investing and financial planning is an individual practice. What is right for one person can be dead wrong for another.

You may also hear or read the warning, "Past results are no indication or guarantee of future performance." Most investment prospectuses will issue this warning. The rationale for this type of warning is to prevent investors from investing their hard-earned funds in over-touted investments that may have experienced good performance in previous years but might be highly inappropriate for that investor.

Popular funds may or may not do well in the future. We don't recommend the purchase of funds simply based on previous trends, performance, or popularity. If a fund has performed well in the past, based on low expenses and appropriate management operations, it might be a good match for your needs. Rating services should only be relied upon for quantitative evaluations, not predictions. Things like fund expenses, historical volatility, trading volume, yield, etc., are better values.

Markets tend to be efficient in pricing. One person's opinion of where the market will go in the future is just an opinion. There are NO good deals, just good choices based on research. A good deal is when your grandmother sells you her house for the same price she paid for it 50 years ago! Publicly traded securities sell at a price the buyer determines is fair and equitable, not one penny more. This includes spreads, markups, premiums, and discounts.

Investments tend to become popular during trends and fads. There are times index funds are touted for their low cost; at other times, managed funds are, due to their different holdings and investment techniques. We encourage you to remember that your investment needs may be very different from those of your neighbor or co-worker. A much younger person might be fine investing in an "all stock" index fund over the long run; however, a retiree might be more vulnerable to the market and need to keep some allocation in cash and/or bonds. No one allocation will always beat any market. Allocating among several types of investments is only intended to reduce the risk of all your holdings being in the "wrong place at the wrong time."

Because investors are emotional creatures, the SEC, a government agency, attempts to protect investors from overzealous investment salespeople and companies--hence all the disclosures and paperwork. We must advise you, however, to seek professional advice to determine which parts of this book relate to your situation. You should always research as much as possible before investing your money in any venture or product. Carefully read the current investment prospectus before investing.

Fiduciary

We believe that when seeking advice, you should consider speaking to a specialist who acts as a fiduciary in areas such as investments, insurance, banking, real estate, wills, trusts, retirement plans, and health care. A fiduciary should always act in your best interests. This person should be held to a high standard of care and follow a code of ethics

Examples of what an adviser should do:

Remain loyal to their clients:

- Provide advice that is in the best interest of his or her client's objectives, needs, and circumstances
- Provide a reasonable, independent basis for investment advice
- Safeguard the client's confidential information

Examples of what the adviser should not do:

- Engage in any fraudulent, deceptive, or manipulative conduct
- Scheme to defraud any client or prospective client

- Mislead a client, including the use of misleading material or purposely omitted material facts, whether in verbal or written statements.
- Engage in transactions, practices, or courses of business which are fraudulent or deceptive
- Practice price manipulation
- Favor the interests of one client over another

For investment services, a client should be made aware of how he or she will be paying for them. That payment should not be made on a one-time "point of sale" of a product where commissions are assessed.

We give this warning several times throughout this book, always run a background check on any person, adviser, or company you work with. You might be shocked by what you might find. IRS fines, Industry related violations, drunk driving, and even non-financial related felonies.

Go to   www.brokercheck.org

Our opinions, comments, and warnings

Some insurance products claim not to charge you a commission or fee, maintaining that "the company pays the commission!" If you believe this line, I have some "swampland" in Florida to sell you! If you leave the insurance contract early, the company immediately charges you a very large surrender fee. This surrender penalty reimburses the company for the commissions they paid the insurance agent upfront. Therefore, although you did not pay a commission directly to the agent, your money is held as "collateral." If you leave the investment within the surrender-penalty period, you will pay. Also, along the way, the insurance company is making what is known as a "spread" of your money. This means they are earning much more than they are paying you.

Many salespeople generate elaborate hypothetical printouts that project possible future performances of annuity contracts showing various growth rates. Since the fixed annuity and index annuity is not a security, the salespeople don't have to follow the very strict rules imposed by the SEC and FINRA.

These projected returns--which would never be allowed in the securities industry, in our opinion--mislead the investor by touting fantasy returns. Unlike the real estate industry's acronym, IRR (Internal Rate of Return), which involves advanced calculations that take into consideration rental income, expenses, appreciation, depreciation, and other tax benefits, these insurance sales pieces project what we call the "insurance IRR," or "Imaginary Retrospective Return."

Hidden costs, fees, and commissions are why we suggest you do your own investing or utilize the services of either a fee-only adviser, who charges hourly or a fee-based adviser, who charges a percentage of assets under management. This way, you know what you are paying for, getting service on a pay-as-you-go basis. If you don't like your fee adviser, you can fire them at any time.

Please remember, the general advice given within this book is intended as an educational aid. Individual advice is inappropriate without meeting with an adviser and giving specific information regarding your situation. You should seek objective, expert opinions from people who have no ax to grind and no conflict of interest.

If using the services of an adviser, we believe that he or she should follow a standard of ethical behavior. The adviser should have a good knowledge of securities laws and regulations and adhere to a code of conduct that is defined within his or her respective profession.

The adviser should give independent advice based on your needs alone, doing so without conflict of interest. The adviser should fully disclose how she will work for you and should disclose all fees, expenses, and costs related to your needs. For your investments, the adviser should construct a custom-tailored personal portfolio designed for your situation, instead of relying on one generated from a computer program designed for the masses.

Investments and portfolios should be suitable for your needs and risk tolerances. The adviser should perform annual reviews and updates, as well. We believe your financial adviser should not also serve as your accountant, attorney, real estate agent, or life-insurance salesperson. That would establish a conflict of interest and develop opinions that are less focused and fewer opinions.

It may be convenient to have an "all-in-one" office location (CPA, attorney, insurance agent, and financial adviser) to obtain advice, but everyone advising you is then from the same business family. Instead, you should get multiple, non-related referrals from stand-alone professionals. This way, the professionals are checking on each other's work, which will better ensure that you are getting objective and appropriate advice.

One example would be if your attorney were to sell you life insurance to satisfy his or her recommendations for your estate plan. Another example would be if your accountant were to sell you annuities to help reduce your taxable income. These recommendations would be tainted with extreme levels of conflict of interest and self-dealing.

We believe one size does *not* fit all. Investing is personal. What you might need could be completely the opposite of what another person needs. You should be consulted individually and interviewed in detail before constructing a plan and portfolio tailored to your needs. An estate planning attorney is the only person who should construct advanced-level legal documents such as trusts, wills, etc. A qualified tax professional should be the only person to do advanced levels of tax planning. Only experienced insurance agents should be selected to plan complex risk-management plans, and investment advisers and financial planners should be the ones to tie everything together.

If you are a trustee named to a parent's trust and you invest money for them, you must be aware of the appropriate "prudent person" rules when investing for this trust and its beneficiaries.

You could be held liable for losses since you now have a *fiduciary* responsibility to act in the best interests of the trust and any other beneficiaries. For example, if you were a day trader and lost substantial amounts of money, beneficiaries could sue you. A fiduciary is responsible for acting in the beneficiary's best interests, which means within his or her suitability standards. You must consider all the basics, the beneficiary's liquidity needs and income needs, the trust's timeline and ability to recover from volatile marks, growth for future contingent beneficiaries, diversification, taxes, etc.

This is one area where taking the DIY approach could get you in trouble. We find that elderly people who value their independence are frequently frustrated with being asked by their adult children about what they are doing. These adult children are concerned for their elderly parents, fearful they might be taken advantage of. The elderly parents, however, are frustrated with the intrusion of their children in their financial affairs.

By having an adviser act as a fiduciary, the adult children can rest assured that their parents are being cared for. They will know their parents are being treated ethically. The elderly parents can, in turn, feel independent while depending on the adviser for an unbiased opinion and advice. For this reason, it is usually a good idea that the adviser maintains a close relationship with the adult children, as well as the client. This will help everyone feel more comfortable with the process.

For contacting regulatory agencies about the background of an adviser, go to

Financial Industry Regulatory Authority (FINRA), (301) 590-6500: http://www.finra.org

Securities and Exchange Commission (SEC), (800) SEC-0303: http://www.sec.gov

Introduction

Things to Know Before Getting Started.

Everyone has different goals, objectives, desires, fears, and risk tolerances. Why on earth should your investments be managed by strangers who have never talked with you? If you hire an adviser, he or she should understand everything there is to know about your liquidity needs, risk tolerance, goals, and objectives. That adviser should manage your money themselves, not farm it out! Many advisers and investment companies--including, and especially, the Robo-advisers--place your money in predetermined portfolios with preselected investment funds and allocations. That approach is not very individualized or personalized at all!

We recommend that you or your adviser create and construct your financial plan and investment portfolio. You should plan to match the exact funds and allocations that meet your needs. As time goes by, revisit those investments and allocations and adjust them, not based on market projections but rather on your risk levels, goals, and liquidity needs. You should not be utilizing "automatic rebalancing" by some algorithm made for the masses. Rebalancing should reflect your current needs and desires, as compared with your portfolio's current allocations and whether they have changed due to the market's movements.

Wisdom tells us to buy low and sell high, but emotions tend to get in the way. There is an emotional cycle that tends to take over that prevents us from making logical decisions to protect our assets.

The emotional cycle starts with "optimism." As the market moves upwards, you will advance to the next stage, "excitement" (the news is good!). Halfway up the first wave of success, you reach the stage called "thrill" (investors are excited!). At the peak of the first wave, you reach the "euphoria" stage (things are great and non-investors are wanting in).

After the peak is reached, however, the market and emotions begin to decline. As we start to fall, we reach the "anxiety" stage. New investors thought things would keep escalating, but they were mistaken. After witnessing this decline, "fear" kicks in, the fear that things will keep getting worse.

After fearing the reality that things are not so wonderful, "desperation" kicks in, and a few sleepless nights occur. As these emotions pile up, "panic" sets in, and the investor decides to exit the markets just to stop the bleeding. After exiting the market cycle, "regret" begins to develop. The investor knows subconsciously that he or she should have "hung in there." "Despondency" and "depression" begin, causing the investor to complain to others and make promises to himself or herself to stay away from volatile markets in the future.

After hitting the bottom of the crash, wise investors, new investors, and those who had faith begin to experience "hope," realizing that markets don't stay down forever. Low stock and low fund prices compute to higher yields and better buying opportunities if investors think long-term. Next, "relief" comes back for those investors who stayed invested and invested more money at the bottom of the last wave. As the market begins to recover, "optimism" grows around the world, and the cycle starts all over again.

You need to understand your emotions and invest accordingly so you can avoid selling at the bottom and buying at the top. Remember, the risk is the potential for permanent loss; volatility is only the risk of temporary loss.

The stock market crash of 1929, the oil market crisis in the mid-1970s, the real estate recession of the early 1990s, the high-tech crash in early 2000, Y2K, 2001's 911, the derivatives debacle and subsequent market crash in 2008, and the Coronavirus in 2020--all brought out the scary reality that anything can happen.

Before the crash, markets were up, and the buyers were lined up to buy. Everyone seemed to be an expert. Many chose to buy because they expected predictable gains. After the crash, some walked away with all the money, and others walked away with empty pockets and a bad taste in their mouth.

Developing your goals to begin the process
Understanding what your personal goals are is extremely important when creating a financial plan that will support you over the long term. You should never copy someone else's goals. They may be happy with them, but their goals may not apply to you at all! You must ask yourself what is most important to *you* and create a financial plan that revolves around that.

Here are some of the many goals and concerns you might have or perhaps should be thinking about, before investing. The importance of each goal is based on your situation. Your goals will determine your personal financial, estate, and investment plans. If you don't have a goal or destination, how will you or your advisers be able to determine the direction of travel? Each of these goals may require the opposite direction of travel than the others. First, determine your goals and objectives, evaluate your resources, and *then* create your plan!

List of possible goals

Maximizing Retirement Income—Some studies show that with people retiring at younger ages, the actual cost of living might be as high as three times what was originally planned. Thus, many retirees go on a search to maximize their investment income.

Reducing Income Taxes—For those who are fortunate enough to earn high levels of income, reducing taxes can be a major concern. Decisions to borrow money to purchase real estate are sometimes based on write-offs rather than cash flow. Tax-exempt, tax-deferred, and capital-gain-producing investments are chosen for their tax benefits rather than their rate of return. While the tax benefits might provide short-term satisfaction, we need to look ahead for long-term results. Tax efficiency should override simple tax deductions. We will learn many strategies to choose from.

Inflation Protection—For those concerned about inflation, the need for the continued growth of investments may be a priority. Growth-

3

oriented investments like stocks and real estate may help protect from inflation, but with the trade-off of added risk and market volatility in the short term. The prices of the goods and services will likely follow inflation and increase over time. Both this and the statistical chance that you will likely outlive your parents require that you invest for future price increases.

Funding Your Children's Education—To manage the rising cost of college education, parents and grandparents must plan early. Some families have gone so far as to begin saving before their children are born. Putting money in a grandchild's name could be a mistake if he or she does not choose to go to college. Using traditional 529 plans can help, but you could encounter the same problem. Another concern is how much time until a grandchild (or grandchildren) goes to school. These things matter because they will determine the investment allocation.

Safety—For some, safety is the ultimate priority when investing. Safer investments generally produce lower returns. If any risk is too much risk, the investor must save even greater amounts of money to keep pace as inflation rises. Yes, in the long run, safety suffers from inflation. You, however, must find a comfortable level of risk to stay invested over time.

Estate Growth—Again, investing for growth requires accepting certain levels of risk, investing for tax savings and proper estate planning.. As an investor, you will need patience and perseverance, given the unpredictability of future market conditions.

Knowing your risk tolerance and having a plan to deal with any possible contingency is especially important. New investment objectives, time horizons, and risk levels can be constructed to mirror the needs of your intended beneficiaries vs. yourself, as you grow older and plan to pass the assets on. Proper estate planning will need to be addressed. All these efforts are designed to let your estate grow, and thus the future generation's estate to grow, during and after your lifetime.

Financing Travel and Entertainment—Retirees and younger working people may want to plan their future travel expenses. Major travel expenditures must be budgeted ahead of time to maintain the financial integrity of your overall plan. Younger people might begin using credit cards with air miles rewards, paying everything you can on the card, pay it off monthly, and saving the miles for travel. Don't forget to buy travel insurance!

Distribution of Assets—Some people choose to distribute assets to other family members or charitable organizations. One reason that people do this, other than the good feelings generosity creates, is to take advantage of the many tax deductions available for gifting assets. Taxes, legal fees, and other expenses can be greatly reduced or eliminated on gifts given during and after the donor's lifetime.

As a donor, you can now gift retirement assets from an IRA to charities instead of receiving your required minimum distribution (RMD), avoiding taxes altogether. Leaving your IRA to adult beneficiaries where they can "stretch out" the taxable distributions over ten years is another benefit. The act of leaving real estate and other appreciated assets to the beneficiaries can benefit from what is called a non-taxable "step-up in basis." Therefore, planning out how you will distribute your assets should be carefully considered.

Retirement—Most Americans have historically relied on their employers for their retirement compensation. After decades of failed pension plans, corporate downsizing, and government civil service layoffs, employer-funded retirement plans are few and far between. Today, employees and business owners are required to save for themselves. With retirement being one of the greatest concerns of Americans, this goal should be taken very seriously. For someone not yet retired, the obvious practice is to maximize contributions to the employer's retirement plan and, also, contribute to a Roth IRA, as well as paying down the mortgage and investing in non-retirement investments.

For the already retired person, late retirement planning might include reducing the spending budget and investing the money saved through budgeting. Money saved on paying off the mortgage can be invested in a stock fund every month.

Protecting accumulated assets—In addition to growing your estate, the next concern is protecting it. Sure, we all buy insurance to cover our expected risks, but what if the settlement amount from a claim against you exceeds your insurance coverage? Or worse yet, your insurance company finds a legal technicality allowing them to disqualify your coverage! You are left with a "Dear John letter" from the insurance company, informing you that you are not covered for the full settlement--or worse yet, not covered at all.

When was the last time your insurance agent asked you to sit down for a review, planning where you need to go regarding the next level of protection? Insurance agents seldom create an insurance plan after you purchase the original coverage. As your estate grows, your financial activities expand, and your risks increase, it is important to reassess where you are legally and financially exposed.

In addition to insurance, you'll need to sit down with a legal professional specializing in asset protection. Legal strategies that relate to your personal and professional situation can be studied. If you own a business or investments such as real estate, you'll need additional planning that must be created before, not after, you are at risk of a lawsuit. The state in which you own the assets and where you live are both critical and must be considered.

Even though most employee-retirement plans enjoy federal exemptions when it comes to lawsuits, judgments, and bankruptcy, your assets might be exposed. In some states, although the plan itself is protected, the plan distributions may be at risk.

IRAs, annuities, and other assets might have limited or no protection at all.

Let us make this disclosure: We are not attorneys, so these are just ideas for conversation. We have no qualifications to give you legal advice, just planning concerns. You should seek a qualified legal professional before acting on any idea or suggestion. These are just ideas for you or your adviser to research and determine if and how they might relate to you.

The primary objective is *always* to reduce risks and conserve assets. At a young age, when you have many years before retirement, you can take more risks and have more potential for upside growth. However, when retirement is just over the horizon, you cannot afford to take the same risks. Growth is great, but the risk goes both ways. Could you afford to lose 30 percent over a year? Not only would the value of your portfolio go down, but so would the amount of income you could safely withdraw every month.

Our goal is to beat the market on the way down, not on the way up. Conservative investors are the happiest when the market crashes! Why is this? Because when their neighbor's portfolio drops by 15 percent, their nest egg may have only lost 5 percent. This is the protection that a well-diversified portfolio can offer.

Conclusion

Let's recap the most important points discussed here before we dive too deep into The Process itself.

First, it is *incredibly* important to understand your personal goals and the situation that you are in. Another person's goals or allocations may not be suitable for what you would like to achieve. Your adviser should not be placing you into a one-size-fits-all plan.

You must learn to observe and control your emotions, not letting them drive you away from your plan. Understand the emotional cycle of the market, and don't let yourself get swept up in fear or inflated optimism.

Remember that you are trying to reduce risks and *conserve* your assets so that you can survive, happily retired without running out of funds before the end of your life.

Now that you understand some key concepts about investing and preserving what you have built within your lifetime, it is time to learn The Process and each task that comes with it.

Remember, financial planning is a **job!** This will be no small task. You must make sure to anticipate and account for every possibility, including medical emergencies and future expenses that you may not have yet incurred.

Now, let's get to work...

Phase I Financial-planning process

The Diagnostic Reports
(Examining your financial past)

It's important to look at what you have already established in your finances, insurance coverages, estate-planning documents, tax strategies, investments, and portfolios. After reviewing these areas, the necessary corrections or additions can be made. To save time and expense and avoid redundancy (you may have just returned from your Estate Planner's office), we'll break down each area individually. When there are weaknesses or necessary corrections discovered, we will dive deeper into that section. Each area of review is referred to as a "diagnostic review." There will be a diagnostic for each category.

Let's face it, you are all grown up now and don't need to be lectured about saving money and spending less. However, there are always areas and issues that will need to be reviewed and updated to meet your changing needs. You will need to review your overall cash flow and general expenses that you have had in the past and those you plan to have in the future.

Questions to answer:

Will you need additional income today, or can we invest in growth for more income in the future?

If retiring, should you take the fixed-income retirement annuity, if offered, or should you keep your investments invested for future growth? Will you leave the funds with your previous employer, or will you take possession of your nest egg by rolling the funds into a self-directed IRA (SDIRA)? Should you manage the funds yourself, or should you hire a professional manager? Should you begin withdrawing income to supplement other retirement income, or should you allocate the funds for long-term growth? Should you refinance your home, or should you pay down the mortgage?

Should you take Social Security at 62, or 70? Should you: activate or delay your benefit if you qualify for half of your spouse's benefit? Pay off the house? Sell your home and move to a retirement community? Move to a retirement community and rent out your house, avoiding capital gains taxes and commissions?

These are just a few of the many questions that must be addressed in your financial plan. As stated before, it is incredibly important that this plan is tailored to *you*, since your personal goals may not line up with the standard investor.

The other elements of the planning basics are outlined in the individual diagnostics. Review them and see if you are missing anything, and only then move forward to the investing process.

An in-depth, extensive financial plan is especially important if you have a complex estate, own a business, or have complicated investments and business structures.

If you need to opt for the traditional route, you will follow these steps:

I. Create a client-professional relationship with a fee-only financial planner

II. Collect and share all your financial information with the planner

III. The planner will analyze and evaluate your finances and status

IV. The planner will develop and present a detailed financial plan

V. You will implement the plan and recommendations

VI. The planner will monitor the plan and support you along the way

A comprehensive financial plan could be a hundred pages of detailed analysis and recommendations. To cover all the bases, the planner may cover some very basic and elementary concepts; to some clients, these concepts can be a little uncomfortable, but they need to be addressed. This book attempts to condense the concepts of a financial plan and reduce your time in the process.

A full, detailed financial plan is the ultimate planning tool if you have the need and the time to dive into all the details. The ideal process would be to have your financial planner, CPA, estate attorney, civil attorney, business attorney, casualty insurance agent, and estate-planning insurance agent all sitting across from you throughout the planning process. Therefore, you need to do your homework, if planning your finances. The adviser is not allowed to give specific advice unless licensed in the respective fields, but he or she can look for and point out areas of concern.

The adviser's job is to create the plan and refer you to qualified professional help for tax, legal, and insurance needs. According to the National Underwriter Resource Center's publication, *The Process of Financial Planning: Developing a Financial Plan, 2nd Edition*, a comprehensive financial plan outline should look like this:

Cover letter

    I. Letter to client
   II. Copy of the original client engagement letter
  III. Table of Contents
  IV. Other introductory material, like:
      a. Mission/vision statement of the adviser
      b. Statement of principles or core values
      c. Ethics statement
      d. Privacy statement
      e. Investment policy statement
   V. Client profile, a summary of goals and assumptions
  VI. Executive summary or observations and recommendations

VII. Individual core content planning sections
  a. Cash-flow analysis
  b. Net-worth analysis
  c. Tax analysis
  d. Insurance risk-management analysis
      i. Life insurance
      ii. Health and disability insurance
      iii. Long-term care insurance
      iv. Property and liability insurance
      v. Umbrella or excess liability insurance
      vi. Other insurance needs
  e. Investment analysis
  f. Retirement analysis
  g. Estate-planning analysis
  h. Specialized analysis
      i. Educational funding
      ii. Planning for special needs
      iii. Refinancing scenarios
      iv. Saving for special objectives
VIII. Implementation and monitoring section
IX. Client-acceptance letter or client-engagement letter
X. Appendices
  a. Calculations and projections
  b. Educational materials
  c. Etc.

As you can see, the financial-planning process is quite lengthy and deep, not to mention very expensive. Let's break things down into a more workable strategy that is designed to pinpoint a specific area that needs your attention, referred to as "the diagnostic process."

By completing a diagnostic, you will be able to simplify the process, reduce your workload, and do the work yourself. If you hire an adviser, you'll have very good knowledge and context regarding what you should receive for the fee charged.

We will look at diagnostic studies covering the following areas:

Current and future cash flow

Insurance

Estate Planning

Taxes

Investments & portfolios

So, let's get started with the process...

Personal cash-flow diagnostic:

The personal cash-flow diagnostic refers to "income and expenses" as you enter or continue retirement. For example, ask yourself, will your income increase in future years when you start Social Security? Should you pay off your mortgage with savings? Will you be required to start your retirement distributions? Do you expect to inherit money from relatives? What if your income might go down in future years? What if a primary spouse dies and his or her pension stops?

Countless concerns may need attention in the future as you age, and your living expenses increase. You'll recall hearing from other advisers that our real concern for you is "living too long." We tend to complain about living too long, but no one wants to die. Therefore, we must plan. People are living decades longer than expected, causing catastrophic reductions in their estates. It would be devastating if you depleted your entire estate before you passed!

With the above in mind, for this stage of the Diagnostic process, you need to do the following:

Create a list of current living expenses you have today and try to predict how much they might be in the future. Some bills are due monthly, others due quarterly, and a few due yearly. So, let's separate them and add up the combined total.

Combined monthly living expenses multiplied by twelve ....$____
Combined quarterly living expenses multiplied by four..............$____
Semiannual living expenses multiplied by two............................$____
Annual expenses that tend to get forgotten...............................$____
Combine the above totals to determine your annual expenses $____
(Don't forget your property taxes, income taxes, etc.)

Simply divide by twelve months for more specific projected monthly expenses.

Through planning, your future income and expenses can be estimated. After you determine your regular day to day expenses, look ahead and determine if there are future expenses for which to prepare. It might be a new roof, unexpected travel expenses if a relative became ill, dental implants, vacation travel, grandchildren's college assistance, future home health care, etc.

You will always need to adjust to the fact that you are aging, so get over it. Think about it: you always wanted to live a long, long life. Now you're going to need to pay for it! It's like this: Over time, prices go up; even the cost of cemetery plots rises. And what do you think this is blamed on? You guessed it: the cost of "living."

So be very cautious when looking at insurance products and annuities for income. Social Security is the only truly legitimate annuity. Everyone pays into the program in hopes of living off their well-deserved income at a later age. For those who live long lives, they are guaranteed income for life, for those who don't they allow others to live off their contributions after they die.

This stage is where you think about future cash-flow opportunities and make strategic decisions. Some people decide to take Social Security Income early, if they need the income badly enough or if they don't expect to live that long in retirement. Others use their IRA funds to live off until they turn 70 and can cash in on a third more Social Security income—a very good idea if they live beyond 77 and expect to live a long time.

This diagnostic is all about income and cash flow. So, do you know what your yearly income and living expenses will be for, say...

This year?

Three years from now?

Five years from now?

Ten years from now?

Twenty years from now?

Remember, unless you have a sizable monthly lifetime pension with substantial future increases, you will need about twenty times your desired annual income invested to meet your minimums. This guesstimate could end up being a low figure.

So how much of your discretionary income should you invest? Sarcastic answer: All of it! If you save too much, we can handle that problem in the time it takes you to write a big check to a charity. If you don't save enough, it could take the rest of your life to figure out how to survive in an ever-increasing-cost-of-living environment. These are all concerns to address since your investment decisions will be affected by your present and future income resources.

To protect your income and assets, you'll need to spend money on insurance. Everyone's insurance needs are different, so the next diagnostic covers all the areas you'll need to learn about or have an adviser review. Remember, your investments are at risk if inflation wipes out your buying power; but what if you get sued by someone and your insurance is insufficient? What if you need long-term care and don't have enough income or assets to cover the cost?

Reviewing, analyzing, and projecting your future income and expenses are essential. Plan for the worst that could happen and enjoy the best of what you have created and planned for.

Remember, beware of investment programs and insurance products that promise no risks, minimum income, and are tax-free, at that. These are abusive insurance schemes. One popular program is referred to as Life Insurance Retirement Program (LIRP). It encourages you to convert a taxable IRA account, pay the taxes, and roll it into a Roth IRA, and buy life insurance and annuity products. LIRP salespeople go as far as encouraging you to take out a mortgage on your home to buy these questionable products. Remember the saying "There is no such thing as a free lunch."

For your Social Security Income benefits information, go to ssa.gov, create an account, and discover your future benefits.

Insurance Diagnostic:

Reviewing the overall risk to your financial security is imperative. What's the point of working a lifetime accumulating enough income and assets to carry you through retirement, only to have an unforeseen accident occur, someone getting seriously injured, and you ultimately being found responsible? Do you have adequate liability insurance? Is your car or home insured for not only the full replacement cost but the maximum levels of liability coverage?

If you are a business owner, are you taking advantage of tax-beneficial medical insurance plans with tax-deductible contributions? Are you taking advantage of tax-deferred cash reserve accumulations? Do you have the proper liability, errors and omissions, and malpractice coverages?

What would happen if you or a relationship partner experienced an unfortunate brain injury or illness? Who would pay the long-term care expenses which are not covered beyond a few months by traditional medical insurance plans or Medicare? For the younger investor, a disability can fully destroy plans to make a living and contribute to a retirement plan. Do you have disability insurance?

For young families, do you have proper life insurance? For wealthy older investors, do you own insurance to cover the high cost of estate taxes? The current estate-tax exclusion will sunset in future years.

If you travel, do you buy travel insurance? If injured, can you imagine having to charter a plane to get home for specialized medical care? It happens, so buy the coverage when traveling outside of the US.

These are just a few of the questions and concerns an adviser will review with you to determine if you are properly insured or whether you need the insurance at all.

A real concern for seniors is the risk of living longer and developing disabilities that might not be covered by insurance. This type of expense has been known to wipe out the estates of many Americans.

Anyone of these risks can drain the assets for which we have worked a lifetime, so leaving any such risk uncovered can be disastrous. Let's look at some of the risks that we face and then learn how to manage them by using insurance policies and legal documents.

Warning! This part can be very boring, but if you ignore the protections afforded you by having insurance or buying the wrong coverage, you will waste your precious resources and money. Not buying the right coverage could destroy everything.

Remember this quote by Hunter William Bailey: "The best you can ever hope for from insurance is that it was the *worst* investment you ever made!" What is meant by this quote is that hopefully you never became seriously ill or disabled, never had an auto accident, never had a lawsuit or business dispute, and of course never died? *We love to hate insurance, but we would not be caught dead without it! (Get it?)*

What you need to know about insurance

Medical Insurance

Who would pay your family's medical bills if you or a family member were ill or injured? Most people who have medical insurance obtain it either through an employer or if retired, through Medicare. The risk here is that the coverage you have will not be adequate to cover medical expenses for serious illness or injury. It is vitally important to be familiar with what your policy will and will not cover. Don't wait until the last minute to find out your policy won't cover a problem.

Two such concerns might be maternity coverage for the beginning of life and long-term care for the end of life.

Insurance Policy Considerations

Exclusions—What's not covered?

Deductibles—How much do you pay out of pocket before the coverage kicks in?

Co-Pay—What percentage of the bill will you pay after the deductible?

Medication Coverage—Some drugs may not be covered by your insurance. Your insurer may cover only generic brands.

Maximum Coverage—How far does your coverage go?

Travel—Are you covered in another state or another country?

Portability—If your employer provides coverage, can you take your coverage with you if you leave that employer?

Medicare—Be sure to study all the options and levels of coverage. Why pay for supplemental coverage you don't need?

Long-Term Disability Insurance

If you have not retired yet, what would you do for income if you became disabled and unable to perform your job? Who would support your family? If you have younger adult children that are working, we suggest you encourage them to buy all the disability insurance they can buy. Instead of making their IRA contribution to them as a gift, it would be more important to pay their disability insurance premium for them, if necessary.

Vacation pay and sick leave may get you through for a short time, but what if you suffer an extended disability? What would you do if you were disabled and the owner of a small business? Rent, utilities, supplies, repair bills, staff salaries, and other expenses still need to be paid. How long would your business last if you, the sole provider and producer, were disabled? Disability insurance is designed to replace part of your regular income. It will cover around two-thirds because the insurance company doesn't want to encourage you to fake a disability if you earn more disabled than working.

(Considerations)

Elimination Period—How long must you be disabled before coverage begins? If you have adequate cash reserves and other liquid backups, can you afford to extend the waiting period before coverage? The longer you can pay bills on your own, the cheaper your insurance premium.

Benefit Period—How long will the coverage last? The longer the benefit period (the time when you're unable to work), the higher the premium. For example, if your policy has a one-year benefit period, the premium will be lower. If, however, you choose disability coverage, an income that will last until age 65, you will pay a much higher premium.

Benefit Amount—What is the total amount of monthly income you will receive? Most people purchase coverage of about two-thirds of their normal income. Benefits from a disability policy are generally tax-free.

Integration Clause—Will other benefits like Social Security reduce your benefit? Many policies maintain a provision that if you qualify for other coverage such as Social Security or State Disability Insurance (SDI), the benefit amount of your policy will be reduced by the amount of any other benefit you are qualified to receive.

Definition of Disability—If you can't do your specific job but could perform other work, do you still receive benefits?

Your Occupation—Policy provision allows you to pay a higher premium and protect yourself against the inability to perform your normal functions within the parameters of your specific job. With this policy, if you are unable to perform your job but could do a different job, you would still receive benefits.

Optional Riders—What other riders (options) can you add to your policy? This is where the insurance company makes a lot of extra money. Thus, avoid insurance agents selling you an optional rider. Do your research and determine if you need one. If you do, that extra expense could be well worth it; if you don't need it, you are simply falling for a sales pitch.

21

Long-Term Care Insurance (LTC)—You've likely heard of families driven into bankruptcy over the cost of nursing home care. Some older married couples have been forced to divorce to qualify for state aid. You must self-insure with your investment drawdown plan or purchase insurance.

(Considerations)

Medical Exclusions—Most policies will exclude coverage, or decline to insure you, for certain pre-existing medical conditions. Make sure you know what your policy does and does not cover.

Maximum Daily Benefit—How much will your policy pay each day you are in a care facility?

Elimination period—A period before your coverage kicks in.

Inflation Rider—Will your coverage increase with inflation?

Home Health Care—Does your policy provide coverage for care at home? If you qualify for such coverage, what daily benefits will you receive?

Adult Day Care—Some policies provide a reduced benefit for adult day care coverage. Again, be aware of how much coverage, if any, is available and for how long.

Benefit Period—Some policies have benefit periods as short as one year, while others are for life. The longer the benefit period the higher the premiums.

Life Insurance

What we don't want to do is pay for coverage we don't need. The goal is to accumulate enough wealth so that some types of insurance policies can be dropped. Policies such as life insurance, disability, and long-term care will, hopefully, be replaced with your ability to cover the losses with your substantial estate in later years.

In the meantime, Life insurance is necessary if a person does not want to leave family or friends with financial burdens upon the "breadwinner's" death. These burdens can include the costs of final services, unpaid medical expenses, unpaid bills such as household expenses, a college education loan, or mortgage.

Types of Life Insurance

Term Life Insurance—Term life is "pure" life insurance coverage. If you die during the life (term) of the policy, the insurance company pays. It might as well be called death insurance, as you must die before your beneficiary collects. With term insurance, you are buying coverage on your life, for the agreed term. If you buy a one-year level term policy, your premium and coverage are set for the next year. A twenty-year term premium stays the same for twenty years.

Annual Renewable Term (ART) Insurance—ART insurance is simply ordinary term insurance for which the premiums are determined by age. With ART insurance, each year that you age (which increases your statistical chances of dying), the annual premium automatically goes up.

Level Term Insurance—Level term insurance premiums are guaranteed not to increase for a specified term, such as 5, 10, or 20 years.

Permanent (Cash Value) Insurance—These insurance policies come in a variety of forms, such as whole life, variable life, universal life, and variable universal life. Unlike term insurance, they are designed to protect you for the rest of your life. These policies require you to invest additional dollars beyond the basic cost of insurance. This cost over time is excessive. Unless you require life insurance at a very old age, low-cost "term insurance" is usually recommended.

Homeowners Insurance

Of course, protecting our homes is on the minds of most Americans. What is often not considered is the risk our homes can pose to all our other investments. What if someone's child was injured on your property, perhaps in your swimming pool? What if that child drowned?

Does your homeowner's insurance provide adequate coverage? If not, your investments could be claimed in a large settlement. See your insurance agent and insist on coverage for all possible risks at the maximum levels possible. Find out the upper limits you have and what's not covered. Ask what the coverage for medical bills will be, for accident liability, fire, earthquake, flood, etc.

Auto Insurance

A risk even greater than your home, your car can place you in an expensive situation if you are involved in an accident. Before you ask about the replacement coverage for your automobile, you should ask, "How much is the liability coverage?" Replacing the car will be the least of your worries if someone sues you for several million dollars. As we age, driving becomes riskier—we might hit the gas thinking it is the brake!

Also, make sure you have adequate uninsured motorist/underinsured motorist coverage. This coverage will bring an uninsured party who caused the accident up to your level of insurance coverage to cover you.

Liability Insurance

Liability coverage is sold for most types of risks. Business owners and manufacturers must have this coverage. Doctors have malpractice insurance, while lawyers, accountants, financial planners, and others have errors and omissions (E&O) coverage for professional mistakes. Individuals need to purchase an umbrella liability insurance policy to add to their home, rentals, auto, and personal coverages.

Remember, insurance companies are in the business of making and conserving money. If they can avoid a claim by investigating your negligence or loopholes in your coverage, you can bet on the fact they will do so with a vengeance!

Proper asset protection can be achieved through both insurance coverage and legal entities. For now, however, follow the rules, the laws, and common sense. Also, buy all the liability coverage the company will sell you. Dot your i's cross your t's and let the insurance company cover the rest. Our next diagnostic will cover various legal programs available to add protection to your assets.

Estate-planning diagnostics:

Full Disclosure! The information and opinions that follow are for educational purposes only. You need to seek advice and counsel from a qualified estate and asset-protection attorney specializing in the areas we will discuss. We hope to stimulate your thought process and imagination by listing several ideas you might consider researching. We are not attorneys, so hence the disclosure. Planning is one phase but acting requires confirmation you are doing the right thing; so, seek advice from a qualified professional when it comes to legal matters.

Beyond the basics of cash reserves, cash flow, investments, taxes, and insurance coverages, estate planning is a high priority. Make sure you have people in place with legal authority to take care of you when you are incapacitated. The concern for who would care for your loved ones after you die also requires close attention to the details in your legal documents.

You will need to ask yourself many questions, such as: Do you have a will to pass on your possessions upon your death? Do you have a durable power of attorney for health and financial concerns, which allows someone you trust to sign for you if you are incapacitated? Do you have a trust to avoid probate regarding the big assets you own when you die? If so, is it the right kind of trust for your situation?

26

Reviewing your will is also very important. This is done to confirm that all your appointees, legal advisers, and beneficiaries are current, and to ensure that items that would pass to various beneficiaries are still appropriate and that you have not changed your mind.

The durable power of attorney is probably the most important document every American should possess. There is a risk that we all could be incapacitated. What would you want to be done? What if you recovered? Who would you trust to manage your affairs while you were unconscious?

The living trust seems less important if two people own assets in joint tenancy with rights of survivorship, where one would inherit everything if the other died. But did you know that tax implications can occur? When both parties purchase an investment that appreciates, and if the investment is held in joint tenancy and one-party dies, and then the survivor sells the asset after inheriting the decedent's half, then tax concerns develop. The decedent's half passes tax-free (step-up in basis), but the survivor must pay taxes on his or her half of the gain when the asset is sold. Serious probate issues can arise if both people die at the same time, such as a car crash, etc.

A trust is especially important if you are an individual owner of investments, retirement plans, real estate, your home, etc. Having the right person manage your estate after you die is critical. Also, if you die without a proper trust, the state could require probate take place, which could last for years and cost tens of thousands of dollars.

Having this document is imperative, but there are mistakes you might make. They include forgetting to change the title of your non-retirement assets to the name of the trust; forgetting to name the trust as the beneficiary of retirement accounts, where appropriate, leaving you in the position of lacking individuals to pass them on to.

For example, if you have a large taxable retirement nest egg and leave its proceeds to your living trust as your beneficiary, instead of a living human being, taxes might be due within five years. Instead, if you made a person the beneficiary, they could choose to take money out of the retirement account for over ten years, stretching out the tax liability over time.

The other side of the argument to this concept is that the beneficiary gains direct control of the plan and its assets. In some cases, this could be a big mistake--for example, if the beneficiary is a spendthrift, a drug abuser, or is in the middle of civil litigation.

You can gain control and spread out the tax liability over time with proper planning through a trust attorney.

With these concerns in mind, you need to review all your estate-planning desires and confirm that your investments and your overall plan are in line with your wishes. Let's review some of the documents to consider in greater detail.

Wills

Many Americans establish a will with the thought that everything will be in order upon their demise. If you die with assets that exceed your state's estate size limitations (in some states, it can be as low as $30,000.00), your estate may be required, even though a will exists, to go through a lengthy and costly probate process.

Many people with small estates and beneficiaries listed on most of their accounts have a less need for trust. Therefore, your will is the focus of most of your needs. You can include a provision in your will, however, allowing for a trust to be established after your death. This is a provision you will need professional assistance with, but it is referred to as a "trust will." Let's make light of reality: Instead of referring to the phrase "when a person dies," let's use the phrase "when the will matures!"

Trusts

Revocable Living Trust—The living trust is the most common estate-planning document utilized for avoiding probate. This document lays out in detail what is expected to happen with your assets after you die. It helps your estate avoid probate, as well as detailing how you want your assets dispersed. It does not, however, eliminate income taxes nor estate taxes for the very wealthy.

When your trust is established, your signatures should be notarized, as well as copies provided for your important representatives and family members.

One problem that becomes a concern almost immediately is a scenario in which not all your assets, such as individual investments and rental real estate, get changed to the name of the trust. If an attorney does the trust, he or she will assist in changing the title to your home, but many other assets can be missed. All non-retirement assets should be considered to be titled in the name of the trust.

If married, your spouse will usually remain as the surviving trustee of the trust, if you die. This works well if your spouse owns an equal share of all the assets. He or she would simply refine the trust instructions and move on with life. What if, however, your marriage was of short duration? What if most of the assets were yours before marriage? Do you want your new spouse to inherit and control all your assets? This one simple concern illustrates the importance of seeking qualified advice with a practicing professional.

No one trust fits all. Make sure you detail all your needs and desires. If you have an attorney establish your trust, make sure he/she listens, and documents your wishes. Read the final legal documents and make sure those wishes were translated to the final trust. Attorneys are notorious for not listening to you and creating a boilerplate trust with generic elements that have no relation to your ultimate wishes, so read everything.

A/B Trusts—These are presently obsolete but a time bomb with the loss of the step-up in basis for the B side of the Trust. The B side gets a step-up in basis at the time of the first spouse's death; the A-side can grow and step up later when the remaining spouse dies. This trust separates the assets for rich married people, to pay fewer estate taxes. The A/B trust would break the assets into two sides of trust, which would allow each side to have its tax exclusion. Although new tax law increases the estate exclusion to over $11 million per person, if

Congress does not decide to extend it, the exclusion will revert to $5 million-plus by 2026. See a qualified estate attorney--if you have one!

Special Needs Trust—We have all heard of this trust. It is designed to hold assets for the benefit of an individual who is not capable of managing the assets by himself or herself. Some other person or company is designated to manage the trust's assets and pay out income for the benefit of the beneficiary. This trust also allows some people to receive trust income but not be disqualified from receiving other public assistance.

Charitable Remainder Trust (CRT)—Many individuals consider opting to utilize CRTs to avoid federal estate taxes, capital gains taxes, and probate fees. When we talk about this in our financial workshops, however, people immediately take a step back and become concerned.

The CRT can provide the following benefits, however:

- A tax deduction over several years, representing the portion of the assets donated to the CRT.

- Normal use of the asset within the trust. For instance, an individual could continue to reside in a home until death.

- Assets that have appreciated to a high degree can be donated and sold while held inside the trust, avoiding capital gains taxes. Next, after the sale, 100 percent of the proceeds can be invested in bonds and cash investments, providing more income than if the donated asset had been sold before being donated. You, in turn, receive that income, and the charity keeps the donated asset after your death. The income can be tax-free if the post-sale proceeds are invested in tax-free municipal bonds.

- Life insurance can be purchased on the life of the grantor with some of the income from the trust. This death benefit can be paid tax-free to the family, replacing the original amount gifted to the charity.

By reviewing all the investments and documents, a more efficient plan can be developed to ensure everything is in sync.

Asset Protection Plans & Trusts—There are various irrevocable trusts established to keep the assets out of the hands of the beneficiary by separating ownership. This separation reduces the chances a creditor can lay claim to the assets in the trust since the beneficiary does not own them. The creditor might try and take the income normally due to the beneficiary, but the trustee can stop income distributions, making it exceedingly difficult to claim. Certain retirement plans can block the creditor from liquidating assets.

Conservation Easement or Land Trust

A conservation easement, also known as a land trust, is a restrictive covenant that allows a landowner to limit the type or amount of development or conserve and protect natural resources on the landowner's property while retaining private ownership of the land. The conservation easement is signed by the landowner, who is the easement donor, and the land trust or conservancy is the party receiving the easement. The land trust or conservancy accepts the easement with the understanding that it must enforce the terms of the easement in perpetuity.

After the easement is signed, it is recorded with the County in the record room and runs with the land and binds all future owners of the land. The most distinguishing feature of the conservation easement as a conservation tool is that it enables users to achieve specific conservation objectives on the land while keeping the land in the ownership and control of the landowner for uses consistent with the conservation objectives. The landowner can specify future uses of the property for his or her benefit and receive significant tax benefits for establishing this arrangement.

Durable Power of Attorney (DPOA)

Two different documents are required, one for medical and another for financial/legal issues.

Medical DPOA (Living Will)

We cannot stress enough the importance of the medical durable power of attorney (DPOA). If you were to be injured or incapacitated, this situation would be very difficult for your family. We've heard a lot regarding the right-to-die issue. Many Americans prefer not to have costly life-support systems hooked up to their near-lifeless bodies. Communicate your wishes before you are unable to do so. This can be done by having a signed, notarized, and witnessed document stating your wishes. If you don't, you can count on the fact that you will be kept alive longer than you may have wished.

Financial/Legal DPOA

Financial DPOA deals with financial and legal matters. Let's say, for example, you are in the middle of refinancing or selling your home, and you become incapacitated and unable to complete the transaction. The deal could be delayed or fall through. The financial DPOA allows a trusted individual to manage your estate while you are incapacitated. Some examples: situations like signing for you regarding selling or refinancing your home, rebalancing your investments to match your changing situation, paying your bills and obligations.

Both medical and financial DPOAs are critical. There must be two DPOAs for every individual. Couples will need a total of four.

Homestead Exemption

Some states provide an exemption of part or all your home's value as protections in the case of a lawsuit. Some states also increase that amount of protection when you turn 65. For example, in Florida, the entire home is protected, regardless of size and value. In California, the amount of exemption goes as high as $175,00 at age 65.

The Prenuptial Agreement

Although many people laugh or scoff at the idea of prenuptial agreements, it is a very important legal document. It allows individuals, upon dissolution of a marriage, whether due to death or divorce, to maintain their individuality, ownership, possession, and rights to distribution of assets that they have accumulated before the marriage.

Retirement is a primary issue in dealing with middle-aged or older people who marry, especially those with past marriages and children. It is critical for both spouses to have a clear understanding of which assets are to be held separately or jointly.

Again, when establishing a legal document, especially a prenuptial agreement, we highly recommend that you seek qualified legal counsel, preferably someone who has no prior relationship with you or your spouse. Once a prenuptial agreement is established, each spouse must have his or her respective legal counsel review the document. Finally, when complete, make certain all proper signatures are obtained and notarized and assets are in the correct registrations.

Qualified Retirement Plans (Provide Asset Protection)

401k, defined-benefits plans, tax-sheltered annuities, thrift Savings Plans (TSP), deferred compensation plans, etc.

These are qualified accounts. Think of the word "qualified." The contributions to the plan "qualify" to be deducted from your overall income. Contributions to a "nonqualified" plan are not tax-deductible.

Most of these retirement plans provide some asset protection in lawsuits but are primarily thought of as plans that provide a tax deduction for contributions.

Plans covered by ERISA (Employee Retirement Income Security Act) provide minimal insurance for plan failures. Strong regulations are in place, designed to protect future retirees from lawsuits levied by creditors. ERISA, however, offers no market protections from failed investments, volatility, and market crashes.

Warning! Be careful not to combine an old contributory IRA with a large rollover IRA. The rollover IRA represents old assets from your old ERISA plan, which, in many states maintains its creditor protection after rollover. When you combine the two you could lose that protection. Do your research and ask questions before combining any accounts.

While they are employed and contributing every month, employees will encounter all types of market conditions. The purchases will dollar-cost average (DCA) into the market through highs and lows and all things in between. Getting the average price is not guaranteed to be the best price, but it does mean getting a bargain when the market is in decline.

Employees must remind themselves that they are buying when everyone else is selling. They contribute and get a tax deduction. This, of course, is very powerful when reducing their taxes during high-income years. More valuable, however, is the fact that the principal is usually covered under this ERISA plan. ERISA provides protection of the principal from creditors if employees are sued. The income, however, can be assessed by creditors in some states, so proper planning is a must.

California Private Retirement Plan (Non-qualified asset-protection plan)

California created a special class of retirement plans for businesses and unions back in the early '70s. It allows setting aside certain assets for one's retirement and exempt them from creditors. The federal government copied the basic structure of the plan and came up with the ERISA plan structure. It was also designed to protect retirement assets from creditors, and it established certain rules and tax benefits.

The California Private Retirement Plan (PRP) predating the ERISA plan was not designed as a mandatory or tax-deductible plan. The PRP allows a business owner to establish a plan without mandatory employee contributions. The business owner can contribute to existing assets all at once. For example, a rental property might qualify as an asset to be put in the plan.

There must be a legitimate plan and trust established. You will need a plan administrator and trustee, but there is great flexibility if you do things right. This plan is not limited by other existing ERISA plans, just proper retirement planning, actuary calculations justifying the need for the plan itself, and plan regulations. As with the employer-provided ERISA plan, the assets in the PRP are exempt from creditors.

There are very few owners/beneficiary tax benefits. All taxes and real estate property tax deductions pass through to the beneficiary like an LLC, partnership, or sole proprietor.

This plan can be very popular since it does not require that payments be contributed for any employees--hence, the reason there are no tax deductions for the contributions, just creditor protection.

Disclosure: This plan should not be constructed with asset protection as your only objective. It must represent your need to create a retirement block of assets designed for your retirement. Do not attempt this process yourself. There is a strict protocol you must follow. You must be willing to give control over to a qualified attorney, administrator, and trustee.

Irrevocable Stretch IRA Trust

When you own a sizable IRA and wish to leave it to your living younger beneficiaries, other than a spouse, they will inherit it if you list them as beneficiary.

This distribution is added to their ordinary income that they are already earning from their employment and other investments, causing income taxes to increase. By electing the beneficiary "stretch" provision, the beneficiary can withdraw the funds over ten years, spreading out the tax liability. The problem here is the beneficiary now has control over the principal and can pull it all out at once, pay the taxes, and deplete what you worked a lifetime for.

Also, there is no legal protection on the asset, like you enjoyed, so a future lawsuit could harm the account. In comes the irrevocable stretch IRA trust. Here, a qualified attorney drafts a special trust designed to inherit the IRA proceeds, with the primary purpose being to set up a future income for your intended beneficiary. This beneficiary is entitled to the income payout over ten years but has no control over the original principal.

Your beneficiary is only entitled to future income or needed disbursements. A divorce, lawsuit, or bankruptcy would have very little effect on this plan.

So, the benefits of this "legacy trust" or stretch IRA trust are that the beneficiary cannot take control of this stretch IRA trust. Income from the trust is controlled by the trustee and paid out over a maximum of ten years. Creditors of the beneficiary cannot access the "corpus," or body, of the trust. This would substantially increase the taxes due to the distributions, so stay on top of the current tax laws.

Limited Liability Corporations (LLC)

This form of business structure is primarily designed to protect your other partners if you are sued. It keeps the liability confined to that business LLC; so, a large lawsuit cannot infect other outside businesses or real estate properties of shareholders. A multiple property LLC might save money in filing fees and attorney costs, but if something happened with one property, causing a lawsuit, the other properties are vulnerable to collections. Separate LLCs would insulate the other properties not held in the same LLC since only assets held by the LLC are vulnerable to collections.

Each state is different with its tolerance for business structures and legal vehicles that provide asset protection. Simply doing an LLC does not eliminate liability. Owning an LLC in a state you don't reside could result in loss of the asset protection, so seek help from a qualified attorney specializing in that area of law.

Charitable Limited Liability Corporation

Like most LLCs, this structure usually has at least two partners: the primary--and largest--owner and a minority shareholder, which is a charity. Since many states frown on single-owner LLCs because there are no other partners to protect, adding a charity tends to add legitimacy. Mark Zuckerberg, it is rumored, owns his Facebook stock in such an arrangement.

Family Limited Partnership (FLP)

Normally designed as a family business tool, allowing family members to share ownership of the family business, it is believed certain asset-protection benefits exist. This is because assets in a family limited partnership would be difficult to sell. A buyer who doesn't want restrictions and lack of liquidity will be less interested. These very issues are believed to protect partners in a lawsuit since the creditor might be uninterested in going after the assets.

We would caution anyone to find a credible attorney who knows how to structure such a partnership. The IRS and state courts frown on partnerships if it looks as though they were created only for asset protection.

Tax Diagnostic:

(The following suggestions and ideas are general in nature and should not be construed as specific advice with regards to your individual tax situation. Always consult with a tax professional before implementing any tax strategy to make sure it is appropriate for you.)

Reviewing your current and expected tax levels is done to determine in which direction to take your ultimate investment plan. Low taxation plans can be developed if taxes are high. Nontaxable, tax-deferred, or lower-taxed investments, such as municipal bonds, index funds, tax-managed funds, can be combined to limit your tax exposure. You can also instruct your adviser, or yourself, to perform "tax harvesting"--selecting the best assets to hold long term and deciding which assets to sell in the short term when you need cash and have losses or deductions to offset the gains.

You will want to consider any appreciated assets, such as stocks, real estate, or businesses that hold accumulated deferred capital gains. We will ask questions such as would selling the assets when the need for cash arrives and paying the capital gains be wise? Or should you do a non-taxable exchange? Or should you simply wait to leave the asset to your beneficiaries, free of capital gains, by using the step-up in basis at your death? This tax-free benefit would be lost if you put the beneficiary on the asset as a joint owner; hence, the need for proper planning.

You will also need to review any previously purchased tax-deferred annuities where the gains are taxable at ordinary income tax rates when cashed out. Questions: Is your old annuity charging high fees or withdrawal penalties? Are there ways to access the cash over time, spreading out the tax liabilities? Which beneficiary could you leave it to who has the lowest tax bracket?

In some cases, you can plan to take taxable withdrawals in later years, in hopes of offsetting the taxable withdrawal with deductible long-term care expenses. You'll assess whether tax-free bonds are better than taxable bonds. Or if you are feeling charitable, simply contribute appreciated assets directly to a charity, and you can avoid the taxes altogether. Remember, with retirement funds, you don't own the whole account. The Government is your partner, and when you take distributions, you will be required to give Uncle Sam his share. If you had a million-dollar IRA, it is sobering to realize that if you were to liquidate it right now, you might own only 65 percent after taxes!

We have a saying in the industry when it comes to IRA distributions, and especially capital gains taxes: "You don't go broke taking your profit." By reviewing all the investments, a more efficient plan can be developed to ensure everything is in sync. Remember, consult with a tax professional or financial adviser before selling, withdrawing, or exchanging any large non-retirement plan investment positions. Your actions might trigger a taxable event.

Do not fall for all those advertisements suggesting you convert your retirement plans to some so-called "tax-free" lifetime investment plan. You would be pulling money out of your IRA and paying significantly high taxes. All this just for the privilege of investing in a whole life insurance policy where the agent earns up to 15 percent commission on your purchase. After that, you will be charged significant life insurance rates. The earnings on your deposit will likely pay for the insurance, so you will not be billed directly but will be led to believe there are no future premiums. All the while, your money is making the insurance company most of its profits. Any earnings you do make can be borrowed out, free of taxes since it's a loan, but you must die before it is repaid with your tax-free life insurance--kind of like a reverse mortgage on your home: non-taxable income by way of a loan, but if you sell the house during your lifetime, those loans must be paid back, and some of them will be taxable unless...you guessed it, you die.

Pulling money out of an IRA, paying an extremely large tax bill, just to put your money into a high-expense life insurance policy is rarely worth it. Even Roth IRA conversions can be dangerous if pulling money out of a taxable IRA or 401k all at once. You need to plan out every move. What is your reason? Will you be in a higher tax bracket in future years, or do you believe the political environment might change, causing future taxes on the gains?

There are particularly good reasons to convert but doing the conversion incorrectly could be a real mistake. The good reasons to convert are the ability to pay taxes during lower income years, or if the market crashes allowing for a transfer of funds that are at a very depressed price. Once transfer to the Roth (although a taxable event) may provide a unique opportunity. Many investors convert over many years, spreading the tax liability. This allows for tax-free growth afterward with the new Roth IRA. The final benefit goes primarily to your beneficiaries. They get the pleasure of inheriting an otherwise taxable investment, tax-free. Plan the conversion first and enjoy the benefit later.

Later, we will look at the basics of tax-advantaged investments and evaluate the inherent risk involved. We will explore the difference between tax deductions and tax credits, and between a qualified and a nonqualified retirement plan. Finally, we will compare tax-exempt income and tax-deferred income, and we will finish with a variety of ideas that will be beneficial to you in the overall planning of your retirement program.

Spending money or making investments just for their tax deductions is not beneficial. This will only return to you the amount of taxes that would have been owed on the number of dollars spent. Let's look at how taxable income is affected by various tax deductions:

If you earn $1 and are in an average tax bracket, state and federal government combined, that combined tax rate would be approximately 30 percent. You claim that dollar as taxable income and pay $.30 in taxes. You will be left with a net income of $.70.

If, on the other hand, you earn that dollar and invest it in a 100 percent tax-deductible investment, retirement plan, or allowable business expense, you will pay no taxes. By deducting the dollar and committing it to long-term investment, you no longer have the dollar to spend today, but because you don't pay any tax on that dollar, you have saved $.30. You've given up the current use of 70 percent of your dollar to an investment that may drop in value or even lose its entire principal.

You can reduce this risk of loss, however, by choosing a very conservative retirement plan, which would allow you to still receive the 100 percent deduction. Regardless, by investing in a 100 percent tax-deductible investment, in a 30 percent tax bracket, you've immediately made $.30 on your $1 investment! Of course, when you pull that one dollar out of a retirement plan, you will pay taxes on it. Thus, you have only deferred the tax, but meanwhile, it has given you tax savings upfront from the tax-deductible contributions. The retirement money can be expected to grow, tax-deferred, and after retiring, you hopefully will then pay a lower tax rate on the withdrawals.

Additionally, you could earn $1 and invest it in a tax-credit program that allows a 100 percent tax credit. In this example, the investment will return a dollar-for-dollar tax credit. Most investments, however, do not allow a 100 percent tax credit. You might receive a 5 percent, 10 percent, or even a 20 percent annual tax credit for several years, allowing you to recapture your investment over many years. These are rare and risky.

Remember that investing money simply for the tax deduction is not a reason to invest; it is an incentive to save. If we plan properly, tax-advantaged investments can assist in reducing overall income tax liability, provide for future years, and reduce dependency on the government.

An example of a tax-advantaged investment is the purchase of a home. If the monthly rent is approximately the same as a house payment would be, the tax benefits alone should be enough incentive to apply that amount toward a home mortgage. The interest on a home mortgage provides a large tax deduction and in turn, reduces your overall tax liability. Purchasing, versus renting, also allows you to build equity in your home, which can help to create a more stable financial future. As you may have done already, paying off your mortgage not only frees up monthly cash flow available to invest or spend but also, you never pay anyone for the privilege to live in your home for the rest of your life! (That is, except for property taxes and insurance fees...)

Other examples of tax-advantaged investing include individual retirement accounts (IRAs), company retirement plans such as 401(k), 403(b), and pension profit-sharing plans, because they are tax-deductible in the year in which you contribute to them. Regardless of the name of your retirement plan, you can deduct contributions that represent earned income.

It is especially important to be cautious before making an investment which stresses a large tax benefit. Be incredibly careful not to jump the gun simply for the tax write-off. This could cause you to make inappropriate decisions with devastating consequences to your finances. Proper research, planning, and counsel are the three elements you will need. We recommend that you invest in tax-advantaged investments when your financial plan calls for them. "Never let the tax tail wag the tax dog."

Let's put things in perspective. If reducing taxes is a priority, let's take a walk up our "stairway to tax heaven,".

Each step in this illustration takes you up the stairway to efficiently invest for tax reduction

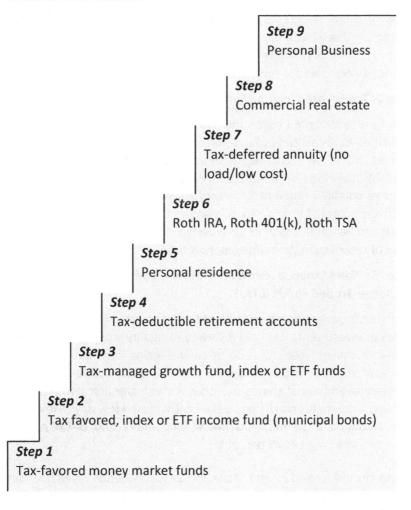

Step 9
Personal Business

Step 8
Commercial real estate

Step 7
Tax-deferred annuity (no load/low cost)

Step 6
Roth IRA, Roth 401(k), Roth TSA

Step 5
Personal residence

Step 4
Tax-deductible retirement accounts

Step 3
Tax-managed growth fund, index or ETF funds

Step 2
Tax favored, index or ETF income fund (municipal bonds)

Step 1
Tax-favored money market funds

Each of these steps is listed in order of importance, building from the foundation up. Utilize the funds at the bottom first, and then build from there as your dollars to invest and your experience grows. Not listed here is one of the most tax-efficient vehicles, the Health Savings Account, or HSA, which is not available to all investors. The HSA provides tax-deductible contributions and tax-free withdrawals for medical needs.

Step 1: Tax Favored Money Market Funds

This fund is utilized for immediate liquidity by check-writing privileges with the mutual fund company. The tax-free money market fund holds extremely short-term, tax-free municipal securities, which should have very little or no volatility in their value. This fund provides tax-free dividends available for reinvestment.

Step 2: Tax Favored Income Fund

This fund is designed as an intermediate-term savings account. The securities in these funds have longer maturity lengths than money market funds do, creating a somewhat higher tax-free dividend available for reinvestment. Tax favored income funds can have an average volatility range of 3 percent to 5 percent, and funds needed short-term could be down by this amount when needed. However, if funds can be left untouched for a period, they may grow with a higher level of return than the money market fund.

Step 3: Tax-Managed Growth Mutual Funds, Index Funds, and Exchange-Traded Funds (ETFs)

This step is designed to be used as a long-term savings account. These types of investments will hold a variety of quality stocks and maintain a low turnover rate to reduce capital gains distribution to the shareholder. You might choose to practice dollar-cost averaging by purchasing additional shares monthly. As with the first two items on our list, these funds can be liquidated within just a few days. However, the volatility of a tax-managed mutual fund, index fund, or ETF growth fund can be as high as 25 percent.

These funds provide very little, if any, dividends available for reinvestment; however, when liquidated, any gains on the fund are taxed all at once at the much lower capital gains rate than, say, dividends from a taxable stock fund or bond fund. These funds allow you to decide when to sell and pay the tax, rather than most managed funds that buy and sell internal securities without considering your taxes.

Full disclosure: ETFs were originally constructed to match a tax-efficient index. Today, however, some ETFs are managed and turn over money just like managed mutual funds; and although they are generally very tax-efficient, make sure you know what their structure and turnover are.

Step 4: Tax-Deductible Retirement Accounts

These plans include IRAs that qualify for tax deductions: Simple IRA, SEP-IRA, 401(k), Solo 401k, TSP (thrift savings plan), deferred compensation plan, pension profit-sharing plan, etc. These are long-term retirement savings vehicles. The gains accumulate on a tax-deferred basis, however, and gains and original contributions are taxable when withdrawn.

The biggest short-term benefit here is the tax deduction of the contributions. For the most part, you can determine when to pay the taxes if you need to withdraw a large portion beyond the required minimum distribution (RMD). With a stretch IRA, you may be able to pass the income on to younger generations over ten years, rather than a lump sum at your death.

Step 5: Personal Residence

Your home usually provides interest tax deductions which can bring your net out-of-pocket expense for housing down near the cost of renting. The tax-deductible interest benefit, the fact that real estate may appreciate, and most importantly, the ability to fix your housing payment for the length of your mortgage make a personal residence an extremely important investment.

Be advised that the rationale for Steps 1, 2, 3, and even 4, 6, and 7 is to provide liquidity of assets. Your residence should not be viewed as a liquid asset, and you should not borrow against the home equity for items that are not extremely important and necessary.

Step 6: Roth IRA, Roth 401(k), Roth TSA (Tax Sheltered Annuity)

The Roth IRA does not allow an immediate tax deduction for dollars going in; however, it does allow the gain to be accumulated on a tax-free basis if held for the minimum period. The Roth IRA provides fewer tax benefits going in than the previously mentioned retirement investments, but at retirement, all your distributions are tax-free and have no required minimum distribution. For those whose earnings exceed allowable limits to contribute to a Roth IRA, they currently can establish what is referred to as a "backdoor Roth." They contribute to a nondeductible IRA, which has no limitations, and then, under IRS allowed time limits, convert it to a Roth IRA. *Consult a tax professional before proceeding with any of these steps!*

Step 7: Tax-Deferred Annuity (Fixed and Variable)

This investment vehicle provides only tax-deferred growth. The fixed annuity is like a certificate of deposit, only it accumulates on a tax-deferred basis. There is no tax deduction for dollars invested and no lower capital gains tax benefit or step-up in basis at death. This vehicle is a good supplement to the prior six investments.

If you like to invest in government securities, corporate bonds, utility stocks, and/or preferred income dividend-paying stocks, this product is for you. You can defer the earnings and provide a death benefit for your beneficiary. The variable annuity is a good investment if it can be offered without the extremely high commissions paid to the sales representatives, insurance agents, and their insurance brokers. Inflated fund expenses, life insurance costs, and living benefit riders will substantially increase your internal cost. Look for a no-load product to avoid these high fees and surrender penalties.

Step 8: Commercial Real Estate

Real estate, such as rental properties and commercial properties may be the ultimate tax savings investments, next to owning your own business. Real estate provides interest tax deductions on loans, property repairs, property taxes, and depreciation of improvements. Investment properties and commercial real estate should be purchased based on the cash-flow earnings potential and not on emotion. A property may sit vacant for a long time, and although you will be able to still use the deductions, the lack of income could be a hardship. This is an investment in a real estate business, and you will take on substantial risk, effort, and expenses. The reward can be substantial in the long run, however.

Step 9: Personal Business

A business will provide substantial tax deductions in the start-up years, which can be deducted from other ordinary income. However, there is a maximum of a few years in which such losses can be taken. A personal business can afford you tax deductions for computers and other equipment, employee benefits, investment in real estate, and other expenses necessary to run an individual business. If successful, a personal business can be the most profitable asset under your direct control.

More About Tax-Deductible Retirement Plans (Qualified Plans)

There are a variety of IRS-approved retirement plans from which an individual can choose. Many of these plans provide an immediate 100 percent tax deduction equal to the amount contributed. These plans are designed to allow employed individuals to divert a portion of their income into a retirement savings plan. The earnings are tax-deferred. Both earnings and employee/employer contributions are taxable when withdrawn.

Potentially taxable retirement plan proceeds should be distributed over your lifetime.

As we have learned, a qualified plan is one that qualifies for a tax deduction when placing the funds into the plan. Although most private-individual and small-business retirement plans allow individuals to withdraw funds before the age of 59½ (age 55 or older), you could face a 10-percent early withdrawal penalty payable to the IRS, and in states like California, another 2½ percent early withdrawal penalty.

A penalty-free lifetime income stream can, however, be created for those under the age of 59½, referred to as Substantially Equal Periodic Payments (under IRS code 72(t) section two). Although taxable, this lifetime income can avoid the early withdrawal penalty if calculated properly, stretch out your taxes, and provide long-term income.

Your Company's Pension and Profit-Sharing Plan

This is your basic two-in-one plan. The employer will contribute to the pension on a regular schedule, and profit-sharing is an optional benefit.

The employer usually contributes to the profit-sharing plan only if there is a company profit.

One possible long-term investment strategy would be to have your monthly contributions invested in the plan's most aggressive investments. Then every two years, move those aggressive funds into the fixed account or a conservative balanced fund, securing any gains. You may be able to take the money with you at age 55 if you leave service, cash it out without penalty, but with taxes owed on the whole amount of your withdrawal.

If you leave your employer, are over the age of 55, and need some cash, this is the time to take it, not after rolling it over to an IRA. The IRA will have early withdrawal penalties up to age 59½. While working, you may be able to borrow from the plan for certain expenses and needs. You must, however, pay the loan back before leaving service, or the loan will become due and taxable.

401(k) Plan

The 401(k) plan is offered by many employers, with some employers matching a portion of their employees' contributions.

Your employer will take money out of your paycheck (generally 1 percent to 20 percent of your earnings) and place it directly into the plan, along with any employer matching contributions. Here again, you get to defer your taxes and claim a lower taxable income. The 401(k) plans usually provide you with several different mutual funds from which to choose. So, continue practicing dollar-cost averaging by investing regularly, and rebalance occasionally.

Of course, like many plans, you can transfer your money into a rollover IRA when you leave your employer. Remember, your early withdrawal penalty age, however, will rise from 55 to 59½. Benefits of the 401k are not only tax deductions when you are putting money in, but your employer's contribution is free money. The funds can grow tax deferred. You are forced to invest through down markets, allowing for lower purchase prices. Sure, you must take a small amount at age 72, but you can leave your funds to your beneficiaries, who can continue to use them. A spouse can stretch the income over their lifetime and non-spouses over ten years.

A Roth 401(k) is good for young investors who don't require maximum tax deductions from a standard 401k plan. The Roth version is a wonderful non-tax-deductible contribution. This is because although the employee did not gain a tax deduction for his or her contributions, all his or her earnings and contributions will grow tax-free and forever! Young people can purchase a home with a thirty-year mortgage and take the deduction for interest, let the home grow in value, and contribute to the Roth 401k. So, let the mortgage deduction provide the tax benefit and Roth provides tax-free growth for future tax-free income. These young people might even qualify to contribute to a tax-deductible IRA on the side.

Employee Stock Purchase Plan (ESPP)

While these plans are beneficial, you could be risking your investment if your employer files for bankruptcy. With most ESPP plans, the employer usually matches a percentage, if not all, of your contributions. We do advise people to take advantage of these programs, but due to the risk from lack of diversification, invest only after you've exhausted all other retirement contributions, such as to 401(k) and IRA plans.

403(b) Tax-Sheltered Annuity (TSA) Plan

The 403(b) or tax-sheltered annuity (TSA) plan is an individualized deferred compensation plan. Individuals who work for a nonprofit organization and/or school district can place funds that they earn into a long-term retirement annuity. They may deduct those dollars from their taxable income in the year in which they make the contributions.

Like other qualified plans, the account cannot be accessed without a penalty until age 59½, unless you are legally disabled, and you must start taking distributions from the account by the time you reach 72. The 403(b), or TSA, is a wonderful tool for teachers and nonprofit employees, used to supplement their retirement plans by monthly payroll deductions. This plan is strictly contributory by the individual. The employer allows the individual to choose which investment will be placed into the TSA, and although some organizations only allow one account, many school districts will allow 20 or 30 different investments (*subaccounts*) inside the annuity. Remember to continue contributing regularly and rebalance occasionally. Watch out for commissions, high fees, and early withdrawal penalties.

Deferred Compensation Plan (DCP)

This plan allows employees to place part of their earnings aside before taxes and defer the use of those assets until retirement. Like most retirement plans, the funds are not taxed until withdrawn. Also, like other plans, it may provide a variety of investment funds to choose from, in which to invest. Unlike other plans, however, your money can be commingled with the company's assets. This means that if the company goes out of business, your deferred compensation, which hasn't been paid to you yet could be lost with the demise of the company. Therefore, maximize any other retirement plans first.

Capital Gains Taxation on Non-Retirement Plan Assets

Buy and Hold

When buying and holding individual securities such as stocks, bonds, tax-managed mutual funds, index funds, and ETFs, you may not avoid taxes altogether, but you can defer them. If your stocks are down and your taxes are high, you have the option of selling them and taking a loss for tax purposes. With most actively managed mutual funds, however, the portfolio manager only cares about the mutual fund's overall performance. Buying and selling securities within the fund, also known as *turning over the portfolio*, produce tax liability and costs that are passed onto you. There are some internal tax deductions that the mutual fund company takes, but for the most part, you will be stuck with the tax burden.

As a result, we recommend that high-turnover mutual funds be held inside retirement plans because the gains generated from the mutual funds aren't taxable until you start withdrawing profits from the plan. (Gains are taxed as ordinary income coming out of a retirement plan.) If taxes are a big issue for you, hold mutual funds that have low turnover ratios. Funds like tax-managed/efficient mutual funds, index funds, and exchange-traded funds have low turnover and allow for less taxable distributions from year to year.

Outside of retirement funds, most investments that qualify for the favorable and lower capital gains tax rate also provide the step-up in basis at death. This is very important for your beneficiaries since they will not have to pay taxes on the appreciated value of the asset after your death.

Tax-Deferred Transfers & Retirement Plan Rollovers

Employer-sponsored retirement plans today are becoming more and more portable. These plans provide employees with the ability to move their accumulated funds when they leave employment. You should *always* check with your HR department to confirm you won't lose any benefits, like health care, if you take your pension or retirement annuity funds in cash or as a rollover. After confirming your funds are portable without problems, let's look at the rollover process.

We recommend that you transfer your funds to a rollover IRA. This option provides you the ability to maintain complete control over your invested assets. Many employer-sponsored plans focus on growth funds, offering fewer income funds--such as floating-rate securities, short-term government funds, intermediate government funds, GNMAs, and preferred stock funds. With sound advice and research, you will be able to properly allocate among several different investment choices and thousands of funds.

So, when you retire with a plan through your employer, you will have the option to leave the money in the plan, accept their annuity income option, cash it out, and pay taxes or roll it over to a self-directed IRA.

When leaving your employer, be careful to research your options. If they allow you to leave your money there, check your fund options. Today, most plans offer many different funds with reasonable expense levels. The one concern, however, is that most plans offer funds designed for growth and fewer funds designed for stability. This makes perfect sense since most people contributing to their retirement plan buy shares each month for growth and accumulation of shares, practicing dollar-cost averaging. These plans are not usually designed for retirement income planning.

If you decide not to move your money and take the cash, instead of rolling it over, federal and state taxes will apply, in addition to early withdrawal penalties if you are under retirement age.

Remember, once you roll your money to an IRA, your minimum age to withdraw money without penalties goes up to 59½. So, if you need money when you retire and are over 55 but under 59½, you might ask your employer if you can withdraw the money you need in the short term before your rollover is complete. (Taxes will apply)

If you are working with an adviser or registered representative salesperson, they are required to disclose the facts regarding your existing employer plan and to point out any benefits in rolling over your funds to their investment plan. Are their fund fees higher or lower than what you are currently paying? If there is a commission on the new account, that must be disclosed. If there is an adviser fee, it must be disclosed and justified. An overall description of what you are being offered must be laid out and in your best interest, to justify the rollover and transfer of funds.

Again, remember: You should not transfer your existing retirement funds from your employer's plan to an IRA unless you or the adviser can add value. If you will be managing your new IRA rollover account, the flexibility and greater fund choices of low-cost funds could easily justify the transfer.

If, however, a broker is going to earn front-loaded commissions, or an adviser will get management fees, the future benefits should be apparent. The problem with a broker is that they get paid five to ten years of service fees in advance by way of their commissions. A fee-based adviser, on the other hand, only gets paid monthly or quarterly and can be fired at any time, without penalties or commissions being charged to you.

We see no benefit to paying commissions on investment funds. If you hire a fee-based adviser, it's only because you don't have the interest or time to do it yourself. You should be aware of the administrative services and adviser's experience that can make a difference when managing your money. Can you do it yourself for less cost? Yes. Could you be traveling the world free of stress, not worrying about the details of managing your investments? Yes, if you hire the right adviser.

As we previously mentioned, at retirement, you may have some or all these dilemmas and choices: deciding to purchase an annuity offered by your company, or leaving your funds with the old company plan, or rolling over to a self-directed IRA. Let's look at each option and weigh the benefits:

Purchase of an annuity—If you chose the annuity, you will be quoted a variety of income options. Each one will provide a different monthly payment amount. The first and highest payment is quoted on just your life. It is the highest payout but will stop after your death, only guaranteeing* you were paid for a minimum period (period certain). This means if you have a period certain of, say, five years, it guarantees that if you died after the fifth year, your beneficiary gets nothing. Even if you live a long time, the income level does not go up with inflation, so in exchange for a guaranteed payment, you give up the ability to get your principal back.

*Guarantees are based on the claims-paying ability of the issuing company.

Other options might offer your beneficiary 100 percent, 75 percent, or 50 percent of your original income payment if you die. The higher the residual guarantee to your beneficiary, the lower your lifetime income payment. Thus, regardless of what you do, it will cost you. Taking the highest income option for yourself could leave your beneficiary a lifetime without income. Therefore, if you are married, your spouse will be required to sign off on your decision.

Some unscrupulous insurance agents have advised retirees to take the maximum annuity payment, and then if the retiree dies, the insurance coverage they sell you will be there for your partner. The problem is that if the insurance gets too expensive; ultimately, the policy could lapse. So, take your time, get several opinions from advisers that have no conflict of interest.

Leaving the funds with the old plan—Current laws and regulatory requirements are bringing the 401k fund expenses down and increasing your fund options. So, for the most part, most large company funds are probably good. If you are a federal worker and have the thrift savings plan, you have the lowest cost index funds on the planet. If the plan has well-managed funds, hopefully, they are of high quality, have low fees, and rank well in their class.

Rolling over to a new self-directed rollover IRA—You might be an investor who likes the availability of trading online. You might enjoy having tens of thousands of securities to choose from. If you are an advanced investor, you will have many tools available to manage your own money.

To remind you, your old plan might have many great "equity" funds intended for the younger-aged investor, who needs a large inventory or stock-related funds. This makes sense since they are investing each month. If the market "tanks," they are buying into the decline and thus taking advantage of a correction. This works for new purchases and old money not needed for several years. For retirees, however, a large decline can be devastating, since they are no longer buying and have less time to wait for recovery.

The old plan might also offer automatic-allocation funds called "target funds". As you get older, these funds slowly transition your allocations to bonds. The big problem here, though, is that the fund invests in intermediate-term and long-term bonds. If interest rates rise, bonds fall in value, and you could have a permanent loss. Not a problem if you are buying on the way down. It is a big problem if your money is sitting idle. Remember this saying: You can't "target" target funds! Meaning if you need to liquidate shares for a lump sum and stocks are down, you must liquidate whole shares. You can't liquidate the part that's not down in value like you can in a managed portfolio.

These plans do not provide a large inventory of downside protection funds, as we will see. A declining market stings more for the retiree since they are not able to continue reinvesting the new contributions into the market at lower prices. The final accumulated portfolio drops all at once with no "new money" recovery options.

So, your old plan might be great for the investing employee, but if you are a passive retiree, you may need many more conservative funds to choose from. You might want more money invested in bond funds, a form of "loanership." If interest rates rise, however, your long-term bond fund might drop significantly. So, to build a large position of fixed assets such as bonds, and even money market funds, to create estimated sustainable income (ESI), you will need many more choices than your old plan offers. For example, you might need a variety of income fund options from a variety of different fund companies. See the following list.

Funds your old plan might not offer:

Income-Producing Funds

- Money Market Funds
- Ultra-Short-Term Bond Funds
- Floating-Rate Income Funds
- Short-Term Bond Funds
- High-Yield Short-Term Bond Funds
- Multisector Bond Funds
- GNMA Funds
- High-Yield Bond Funds
- Emerging Markets Bond Funds
- The Developed Market International Bond Funds
- Utilities, Energy, Commodities, Real Estate, Preferred Stocks, etc.

In addition to the different index and exchange-traded funds holding the same securities as the funds listed above, the market also offers new ETFs every year. A few of these ETF options may include the following structures:

- Low-Cost Index Funds
- Smart Beta Funds

- Strategic Beta Funds

- Multifactor Funds

- Minimum Volatility Funds

- Low Volatility Funds

- Although not recommended, leveraged ETFs

We will go into greater detail in future chapters.

These options might be a bit intimidating, so the assistance of a qualified and well-respected financial adviser who is a fiduciary might add another component not generally available with your old plan. An adviser should follow all the steps we have outlined in the diagnostic reviews. This is the first of three steps that need to take place when you retire. The second step is the reallocation of those investments to match your retirement needs.

Managing your retirement portfolio should not end once you have reallocated the funds to match your retirement and passive investing needs.

What your adviser should be doing to justify a rollover IRA:

Complete all the diagnostic reviews for retirement cash flow, insurance needs, tax analysis, estate-planning documents, investment reviews, and old portfolio analyses.

After you have rolled over, and thus reallocated your lump-sum retirement portfolio, you or your adviser need to follow the portfolio closely along with the following schedules.

Daily—watch potential changes to interest rates & regulations

Weekly—review various fund alerts about your funds

Monthly—shop for lower-expense funds and funds with newer strategies

Quarterly—monitor existing funds in your portfolio

Biannually—rebalance over-weighted funds occasionally

Annually—review your financial, estate & investment plan.

We will discuss these necessary ongoing monitoring standards later in this book. For now, however, let's learn the actual process required to roll over your funds in the first place. We will also review the other decision you might face, converting your rollover IRA to a Roth IRA.

You've decided to roll over your previous retirement funds to your new rollover IRA plan. Here are the steps you should expect to follow:

Rollover Steps

1. You decide on (or are informed of) separation from service.

2. Request the plan rollover forms and instructions from the employer's human resources department.

3. Establish a new brokerage IRA account at a well-known investment company. Request a new account number from that same investment company for this newly established brokerage IRA account that has been set up to receive the rollover funds. Generally, we recommend that you establish a rollover IRA separate from old nonrelated IRA's. The reason for this approach is that you could lose creditor protection on your old rollover funds; and/or, you could encounter tax complications about tax basis of past nondeductible IRA contributions.

4. If you are married, you may be required, as in community property states, to obtain your spouse's signature to waive the option to invest into a fixed, guaranteed annuity sponsored by your old employer. This is usually an exceptionally low payout over the retiree's lifetime.

5. Complete the rollover portion of the request forms provided by your employer, indicating you want your existing investment funds converted to cash and specifying where your money should be

sent, which is your new Rollover IRA. There will be a section on the rollover form for this.

Some employers, however, insist on sending the check to you personally, so be careful. It must be made out to the receiving company, not you. It should only list you as "for the benefit of," then your name.

If funds are sent directly to you, send them immediately to the new IRA custodian. If you cash the check, you'll have only 60 days to get the money back into the IRA. If you don't, you will face substantial taxes, and if under 55--and in some cases under 59½--a minimum of 10 percent in an early withdrawal penalty will also apply with the Fed and additional for certain states.

If you fail to declare the distribution as a rollover, your employer will be required to withhold 20 percent for taxes. That leaves you with only 80 percent to roll over, which will not qualify for a full rollover. You will need to come up with the missing 20 percent out of pocket! You'll get the tax withholdings next year at tax time, but until then, you'll have to fund the mistake.

6. Once you receive notification from your new rollover IRA custodian that your money has been received, you should begin preparing your asset-allocation plan. Your adviser, if you have one, will prepare a plan for you. After you confer with your adviser and review the plan, the asset-allocation plan will be set in place, and new investments will be purchased. So, that's all there is to it.

Remember, this rollover should be done in your best interests. If investing on your own, you would roll over the funds to a company like Charles Schwab, TD Ameritrade, Fidelity, etc. Your new account would continue to be an IRA in the form of a "self-directed brokerage account." You will now have thousands of investment choices. You will be able to diversify among many different investments, as well as investment companies.

If an adviser is assisting you in the rollover, he or she must show there is a benefit to you. Since your old 401k, TSP, or deferred plan most likely offered low-cost funds, an adviser must show their value in your rollover process. That value would be in the multiple planning and monitoring steps outlined in this book. Avoid any adviser or salesperson pressuring you, for any reason, to roll over your funds into their investment.

Do not forget, those tax-deferred dollars will always be taxable if drawn out. Many retirees attempt to convert their sizable rollover IRA into a Roth IRA, hoping to reduce future taxes. One must be incredibly careful, however; you will pay the taxes one way or another.

Converting Your existing IRA to a Roth IRA

We would all love to know our IRA investment is ultimately growing tax-free, not just tax deferred.

This will only happen if you contribute to a Roth IRA or Roth 401k, giving up any tax deductions in the year's contributions are made or after paying taxes on the conversion from the old IRA to the Roth IRA.

Reasons for converting to a Roth IRA:

Once the conversion is complete, the money can then grow tax-free from then on. Thus, consider the following reasons and precautions for converting your new rollover IRA to a Roth IRA:

- You retired and are in a lower tax bracket for a year or two before you go back to work or become a paid consultant.
- You retired early in the year, can defer pension plan payments until the following year, and expect substantial tax deductions which will offset the taxes on the conversion.
- You are working and allowed to do an "in-service" rollover to an IRA, and you expect your salary to rise in future years.
- You were self-employed, are now retired, and can live off your savings for a year or two. By converting part of your Rollover IRA account to a Roth IRA (paying low rates of taxes), you are reducing the amount of future required minimum distributions (RMD) that you will face in later years when you start withdrawing retirement funds, as well as taxable Social Security income.

- You might want to pay the conversion taxes for the benefit of your future beneficiaries so they can inherit the account tax-free.

Reasons against:
- Don't do the conversion if the tax liability will move you up to a much higher tax bracket. Work with your tax consultant and develop a plan for partial conversions over several years.
- Don't do the conversion if you don't have the money for the taxes set aside. Paying taxes with taxable withdrawals will multiply the tax consequences.
- Don't do the conversion in any year where your tax rates are not less than they were when you contributed to your previous plan.
- Avoid the conversion in a year where you might be selling any investments that will increase your tax liability.

For example, real estate: Let's say you don't want to do a tax-deferred exchange on an investment property; you just want out of the real estate market and are willing to pay the capital gains and recapture depreciation deductions. The sale of a property and a Roth conversion in the same year could cause a large tax problem. Regardless, pulling money out of a tax-deferred account must be planned. See your tax adviser and avoid a costly mistake.

More about Real Estate

Real Estate Tax Deductions

There are a variety of tax deductions available to real estate investors. For example:

Personal Residence
- Loan points on the first mortgage are deductible (at purchase only, not for refinancing).
- Mortgage interest is deductible for most homeowners.
- Property taxes are deductible within certain limits.
- Improvement costs reduce taxable gains at the time of sale.

- Residential partial gains on sale are tax-exempt (single person, the first $250,000; married couples, $500,000).

Rental Properties (excess deductions carry forward to the sale of the property)

- Loan points on the first mortgage are deductible (at purchase only).

- Mortgage interest is deductible.

- Property taxes are deductible.

- Insurance premiums are deductible.

- Maintenance costs are deductible.

- Management expenses are deductible.

- Improvements to property are deductible over time.

- The actual structure on the property is depreciable as a tax deduction; it will be repaid at the sale, however.

- Travel expenses, advertising, so on, are deductible.

- Repairs, not improvements, are deductible upfront.

- Taxable gains are taxed at lower rates.

- Capital gains taxes due to the sale of the property can be deferred using a tax-deferred exchange if buying another property (1031 Exchange).

The investment programs listed in this lesson are tremendous opportunities, not only to provide current tax deductions and tax savings but also to contribute greatly to building your wealth.

Before you spend money on real estate, we suggest you plan your priorities first, identifying the money you must use to fund these programs, coupled with the time to manage them. Albert Einstein once said, "The hardest thing in the world to understand is the income tax." So, do not buy real estate only for the tax benefits. Real estate is extraordinarily complex, especially if you borrow the money to buy it, so be careful. Leverage might increase your gains; it can also increase your losses.

A Word About Tax Benefits:

Remember, there are strings attached! Capital gains rates are given to riskier investments. The tax-deductible and tax-deferred retirement plan only defers taxes. You might be in a higher tax rate at retirement! Worse yet, if you build a multimillion-dollar estate, your beneficiaries might end up paying high ordinary income taxes on your retirement plan, as well as estate taxes on the pre-tax balance. Plan your future by utilizing the advice of professionals. Tax-favored investing is wise; just plan what you do carefully. What you do one year to reduce your taxes could substantially increase your taxes in future years.

Investments & Portfolio Diagnostics:

Before making any recommendations to keep or change existing investments, the adviser must first know whether the investment fits your needs and whether it's of good quality.

In the same way that eating right requires you to look at the label to determine what's in your food, you must also look at the labels of your investments.

You'll look at each stock, bond, or fund individually, regardless of whether it's owned outside, rather than inside, your retirement portfolio. To determine the quality and appropriateness of any single investment, you must review the following components:

Past investment structures, allocations, and category—These days, most investors use investment funds--a basket of stocks, bonds, cash, etc. Their method of investing, asset turnover, managed or passive structure, all allow you greater choice and diversification.

You will, however, need to know which different types of investments dominated the landscape years ago when your old investments were purchased. Real estate limited partnerships were once more popular than they are today. Many of them failed, due to poor planning and outright misappropriation of investor funds. Older mutual funds charged up-front commissions. Some have long-term surrender-penalty schedules and fees. Insurance products were the most aggreges when it came to horrific surrender penalties and high yearly fees. Surrendering just because you don't like the investment could be like pulling a fish hook out of your thumb! Things could get worse with withdrawal penalties and taxes. Planning is critical.

The good news is that you might have far exceeded any surrender penalty on mutual funds or annuities, giving you more options.

Some old fixed annuities might still have what the insurance company considered an extremely low guaranteed minimum interest rate that is fixed for the life of the contract. A typical minimum rate was, and for some investors who still hold those contracts is 4 percent. With the certificate of deposit rates dropping to very low rates, this minimum was a welcome victory for investors. Old variable annuities, however, continue with their extremely high ongoing mortality and expense fee (M&E), marked-up fund expenses, additional but seldom-used living benefits, etc. These old contracts should be carefully analyzed to consider if the future expenses are worth continuing to hold them.

Old annuities and life insurance cash values might be a source of long-term care resources--either by cashing them out when needed and offsetting the taxable gain with health-care tax deductions or researching the possibility of exchanging them for LTC policies. Be careful, however, because wherever there is an annuity-exchange opportunity, there is an aggressive insurance salesperson. So, double-check the facts.

See if you can find a no-load option, and if not, find an insurance agent you trust. That agent, however, should not be your fee-based adviser. If that is the case, he or she should first exhaust every non-commission product available before selling you a new insurance contract, since he or she will be paid a commission, and you will assume a new extended surrender penalty. Full disclosure is required here.

The modern-day investment index fund, managed fund, or ETF— although every fund has its asset mix, we need to know how it performs in business. An index fund primarily buys a group of securities that represent the desired index. A few examples of these indexes might be the Dow Jones Industrial, which holds 30 stocks; the S&P 500; total bond or stock markets; and various specialty indexes such as utilities, preferred stocks, oil, etc.

A managed fund is comprised of a different mix of securities and represents what the manager believes will outperform its benchmark index, using various management strategies. Exchange-traded funds are usually allocated like their counterpart, the index fund. These funds can be traded by the investor throughout the trading day like individual securities, versus at the end of a trading day like a mutual fund.

The concept of funds is to reduce your direct risk of loss, something you might experience if you owned just one stock and it went bankrupt. Let's look at all the various risks we must be aware of before jumping into the "investing shark tank"! We will cover the details in the next couple of pages.

Understanding risk versus reward

"There is no free lunch!" If you choose to pursue higher returns, you need to be aware that there will be a trade-off, whether that be higher risk, longer maturity, market volatility, or some other factor.

Systematic vs. unsystematic risk

We know the markets are efficient, so we want to strategically and systematically place our investment in a category of similar securities. Let's use US large-cap stocks as a group to diversify our risk among several positions and different, but similar, companies. Choosing non-systematic risk, you invest in one stock. You take all the same market risk, with no diversification among other like-kind stocks. If your stock remains healthy and its price rises, your assumptions were right. If it has devastating performance or goes out of business, your gamble failed.

Another concern is the negative relationship between volatility and returns, which is called "the leverage effect." When the stock's return drops, the financial leverage of the company increases, since the debt remains constant and the market value drops.

Remember, markets are efficient at setting stock prices; so why gamble? You can select certain areas of the market to place your bet on, but why take the ultimate risk that your single investment could fail?

Think about this: When is the last time you heard about a company planning to file for bankruptcy protection? The answer is "all the time"; right? When is the last time you heard about a mutual fund planning to file for bankruptcy?

Remember, no two bear markets are the same, so diversification is critical--not the most profitable on the upside, but most likely less harmful on the way down. Although frequent buying and selling are discouraged, not trading at all (no rebalancing) is as risky as trading too often.

Taxes can also be a risk to consider. A tax deduction today might be a tax liability in the future. So planning, timing, and evaluation need to take place to get the most of your financial situation. If handled incorrectly, your wonderful tax deduction today can pop up in your retirement years as an added level of income, which might increase your income and trigger a series of tax increases. You must pay your taxes, but "there's no law that says you need to leave a tip." Taking tax deductions, although a great idea, is a risk if done incorrectly, so consult a tax professional.

Asset allocation goes a step further than just buying one or two funds, and this strategy attempts to balance the strengths and weaknesses of different categories and sectors. Automatic rebalancing is offered by many institutions, but it simply resets your percentages within categories. It rebalances you back to the starting allocations--neither good nor bad. It all depends on your current needs, compared with the updated allocations.

Diversification and allocation give your portfolio strength in a falling market. It's this "sheer" strength that ensures your portfolio is still standing when a storm blows through. By reducing redundancy among your funds, you avoid having all your eggs in one basket. There is a price to diversifying your portfolio, however: You will never beat the market on the way up since you are not fully invested in the same positions that are rising. However, if you are properly diversified, you might have a much better chance of beating the market on the way down. Now, over the long run, stocks have always beaten portfolios with cash and bonds, but when the market tanks and you need to liquidate money, you'll have less affected assets you can sell, and thus can avoid stock-market losses.

If you didn't plan to touch the money for a few decades, the selection would be simple: buy the market. What if however, you need to cash out for some emergency? Or what if you need income? Financial planning requires asset allocation, not pure investing for profits. If you will *never* have a need for safety & liquidity, buy only stock funds! Fixed assets like cash, CDs, and short-term bonds, in our opinion, are not good investments. They do, on the other hand, make good savings accounts.

So, for short-term emergency funding, we have learned we should stay with cash, certificate of deposits, and money market mutual funds. As you seek higher yield and returns through longer maturities, you will need to invest in long-term certificates of deposit and intermediate-term bond funds. If you are willing to risk interest rates rising, another option is to invest in long-term bond funds.

Long-term bonds are sensitive to rising interest rates. If you buy a long-term maturing bond at one rate of return and then rates rise, new bonds will pay higher yields. This will cause a potential buyer of your bond (if you decide to cash out early) to pause and realize that a higher yield could be realized by buying a new bond, rather than buying your lower-yielding bond.

A calculation referred to as "duration" tells us how much a bond should rise or fall in resale value if interest rates rise or fall. Specifically, the bond will rise or fall by duration. So, if the duration were ten years, and the Feds announce an interest-rate increase of one full percentage point overnight, the bond will drop by the duration, a full 10 percent. Trying to sell a long-term bond with a high duration after interest rates rise can be very painful. Bond prices will fall, and spreads will widen when there is a fear of a bond being downgraded. Therefore, maturity, quality, yields, size, and liquidity are important factors when considering the purchase of bonds.

The market, however, might react differently, based on investor emotion, but you should still plan for the worst-case scenario. Don't forget, only about 11 percent of corporate bonds are traded daily, so liquidity is a great concern. Funds that hold illiquid bonds can trade more frequently than the bonds they hold, making them a better bet.

Also, do not forget, you can reduce price volatility by holding bonds until maturity. You can also hold a series of bonds with different maturities. You can spread out the maturities of individual bonds for future liquidity. Using funds, you can also ladder them using short term, intermediate-term, and long-term bond funds.

One other thing to remember: After a few years, many individual bonds can be paid off early by the issuer. This is referred to as a "call provision." You buy the bond at one interest rate, but if rates fall, the issuer can call the bond back and refinance their debt at lower rates. You end up getting your money back and must buy new bonds at lower yields. There are mathematical calculations to determine the actual yield until maturity, based on what you pay for the bond in the open market and another calculation called "yield to call." You might even get a little premium if the company pays you off, but that's little consolation if your old yield was substantially higher than the new rates.

So, when analyzing old investment vehicles, as well as new ones, we must understand the variations, parameters, and factors that make up your investment. Many of these elements will not only apply to an individual investment vehicle; they will be transferred and overlaid onto your ultimate combination of funds in the portfolio. The portfolio of combined funds will absorb and average out these parameters.

You should have less concern for the historical volatility of a single fund, as compared with the historical volatility of the total portfolio. You will be reviewing all the areas of stocks and bonds that make up the thousands of investment funds available today. Combining these funds makes up the portfolio. The portfolio will be allocated to meet your needs and downside risk tolerance.

We will look at the parameters and elements that make up the various funds available to you in the market today. We will also look at all the classes of investments, categories, and sectors to choose from. After becoming familiar with the individual investment parameters and risk metrics, we will look at the parameters to be covered when creating a portfolio with the combination of funds in the "portfolio diagnostic section." So, keep reading and learning.

Investment funds and parameters
(Used for analyzing old investments funds and choosing new ones)

Let's consider the many elements and parameters to look for when analyzing a specific investment fund, such as an index fund, managed fund, or exchange-traded fund.

The idea of a fund is very appealing because although there is no guarantee against loss, you have the following elements:

Internal diversification
Marketability and liquidity
Investment accounting with statements and cost basis
Dividend reinvestment
Government regulatory oversight
Access to markets and sectors historically unavailable
Cash management and dollar-cost averaging
Small purchases through shares
Etc.

Index funds—Offered directly by the fund company itself. You will buy shares of their index fund at the end of the close of the market on a trading day after your money arrives at the company and is processed. As you know, an index fund involves extraordinarily little management. You should look for index funds offered by large, well-known fund companies. Since these large index funds are not actively managed, the fees should remain low. This is a case for "larger is better".

We will need to not only be concerned with the size of the fund and its expense ratio but also the index or sector it is following. Index funds are great when it comes to cost, but in down markets, they tend to be overly sensitive to volatility, since they are "all in." Owning these funds makes it even more important to plan out your portfolio allocation strategy and manage the risk level.

An index fund follows a selected index and will mirror that index by holding the same securities in the same weighting. So a Dow Jones 30 industrial index fund would, of course, track the Dow Jones industrial index, which tracks 30 stocks. Your index fund would mirror the same stocks and the same weightings of its index.

There are thousands of indexes and, thus, funds that follow them, so be careful to understand the index that your fund is following. Does your index fund allocate and weight the securities in the index fund at the same percentages as its index? Or, does it weight the holding differently? In the index fund, if there are liquidation requests from investors, and they cannot be matched with new buyers, the fund must sell a cross-section of securities to provide the needed cash. Rebalancing back to the original weightings is called "index reconstruction."

These transactions can cause the fund to have additional expenses for each security sold. So not only are there trading expenses to meet liquidations but additionally, administrative costs, salaries for staff and traders, rent, utilities--not to mention spreads on the bid price and the asking price. The fund must also hold some cash on the sidelines to meet future liquidations and avoid internal trading, this is referred to as "cash drag, slightly reducing performance when the market rises.

Internal-trading costs and not investing the cash reserves, plus the fund expense, can cause the fund to underperform its index. For these reasons, the ETF's popularity is rising. As we will learn, the ETF is superior to the fund when it comes to lower costs and expenses, as well as providing more transparency and more tax efficiency.

For indexes the funds will follow, here's a list and description, provided by our government, at http://www.sec.gov/answers/indices.htm

Market Indices

A market index fund tracks the performance of a specific "basket" of stocks considered to represent a market or sector of the US stock market or other economies. Think of it as a sports crowd performing the "Wave", all together as a sequence. When the index is up or down the index fund follows in sequence.

Here are general descriptions of a few major market indices. (The SEC does not regulate the content of these indices and is not endorsing those described here.) You can also find them described on their sponsors' websites and in the available information of the funds that track them.

Dow Jones Industrial Average (DJIA)

The Dow Jones Industrial Average is an index of 30 "blue-chip" stocks of US industrial companies. The index includes a wide range of companies—from financial services companies to computer companies, to retail companies—but excludes transportation and utility companies, which are included in separate indices. Unlike many other indices, the DJIA is not a "weighted" index, meaning it does not take market capitalization into account.

NYSE Composite Index

The NYSE Composite Index tracks the price movements of all common stocks listed on the New York Stock Exchange. The index is "capitalization-weighted," meaning that each stock's weight in the index is proportionate to the stock's market capitalization.

S&P 500 Composite Stock Price Index

The Standard & Poor's 500 Composite Stock Price Index is a capitalization-weighted index of 500 stocks intended to be a representative sample of leading companies in leading industries within the US economy. Stocks in the index are chosen for market size, liquidity, and industry group representation.

Wilshire 5000 Total Market Index (TMWX)

The Wilshire 5000 Total Market Index is intended to measure the performance of the entire US stock market. It contains all US-headquartered equity securities with readily available price data. The index is capitalization weighted.

Russell 2000® Index

The Russell 2000® Index is a capitalization-weighted index designed to measure the performance of the 2,000 smallest publicly traded US companies, based on market capitalization. The index is a subset of the larger Russell 3000® Index.

Nasdaq-100 Index (NDX)

The Nasdaq-100 Index is a "modified capitalization-weighted" index designed to track the performance of the 100 largest and most actively traded non-financial domestic and international securities listed on The Nasdaq Stock Market (Nasdaq). To be included in the index, a stock must have a minimum average daily trading volume of 100,000 shares, generally.

Direct indexing

With zero trading costs to investors, many may choose to create their index, or they may choose to modify the most popular index. It's no surprise that advisers are offering this service to investors. Record-keeping and accounting, however, can be a nightmare.

One risk the investment world would run into if everyone invested in index funds is the limited trading in the market that would soon develop. Since buyers of index funds are passive and only do a "buy-and-hold" pattern, the markets would slow down to a crawl. With few stocks being traded in the market, the index, ETF, and managed funds would be negatively affected, not to mention all other stocks. Prices would drop, limiting activity between the buyer and seller. Overall stock prices would drop significantly, declining to dangerous levels and eliminating liquidity. Value in the overall markets would be crushed. For this reason, we welcome traders buying and selling positions throughout the day, thus setting the share prices for the overall market.

Managed Funds—Here, the management of the fund is particularly important. You buy shares from the fund company itself at the end of each day, even if purchased in a brokerage account. Since you will pay a higher fund expense than the index funds, we expect something in return when paying a higher management fee, such as better performance than a certain index or a similar category of funds.

Some managed funds can employ downside bear-market strategies and change their position immediately, if necessary. They can also buy derivatives to offset and insure against certain negative market movements. For example, a managed bond fund's portfolio could be designed with various flexible bonds to resist loss in value, if interest rates rise. Managed stock funds have their styles and techniques, as well. Thus, we need to know what the manager's mission statement is while managing the fund. What is the expense ratio, and is it worth it? Other parameters include, but are not limited to, performance, risk, objectives, etc.

With managed stock funds, the manager has the flexibility to exclude undesirable stocks within an index and keep the best stocks that meet his or her criteria. The manager can design a custom allocation different than its index and, if successful, outperform the index. The techniques and methods, however, could be the reason the fund underperforms its index, so be careful, be specific, and be selective with a high-fee managed fund. For us, it is the downside protection we are willing to pay more for. A managed fund has much more flexibility to buy, sell, and reallocate, depending on its "fund objective." The managers are given the authority to select certain stocks or bonds and to decide when to buy, sell, and when to hold.

There are a huge number of managed funds, so we will list a few fund categories you will hear about the most.

Money Market Funds—These funds require active management because of the ongoing necessity to seek out and buy new securities as their holdings mature. Investments like Certificates of deposit, ultra-short-term government, and corporate securities.

Bond funds—All variations of maturities, credit rating, and yields are managed to provide scrutiny on buying and holding the very best bonds in the desired market. Unlike stocks, the bond fund does not have a large exchange in which to trade bonds. Also, there are many times more bonds out there than stocks. Bond fund investors tend to forget this important detail.

The benefit of the managed fund is that shareholders have a manager who, if qualified, will have sources of where to not only buy the right bonds but where to sell them. Liquidity can cause individual bonds, and thus bond funds, to run into serious declines in value if the market turns against them. Therefore, although a bond index fund can offer much lower expense ratios, a well-managed bond fund might provide better monitoring of bonds held and liquidity when needed.

If there is a serious downturn in the economy, many of the corporate and municipal bond issuers could run into financial problems causing the bonds they previously issued to be downgraded to lower levels. If this happens, the bonds in the mutual funds could fall in value, and--you guessed it--then the funds' price per share falls.

So, for bonds other than Treasuries, future credit re-evaluations, and thus downgrades, can hurt the existing bondholder. For example, if you have a bond fund that holds an average credit rating of BBB-rated bonds, usually considered the "sweet spot" for investors, you have a nice investment. But if everyone else also believes this, the market could become over-purchased, and a "bond bubble" in the BBB-rated bond market occurs.

One might become concerned, because if there is an economic downturn as we recently witnessed in 2020, or a recession begins, the BBB-rated bond issuers could run into financial concerns and those bonds could be downgraded to, say, single-B. If you own a single individual bond and are not concerned, you wait for the bond to mature and collect your interest along the way. If you own a bond fund mandated to hold only BBB-and-above bonds, the fund manager could be forced to sell the downgraded bonds. Consequently, the manager must sell the old bonds at a loss to follow the fund's mandate, and replace them with higher-priced BBB bonds that survived the reassessment of their credit rating. Bonds from large companies that have been downgraded are better known as "Fallen Angles".

So, in this hypothetical example, the manager sold BBB bonds that lost value, only to buy new BBB bonds at a premium. Therefore, we recommend you consider higher-rated bonds for the index funds and use managed funds for the lower credit-rated, higher-risk bonds. It's hoped the bond manager can avoid holding bonds that might be downgraded and protect the shareholders from undue losses.

Stock Funds—Again, there are more funds than we could list here. When an index fund fails to meet your needs, the managed fund can allow you to enter areas of the market that you would otherwise feel unqualified to enter by yourself--areas that require "boots on the ground," like digital currency, emerging markets, foreign bonds, etc.

You can also invest in funds that specialize in alternative investment securities and methods. Alternative investment funds (AIFs) might include areas outside the standard total market index or S&P 500. These include funds like energy, real estate, metals, preferred stock, convertible bonds, and so on. You can even invest in funds that use derivatives, calls, puts, and various other trading methodologies. By using the managed fund in these categories, you are afforded the benefit of letting an expert make the trades, reducing your likelihood of making "novice mistakes." A few of these funds include:

Market-Neutral Funds—These funds hold high-quality stocks the managers believe will do well in upcoming months, at the same time shorting (beating on the downside) other stocks they feel will do poorly.

Multicurrency Strategy Funds—The managers invest in different currencies to capitalize on their relative strength.

Long/Short Funds—These operate very similarly to market-neutral funds, the difference being that long/short funds heavily utilize derivatives to balance their positions. These funds maintain an ongoing effort to stay one step ahead of the market in either direction.

Long/Short Credit Funds—these funds operate similarly to the long/short funds in that they are used to buy and hold fixed-income assets, like bonds, that are expected to do well in the future; they are also used to bet against those bonds that are expected to do poorly.

Non-Traditional Bond Funds—these funds have very few constraints. The manager is given a broad latitude to move from one area of the market to another, whereas other funds have strict guidelines and rules. Be careful, however; we have seldom witnessed success in these long/short or non-traditional funds since they involve high fund fees and bets on the future that don't consistently pan out.

Tax-Efficient Funds—this type of fund is used to manage the portfolio for gain, also managing the tax consequences for the investors, at the same time. They sell some positions that are up at the same time possibly offsetting the capital gains taxes by selling some positions that are down. All this activity is not cheap, however, so the funds' historical performance and other parameters must make the expense worth it.

In specific areas like technology, emerging markets, real estate, and other high-risk and very complex markets, many investors prefer a manager who can travel to the headquarters of the company and confirm that they exist, that they are building the products they claim they are manufacturing, etc.

Take technology, for example, just a handful of tech companies may dominate the market at any given time. Would it be more profitable to hold shares of a large tech index, or to find a managed fund where only the most profitable and most innovative companies are screened, selected, and managed by experts in the field?

For now, there are more custom-managed funds available that might meet your individualized needs since managed funds have been around forever. They are quickly losing ground, however, to the multitude of ETFs coming out every day. As you will learn, conversely, the old managed funds, and even the index ETFs, are becoming less dominant, and the passively managed and actively managed exchange-traded funds are becoming more popular.

Caution is advised, however. We have seen some actively managed ETFs with expense ratios higher than the average managed fund. So why use a managed fund vs. an ETF fund? Well, for a custom design. We have witnessed managed funds holding up during severe market corrections better than index funds. It took us a few years to figure out why! It is like a punchline to a joke: Why did the managed fund do better than the index fund in a market correction? The answer: Because the managed fund is not an index fund--meaning that it does not involve owning the same positions as the index, and thus dodged a bullet. Now, the opposite could be true if the positions in the managed fund dropped more than the index, but you get the picture. If you do not like the averages as offered by an index, a managed fund might be for you.

Remember how we learned about fixed-income bonds which can be relatively illiquid when sold individually because there is no central bond exchange? The problem is even more pronounced with municipals, junk bonds, and senior floating-rate securities. For this reason, there is value in having a team of portfolio managers selecting the purchase and sale of selected bond-related securities inside the fund.

All this activity, however, costs the shareholders the internal trading costs, as well as potential taxes from internal gains, even if you reinvest those gains, so beware. Shareholders might accept the fact that a managed fund has various management activities that might cost more to manage. They must also ask why an index mutual fund charges slightly higher fund fees than an ETF of the same holding. Well, consider the workload of an index fund or managed mutual fund compared with the exchange-traded fund, when you buy those shares. We predict that the old-style "mutual fund" will not exist in ten years because of this workload.

Buying the traditional no-load index or managed mutual fund

First, you decide to buy shares of a managed or index mutual fund, which was created by the fund company itself with its own "startup" money.

Next, you send your money via the computer to your brokerage account to make the purchase. Alternatively, you can buy directly from the fund company, but you are limited to their funds only.

The "behind-the-scenes" process when you buy shares

When buying directly from the fund company or through your brokerage account, they must do the following:

- Document the receipt of your funds.
- Wait until the end of the trading day to calculate the value of the shares you wish to buy.
- Calculate the number of shares your money can buy.
- Create an account or transaction for you in the registration title you wish, all the while copying or scanning and documenting everything.
- Track the activity and document everything in the account--from reinvested dividends, lump-sum distributions, to year-end 1099's, etc.
- Mail you a prospectus of the fund you purchased and update you with any changes to the fund when required by law.
- Send you your first, as well as all future, monthly or quarterly statements.
- Mail you a year-end statement that consolidates all the activity your account participated in throughout the year.
- Create a phone bank to answer any questions you or your adviser might have, regarding the fund.
- Go out into the open market and purchase additional securities representing your added money and the shares you purchased, after receiving your money and issuing your shares. (This all creates additional trading costs.)

The reverse is true if you choose to sell your shares back to the fund company. If the fund lacks new buyers wanting to buy your shares, and if they lack the necessary cash reserves to buy those shares, they must sell securities within the fund to create cash. This not only causes more trading expense and potential losses on the securities sold, for all investors; this might also create unwanted capital gains taxes for other shareholders who own part of the securities being sold to give you cash. Even new investors who just purchased shares of the fund you are selling could be responsible for paying capital gains tax on gains of old shares. If you buy shares through your brokerage account, the fund company must send all this information to that account.

To appreciate what the fund must do when a large group of shareholders wants to cash in their shares, consider this scenario: Imagine you own a real estate property with several other investors. You collectively paid $100,000 for the property ten years ago, and now the property is worth $500,000. If one of the owners wants their money from the investment, the other owners have the following options to let that one owner out of the partnership: They can buy the shares of the selling partner with their cash or with a loan.

If, however, the other owners don't want to buy the selling partner's ownership (shares), the only other option the remaining shareholders have is to find another investor to buy the selling partner out. If they can't find an investor or the cash to buy the selling partner out, the only other option the remaining shareholders have is to sell the entire property outright. By doing this, all the shareholders, including the selling partner, are entitled to the cash, and they are required to pay capital gains taxes. Even if all the shareholders reinvest and buy shares of other properties, they still pay taxes. (For an exception to this, see 1031 exchanges.)

So, when a mutual fund--even an index fund--needs to sell internal securities to create cash, everyone pays. In the case of a managed fund that buys and sells frequently, the same tax liability occurs unless the shares are held in a retirement account; there, the tax liabilities will only be deferred.

This "phantom gain" for new purchasers raises their cost basis so that when they sell the shares, they will have already paid taxes on the gain; but tell that to a new shareholder who is hit with capital gains taxes from six months ago on shares they purchased one week ago! The message here is to watch out for a fund's internal turnover, year-end sales, and excessive investor liquidations requiring internal sales of securities.

Again, when securities are sold with gains, the fund is required to distribute nearly all those gains to shareholders. Even though most shareholders reinvest the proceeds and buy additional shares, this practice does not avoid the capital gain tax owed, come tax time. Exceptions are funds held in tax-deferred or Roth accounts.

If the fund is successful at performing in the manner you desire, there will be taxable gains as a result of the managers' buying and selling activities. Just remember, the capital gains taxes you are paying are not charged twice. By paying taxes as you go, you are reducing future capital gains taxes. You might be asking yourself how you could have accumulated substantial profits on a managed fund and yet end up owing little in taxes when selling. This is because when you sell shares, you may have already paid the taxes over the past several years by way of the previous capital gain distributions. A passive and tax-efficient fund, on the other hand, has avoided internal buying and selling and, thus, little or no capital gains taxes. When the day comes to sell shares, all gains are taxable all at once, since you have not paid taxes on the deferred gains. So be careful of what you wish for.

Like everything in financial planning, there are other sides to this argument. Although the passive fund will suffer much greater deferred capital gains taxes, it will have had less "drainage" from paying taxes over the years. Thus, there is more chance of accumulated gains.

Better yet, if you were holding the shares for your beneficiary, no taxes at all will be due if you die and leave the shares to him or her. This is called the "step-up in basis," meaning there are no capital gains taxes on non-retirement equity assets like stocks, real estate, businesses, and other similar investments, upon the death of the original owner.

Managed funds can run up large transaction fees, administrative costs, bid/asked spreads and missteps, when trying to time the market, so choose them wisely, since most ultimately underperform their index over the long run.

The takeaway here is that managed funds are more expensive; but like a new car with additional options, if you want or need those options, purchase the fund, and utilize the fund's unique structure.

Exchange-Traded Funds (ETFs)—Originally structured like an index fund, the ETF can be bought and sold during the trading day, or what is referred to as "intraday trading," just like stocks. ETFs have five structures: open-ended funds, unit investment trusts (UITs), grantor trusts, limited partnerships, and exchange-traded notes.

You'll have all the traditional stock and bond fund categories, sectors, and indexes to choose from that were originally offered in the form of an index and managed mutual funds, but now in the form of a daily traded exchange-traded fund. We will review the various ETF fund choices in upcoming sections. For now, however, we need to understand how an ETF is constructed, how it operates, and how it trades.

You will buy your ETF shares directly through your brokerage firm where you hold your account. If you have an adviser, he or she will choose a brokerage firm where your account will be established-- firms like Fidelity, TD Ameritrade, Schwab, etc. You will grant your adviser a "limited power of attorney," allowing them the ability to buy, sell, and allocate within your portfolio based on fiduciary standards and your best interests.

The buy-and-hold practice of ETF shares, like low-cost index funds, will pay off in the long run. For managed funds, however, the costs are much higher. Expenses like trading spreads and other risks add to the cost.

With ETFs, you are no longer purchasing shares from the company that creates the fund; you are buying and selling shares from another investor or market maker. Your brokerage account will track your transactions and provide you a statement.

Some of the ways the brokerage firm makes internal profits include spreads earned when you buy and sell securities, earnings on your cash account, fees the funds pay them to be on the trading list, and even the sale of your information to high-frequency traders. The brokerage company that holds your account can also actually lend your securities to others for its internal profit. They may even charge you an "inactivity fee" if you don't trade. You can expect the brokerage company to send you a consolidated brokerage statement and year-end tax records.

Regarding the funds in these brokerage accounts and their disclosure of internal assets: The regularly managed and unmanaged index mutual funds can hide their current internal investment positions for up to four months before reporting them. They must disclose holdings in quarterly reports due every ninety days plus 30 days extensions. The ETF, however, lists what it holds on the fund's website daily, making it much more transparent. Watch for the new ETF registrations coming out that will allow for the "nontransparent" ETF. These funds are also referred to as ANTs, aka actively non-transparent.

More specifically, the ETF website lists what it holds in its "redemption basket" every 15 seconds. This allows for a real-time net asset value (NAV) or (INAV) intraday net asset value assessment of the shares to be published; this disclosure is no longer required, but many funds will post it. The securities in this basket are what the fund distributes to the authorized participant (market maker) who will ultimately attempt to regulate the pricing of the ETF in hopes of avoiding radical differences between the share price and the assets inside it.

The authorized participant must deal with the capital gains taxes while exchanging shares for securities, and vice versa. The fund can choose to distribute to the authorized participant those securities which have the highest pre-tax gains and reduce the tax exposure to the fund's shareholders. ANTs (active non-transparent funds) don't disclose their holdings and methodologies; however, they work identically to standard ETFs.

As we have learned, managed and index mutual funds, on the other hand, are only required to disclose their holdings every quarter, and with that additional 30 days allowed. So, these funds can tend to drift away from their original targets for as long as 120 days without public disclosure. This tendency is known as "style drift," which can change the intended allocations and confuse the investor.

How to buy ETF shares

You can purchase exchange-traded funds, ETFs (and other exchange-traded products--ETPs) using various techniques like limit orders, stop-loss orders, selling short, using margin, etc.

These ETFs usually have much lower management fund expenses--as low as .02 percent, with an average high of around .35 percent. One must, however, be careful not to assume they are lower in cost. We have seen some ETFs show expense ratios as high as 1.4 percent, Yikes! Don't assume anything; do your homework. Remember, free is not always free. There are brokerage firms that will let you buy ETFs for no trading costs; some ETFs might have no expense ratio altogether. These are just loss leaders for the company to get you in the door. Use them wisely, and you will be the one to profit, not them.

ETFs are most likely the wave of the future. Tracking desired indexes while charging extremely low fund fees is becoming a favorite style of investing for many portfolio managers and their clients. Don't, however, assume the fund is an index fund with low fees. As we mentioned, more and more, these days, ETFs are being managed and charging high fees. Be careful to understand what you are getting into. Now let us review the parameters and create a list of the fund elements that meet our guidelines when buying shares.

Elements and questions like:

- How long has this ETF been in existence?
- How large is the fund? Will shares trade if we need to sell?
- Is the company sponsoring the ETF well-established?
- What is the total expense ratio (TER)?
- What is the fund's trading volume?
- What is the price difference between internal securities and share price? Do the shares sell at a discount or premium?
- What is the spread between the bid and ask price?
- What is the index or sector the fund follows?

- What securities does the fund hold?

- What are the allocations of the fund?

- What are the strategies the fund follows?

- What is the yield?

- What is the tracking error or difference between the fund and its index? If the fund is an index fund, you would expect it to mirror the index, minus the expense ratio.

- Is the fund leveraged, meaning does it take on debt?

Fixed-income securities (bonds) have difficulty dealing with pricing and lack liquidity. Unlike stocks, they don't trade on various exchanges. Therefore, many investors buy bond ETFs instead of individual bonds. This is because the fund shares might sell more often than the internal bonds they hold, providing greater liquidity. Remember, not all bonds will have buyers or markets for immediate liquidity, so look at what is held by the fund, and consider liquidity.

Believe it or not, some ETFs fail to gain the assets needed to cover the costs of running the fund. ETF closures happen regularly. There is no risk of loss to the investor, however, since the fund will sell off the internal securities and produce cash in place of the shares, send you the money, and close the fund. The downside to delisting is the potential deferred capital gains the investor might owe.

Remember, funds with large portfolios are likely profitable enough to stay in business. ETFs issued by large investment companies are likely to gain the investor dollars and size needed to stay in business. The minimum-assets amount under management for a fund to survive is approximately $100 million unless underwritten by a larger company. A fund with a favorable ranking in its category will likely do well in popularity and grow to the minimum size needed.

So how are these new ETF funds formed? Authorized participants (APs) are a major part of the ETF construction and operations. AP's provide the needed creation and liquidity. When a company wants to create a new ETF or generate more shares, they turn to the AP's.

It's the job of the AP to acquire the securities that the ETF manager wants to hold. So, if an ETF manager wants to create a stock index fund, the AP will buy the same stocks in the same allocations as desired. The ETF sponsor exchanges shares of the fund with the AP for the desired securities. The AP holds additional stocks in inventory and increases or decreases the holding as the fund needs change. The ETF fund provider gets the stocks it needs to track the index, and the AP gains the same value in the underlying ETF shares, which it can resell for a slight profit. The individual stocks are held in trust.

Let us review the process: The ETF company designs and markets the fund, all the while receiving its management fee based on assets in the fund. It relies on the authorized participant to receive the investor's cash, buy the securities, and exchange them with the fund for fund shares. The ETF will hold the shares in a separate trust account. One minor risk exists, however, known as "step-away risk." If the AP steps away from offering to buy or sell shares or securities, the liquidity of the ETF could be jeopardized.

This is like the following scenario: Let's say you are a real estate property manager and wanted to create a large apartment building investment that other people would own, but that you would manage and earn a living from. You might advertise the investment program and create interest. Since you are not a real estate broker, you would turn to brokers to accept the investors' money and buy the property. Once purchased, the brokers could also help you and the investors sell apartments when needed.

Just like our authorized participant, the property managers might even buy a few apartments themselves to keep the interest up and maintain a fair market value. They, in turn, earn a very small markup or markdown fee, but they keep things moving while allowing you to manage the complex and earn your fee. The actual process is different, but this gives us the idea.

Most popular funds have several APs. An AP's ability to create and sell shares helps to keep the ETF price at a fair level. Usually, the more APs, the more stable the share price.

The authorized participants are designated by the ETF creator. They have exclusive rights to change the supply of the ETF shares on the market and can create shares when needed. They can also redeem shares when the need arises by buying shares from the issuer and selling them on the open market.

So, what does it take to "start your own ETF"? Beyond the SEC registrations and legalities, you just start with a minimum base investment of only $2,500,000 (plus tens of thousands of dollars in startup cost), offering an opening of 100,000 shares valued at $25.00 each. So immediately, you must find that associated participant to supply the needed securities, a market maker to get them to the public, and broker/dealer for the buyer/seller to trade them. Rules and minimum capital requirements, however, are coming down due to the new "ETF Rule" passed recently.

Like a stock, the ETF's price will fluctuate during the trading day based on simply "supply and demand." So, the ETF's share price can rise above or fall below the actual securities it holds. When confronted with this concern, the authorized participant can step in. The AP might buy up underlying shares of an ETF and then sell them on the open market to bring the price of the share in line with a fair value of its underlying securities--while, in turn, earning a risk-free arbitrage profit.

If the ETF share value drops below the market value of the securities it holds, the AP can buy additional shares of the ETF that are undervalued, driving the price back to a fairer value--once again making a profit. This arbitrage effect helps keep the ETF in line with its underlying securities.

Without this ability, investments like closed-end funds are not in balance with the share price. The shares frequently trade for substantial premiums or discounts to the actual securities in the fund.

Similarly, one concern about a thinly traded ETF share is that the spread between the bid and ask price can be significant, and also the shares can sell at a premium or discount since they lack demand and multiple APs.

This is a reason many day traders fail. They buy high risk, thinly traded stocks, and ETFs which maintain large spreads. Remember, when you buy, you pay a higher price; when you sell, you get a lower price. Thus, spreads can be the biggest reason these traders fail. Do not forget, the managed funds also pay these trading costs. You do not see them, since they are internal expenses and most investors don't take the time to research them, but they are there. When you buy or sell a regular mutual fund, at the end of each day, if spreads still exist, the fund and other shareholders absorb the cost.

Within ETFs, the internal trading costs are born by the AP's. So we should be looking for more favorable statistics, such as average spreads, average trading volume, and minimal premiums or discounts to the fair value of the securities vs the fund's share price. Make sure the shares trade regularly, your targeted index is specific to your desired need, and of course, as we already discussed, the expense ratio of the fund is in line with the market. Also, as we previously discussed, a fund needs to grow to at least $100 million to stay in business. If it falls short, internal operating costs could cause the fund to close. Therefore, keep an eye on the size of the fund and its growth process. We call these funds "zombie funds," since they are near death.

Let's look at our newfound "freedom to trade" in the open market. Rather than buying shares from a mutual fund company where the existing shareholders help subsidize the cost of new securities, the internal trading expenses and taxes on trades of the ETF are born by the AP. This makes sense since they make money on the spreads of the ETF share price.

The real fun begins with your ability to buy and sell ETF shares throughout the trading day. The ETF shares trade like individual securities. In fact, on your brokerage statement, they will be listed as equities or individual securities even if they are a bond ETF. Let us learn about the various and sometimes dangerous trading options available:

Market Order—This order executes immediately at whatever price the market demands; it is the best price at the moment. For this type of trade, speed takes precedence over price. This is no problem for high volume ETFs but can be disastrous for low-trading-volume ETF funds.

Your shares will trade at the best market order or most recent offer to buy them.

Limit Orders—You set a maximum or minimum price at which you are willing to buy or sell a security. We stress the use of limit orders on all trades placed.

Stop Order—A market order that only triggers if the security--ETF, in our example--hits a desired price. Hence the word "stop." The sell stop order is sometimes referred to as a "stop-loss." You can, however, lose money on a bad execution. The stop price is not your trading price. It's just a trigger. When the trade activates, it becomes a "market order."

Stop Limit Order—When the price of an ETF hits the stop price, the trade is activated and is executed as a limit order. It won't fill until it reaches the limit-target price or better.

You will not need these complex orders if you are trading large liquid ETFs with high trading volume and low trading spreads. We highly recommend you learn all there is to know before venturing out into this area of trading. Make sure you are confident with the trades you make and the positions you hold.

We have all heard the story of the adviser who placed a stop-loss order on a very conservative ETF. During a "flash crash," the shares dropped 50 percent, the price at which the shares finally sold. By the end of the day, the share price consequently rebounded to only a 3 percent loss, but the adviser's order sold out at a 50-percent loss before the price recovered. This could have been avoided by creating a limit order. Statistically, spreads tend to be wider in the early morning hours of a trading session. So do your homework or rely only on an experienced adviser.

Borrowing to buy Securities

Buying on margin, buying leveraged funds, and other trading techniques can create more pain than gain if you are not an expert, so be careful. Borrowing money to buy something that can dramatically fluctuate magnifies the risk. Buying leveraged funds is the same thing, but they do the borrowing for you inside the funds. The results are the same: If things go up, you make more; but if they crash, you lose much more. Also, there may be time limits.

Three levels of ETF liquidity

Level one: The buyer and seller are matched on the secondary market. A market maker publishes quotes in real-time that represent the price and number of ETF shares it is willing to buy and sell. The best prices in this publication are known as the National Best Bid and Offer (NBBO) quotations. The difference between the bid and offer (also known as "the ask"), is known as "the spread." You'll buy at the asked price and sell at the bid. The market maker gets the difference or spread.

Level two: Most ETF market makers will publish quotes beyond the NBBO, helping to provide more activity.

Level three: Primary Markets. Creation and redemption activities are utilized. When demand for ETF shares exceeds supply, a creation action ensures that there are enough securities and new shares of the ETF to fill an investor's order. As we have learned, firms authorized to purchase securities to create more ETF shares are known as the authorized participants. It assembles a portfolio of new securities so that the new ETF shares can be created and sold to new investors. The reverse is done when shares need to be sold.

If the ETF shares become overpriced or underpriced, a fund has built-in mechanisms that will attempt to realign the share price to the underlying assets in the fund, the net asset value (NAV). This is not a guarantee, however. We have seen very legitimate funds with very respected companies that had spreads as high as 10 percent, simply because either the fund shares represent securities that are not traded as frequently as others, or there is fear in the market.

Small-cap ETFs might have a large spread, whereas highly traded S&P 500 shares might have no spread at all! Thus, if trading often, try to stay with funds with narrow spreads, and if you are a buy-and-hold investor, do not worry about the spread; plan long term for overall gain. Buying or selling at the end of a trading day might help you with a more stable price, regarding share vs. the internal securities and price spreads.

ETF taxes–It goes without saying that when you sell your shares of an ETF outside of a retirement fund (where the taxable gain is delayed and taxed as ordinary income when distributed), the gains are taxed as short- or long-term capital gains. So why are ETFs so much more tax-efficient than regular mutual funds? As we discovered previously, selling your shares is done outside of the ETF fund itself.

Consider this example: Say a group of people want to travel somewhere together. They rent a bus and plan out their trip. Because they are in a group (like a mutual fund) they travel in one direction together. If one person (shareholder) wants to get off the bus, they must stop the bus. This is like when a fund is required to sell internal securities to provide cash for liquidations. When the bus stops, everyone stops. When the fund sells internal securities everyone is responsible for their share of the taxes, even if they re-invest the proceeds.

An example of the ETF goes like this. Imagine a group of people get together and want to travel to the same location together. Instead of going together on the same bus, they rent several tiny electric one-person cars. They all drive together in the same direction to the same destination. Only, in this example, if one person wants to stop to go to the bathroom, the other riders can continue their trip without disruption. So, the ETF owner owns his or her shares independent from the other fund shareholders. If the ETF owner wants to get out, he or she simply sell the shares to another investor or back to the market maker, also known as the authorized participant.

You sell your shares to another investor or the authorized participant the same way you would sell an individual security. This way, the other investors in the ETF fund have no tax impact unless they sell their shares at a gain or loss in the open market. To review the process: When you sell your shares back to your mutual fund, the fund can give you cash from new investors to the fund, use its cash reserve to buy your shares back or, as we mentioned, "sell across the board," causing other shareholders to potentially receive taxable gains. Even if the mutual fund has enough cash to buy your shares, investors frequently complain that this practice prevents the fund from being "fully invested," thus producing fewer gains in a rising market.

Also, since most ETFs track an index, they seldom do buy or sell transactions for the fund unless the index provider announces a change in holdings. If the ETF is passively managed by tracking more than one index, there will be internal trading to rebalance the positions that can occasionally create minimal internal capital gains. The ETF can, however, pass along low-cost-basis securities to the AP and avoid capital gains tax altogether. This is done by trading stocks from the ETF to the AP, hence tax efficient.

Fixed-income ETFs, however, have a frequent turnover of the internal bonds since they mature over time, and new bonds must be purchased. Capital gains taxes may not be a problem, but trading costs and spreads can cause the overall cost to rise slightly.

We forget that the ETF, like a mutual fund, may pay out dividends it has earned from the stocks and/or bonds held in the fund. The ETF will also have "cash drag" during the period between when the time the ETF receives a dividend and when it distributes those dividends to shareholders. ETF managers will temporarily reinvest those dividends in cash in preparation for paying out the dividend, which can slightly dilute the upside gain.

These dividends from the ETF fund, when paid out, are usually taxed as ordinary income to the shareholder since they typically represent an interest or dividend income earned by the fund. These dividends then go to a brokerage cash account, or they can be reinvested back into the fund, depending upon the type of brokerage account you have. Funds that are not tax-efficient should be held inside your retirement accounts.

Funds outside a tax-deferred account should ultimately be low yielding, low-turnover, tax-efficient, and/or tax-free municipal bond ETFs.

One technique an ETF can use to create additional income for the fund is to lend out the internal securities (stocks) to institutional investors. We have learned brokerage firms do this with investors stocks inside brokerage accounts for their profit. The difference here is that the ETF does it for the benefit of its shareholders. The borrower of the stock must put up collateral to cover the loan of securities while he or she takes possession and sells them in the open market. Next, the borrower hopes the shares will fall in price, allowing a repurchase of those same shares at a lower price.

This harvesting of the price difference and returning of the original shares to the lender allows the borrower a profit. If the share goes up, however, the borrower is in trouble and must draw from his or her reserves to make up the difference. Either way, the lending ETF fund receives income from the loan, allowing it to purchase additional securities inside that same ETF and thus make a profit for the shareholders. The only risk here involves where the collateral for the loan is held. If, say, the collateral was held with Lehman Brothers back in 2008, it might have put the fund in jeopardy, but this risk is exceedingly small.

To recap, when looking at ETFs beyond the basics, you should consider market liquidity, average spreads, average trading volume, and premiums or discounts. (Does the ETF share trade close to its net asset value, the value of the internal securities?) Be careful with new funds, small funds, leveraged funds, and funds with high fees. Remember to diversify among funds and fund companies, who knows when the next "Black Swan event," pandemic or big crash will occur.

Exchange-Traded Notes (ETNs)—The main difference between ETNs and ETFs is that the ETNs are unsecured debt instruments and ETFs represent ownership in companies. ETNs can be held until maturity or sold in the open market. This risk with the ETN could be 100 percent if the issuer goes out of business. Remember the demise of Lehman Brothers in the 2008 financial crisis? Many of the ETN's they issued stopped trading, resulting in losses to investors of up to 92 percent! We do not recommend you invest in any unsecured assets in any form at all. Let us leave those investments to the day traders, speculators, and rich investors who can afford a full loss of principal.

Leveraged and Inverse ETFs—Not recommended. The new market of exchange-traded funds offers investors the option to trade in funds, rather than just individual securities. This reduces the loss of individual positions falling in price since the funds usually hold several positions. An additional risk, however, exists when the ETF is used to purchase securities with your money but is also allowed to borrow money to buy more securities. Like buying on margin, if the market goes up, ETF managers pay back the loan and keep the profits for shareholders.

If the market crashes and when the loans come due, they lose substantially more than you would have if you had purchased a non-leveraged fund. Inverse leveraged funds use overly complex and complicated methods of gambling. They primarily use derivatives to profit when the market declines. These complex investment tools can not only be expensive; if the market does not go in the right direction within a certain period, they can expire and cause greater losses than just owning the asset. If the market does not decline and goes up, large problems will arise.

Internal parameters for all classes of funds (Index fund, exchange-traded fund, and managed mutual fund data using Morningstar's fund analysis software)

Ok, regardless of which fund structure you decide on, here are a variety of parameters you might consider when screening your funds. As you have read, we suggest diversifying among all types of funds and companies. Here is where we start. Think of these elements as the fund's "periodic table" of factors & parameters:

Investment's historical performance—we will need to know what the historical performance of the fund is concerning other funds in its category.

Investment's ranking—we will need to know how the fund has historically ranked compared with other funds in its category and, if managed, whether this fund has exhibited better or worse management skills in the past.

Investment's historical standard deviation—Think of this parameter as a side profile of a roller coaster: What do the historical ups and downs average out to? Knowing how the fund has performed in bad times is as important as in good times. Past performance and volatility are no guarantee for the future, but it gives us an idea of how the fund performed historically in comparison to its category and various indexes through the ups and downs. This is a "rolling" average.

Risk Metrics: Investment's historical Beta, Alpha, R-squared, Sharpe ratio, and Sortino ratio–These individual analyses and rankings give us a view of how the fund is structured compared with other funds and indexes during different time frames.

Beta–This is a relative-risk comparison to an index, usually the S&P 500. The index has a numerical valuation of 1.0; your fund is compared to this index. If your fund has 50 percent less risk, it will show a valuation of .50 in the report. This will help you determine whether your fund meets your needs. A lower beta than the index and better return would be the desired outcome. If your fund has higher risk levels and lower returns, you might become unsatisfied. It is no surprise that a fund with a higher beta than the market might have higher returns in an upmarket, but in a down market, would fall further. This higher risk level is called the "risk premium": more risk, more return.

There is a factor called "BAB," which stands for "betting against beta". You go "long" (buy and hold) on low beta stocks and "short" (sell) on high beta stocks. Do not forget, these very interesting concepts are great when looking to the past, but there is no guarantee they will be "right on" in the future. They give us a "range of comfort" while creating a portfolio, as though we can count on our creation behaving as it did in the past; but make no mistake, the future is unknown.

Alpha–Alpha measures an investment's return over its beta-adjusted benchmark, an indication of how your fund has performed compared with other funds with the same beta risk levels. Funds that specialize in specific sectors of the economy might add alpha to a portfolio because they are negatively correlated to the overall market. A real estate investment stock fund might add alpha to the portfolio by being different from the overall stock market and providing balance in a declining market. When the overall market declines or underperforms, the real estate fund might hold its share price and add strength. Its high dividend income might also help a portfolio to lessen its losses in a declining market and increase its return in a rising market.

There is a downside to these high alpha funds, however. If their specific sector and class of assets fall on hard times, you can forget about the extra performance. 2008 proved we cannot always count on negatively correlated funds holding their values. Alpha is the average return over an index. So, if alpha is based on a benchmark, is there even such a thing as true alpha? There might just be a difference to an index that makes a fund have more or less alpha. The academic literature calls this a "joint hypothesis" problem, and the search for alpha is the same as the testing for market efficiency. Therefore, if a portfolio manager creates alpha relative to a benchmark by making bets that deviate from that benchmark, by creating alpha, she is doing nothing more than gambling.

R-squared– (R^2) is a statistical measure used for investment analysis and research that investors can use to determine a particular investment's correlation with (similarity to) a given benchmark. ... R-squared reflects the percentage of a fund's movements that can be explained by movements in its benchmark index. A portfolio with a well-diversified and conservative allocation might have an R-squared of 80+, in which case it is hoped it would hold up well if the overall stock market declines, since it would not move in 100% the same way.

Sharpe ratio–This indicates the fund's risk/reward ratio relative to other funds in its category. Funds with a high Sharpe ratio appeal to conservative investors in retirement. An attempt to gain the best risk/reward strategy is hoped to offer a reasonable upside risk and less downside loss. This is a "risk vs reward" calculation.

Treynor ratio–Similar to the Sharpe ratio but uses beta as the risk measure. Beta is a measure of systematic risk. Treynor ratio makes more sense when analyzing a balanced fund or diversified fund--the reason being that the unsystematic risk is reduced due to diversification. For undiversified funds like sector funds, the Sharpe ratio must be used since the fund is exposed to both systematic and unsystematic risk. The higher the ratio, the better it is.

Sortino ratio–This uses downside risk (downside deviation) in determining a fund's risk compared with the market. This strange-sounding parameter analyzes a fund's Sharpe ratio with a focus on the downside performance of a fund. So here, we are interested in the best risk/reward performance concerning a declining market.

Additional Considerations:

Economic moat concept–Developed by Warren Buffett to define companies, as he explains, that have a sustainable and competitive edge over their competitors. This would include stocks like Coke, Procter & Gamble, and Microsoft. These companies deal with competitors every day but secure their position by having a strong brand.

Investment's historical upside and downside capture ratio–These results will indicate how much of the upside and downside of the market the fund has captured over various time frames, compared with its category. For managed funds, this is where you can determine whether the higher fee has been worth it. Did the fund reduce the loss on the way down and/or make more on the way up, when compared with its category of other funds?

Fund turnover ratio (internal trading activities)–This explains how active the fund is at buying and selling various securities inside the fund. High-turnover funds tend to charge higher management fees, and low- to no-turnover funds would, conversely, be expected to charge significantly lower management fees. Index funds seldom have turnover, other than an index allocation change. Managed funds are known for turnover while following strategic management activities and methods that require trading. Exchange-traded funds can be passively allocated with occasional reallocations.

Beware of funds that track an index by holding the same positions as that index but charge a large management fee. What is the point of a fund like that? You might as well buy an index fund with extremely low expenses. Not that turnover is even a good thing, but at least you know what you are getting.

That said, there are, however, a handful of managed funds with high turnover that have beaten their index over the years while charging higher fees. Again, the cost is only an issue if you are not getting something in exchange, so do your research. Is the fund rated high within its category? Good. Has its performance been acceptable? OK. Does the fund give you the exposure you might otherwise have avoided? That is reasonable. A fund's turnover (buying and selling) adds cost to the fund through the cost of trading and spreads. These internal costs, as well as the fund's management fee, can be very costly, so select your high-fee managed funds very carefully.

Remember, the more the trades, the more the internal trading expenses, with transaction costs and spreads. Capital gains or losses can occur when a managed fund reallocates its internal positions. These transactions can also cause you to owe capital gains taxes when you least expect it, even if you are a new investor. If the fund sells appreciated securities at the end of the year, when you just invested, you might get a 1099 for the gains, even though you did not experience any! High turnover equals unexpected taxes and trading costs. Make sure it is worth it.

Fund's total assets held—The total assets held in the funds and total shares held by investors is important to know when an investor wishes to sell shares, either back to the fund company or in the open market. If the fund is small, especially with an ETF, the spreads of the share price could be exceptionally large. The securities in the fund and the size or trading volume of the fund will determine the spreads. Compare their markup in price to a corner specialty store that has exceptionally low sales (trading volume). Their markups must be higher since they do less volume to cover their cost.

Fund's expense ratio compared with its category—What the fund charges as an expense will affect Its net performance. It is important to know what the costs are and determine if the performance, fund structure, and category should justify the fee.

ETF funds' current spreads–As we have learned, this is the difference between what you pay for the ETF shares and what someone will pay you when you sell. With thinly traded ETFs, this spread can cost you as much as 10 percent, even more in bad markets. Therefore, look for heavily traded funds unless you intend to buy and hold for long periods.

ETF fund's premium vs. discounted share price–An ETF is expected to sell for the same value as its internal securities. There are brief periods that, before the day ends, the share price might be greater or less than its internal assets. The authorized participant and market makers are tasked with buying or selling shares to correct the difference.

Fund's tracking error–This will tell you how close or distant the fund follows a designated index.

Time-series momentum–Examines the trend of an asset concerning its past performance. This differs from "cross-sectional momentum," which compares the asset to the performance of other asset classes and indexes.

Fund's performance compared with its index–Although the reason we might choose some funds is that they are not "the index," it's important to know how the fund's performance is, compared with that index, to decide whether the expenses of the fund give value or not.

Manager tenure–with managed funds, the longer the manager's tenure, the better it is, since the long-term performance of the fund can be attributed to the manager managing the investments. If a manager is new, the fund's past performance will have less value in assessing the new manager.

Managers ownership participation–any fund that depends on a manager(s) should be of such value and quality that those managers should invest their own money in it. Morningstar will list the amounts that each manager has invested in the fund they manage.

Fund's bond duration & credit ratings–these are the most important parameters of a fund that holds bonds. The duration calculation tells us how much the bonds in the fund should rise or fall in value if interest rates rise or fall. Duration does not necessarily relate to the bond's maturity, but to how many years it will take to grow to full value. We can understand this parameter by thinking of a zero-coupon bond:

Remember the old E bonds our parents purchased when we were children? Say you buy an E bond for $50 that will mature for the full value of $100. The question is, when will your $50 grow to $100? The answer lies not in when the bond matures, but in how much the bond earns. If it earns 3.5 percent, it will take 20 years to grow from $50 to $100; thus, this bond has a duration of 20 years. If, however, you could earn 7 percent, the time it would take to double in value would be just ten years. Therefore, the duration is less with the bond that earns a higher yield or has a short time until maturity. If interest rates rise, the bond with the lower yield will drop more in value than the higher-yielding bond. A bond with less time until maturity will drop less in value if interest rates rise.

An illustration to think of is that of the side profile of a teeter-totter swing--the one where one child sits on one end of a long, flat board, and the other child sits on the other end. There is a fulcrum in the middle. When one end goes up, the other goes down.

With our example above, think of this image representing the low-end being interest rates and the opposite high end representing long-term bond values. When the Fed raises interest rates, the resale value of the old long-term bonds goes down. If you want less risk of interest rates rising, you move to the middle of the bond's maturity length (imagine a teeter-totter), which would represent intermediate-term bonds; there's even less risk as you move closer to the fulcrum with short-term bonds. Being closer to the fulcrum, they have less yield, but also less loss potential if rates rise.

The credit rating of the bonds tells us how strong the ratings are of the issuer and, thus, the bonds. Rising interest rates can harm the bonds in the fund if they are sold before maturity. Falling credit ratings of the bonds can cause investors to get nervous, thus also reducing the bond's value if sold before maturity.

Remember, there is no bond exchange like stocks. You must find your buyer. For lower-rated bonds, it could be difficult finding a buyer if the market falls. Institutions are not allowed to own them, so a bond bubble could be very harmful to a bond's value if the market collapses. (This type of scenario is called a "bond-pocalypse.") The opposite is true if confidence goes up and interest rates fall.

Fund's yearly yield vs. SEC yield–This gives the last year's total trailing yield of the fund, compared with the SEC yield which gives an annual yield but based on the last 30 days' share price. If the fund's share price had risen in the last 30 days, the fund's overall SEC yield would show a smaller return than the yearly number. The reverse might be true if the yield payout stays the same, but the share price dropped.

Diversification–You will hear throughout this book, and others, the importance of diversifying among several areas when investing. US vs. foreign, large vs. small companies, value vs. growth, stocks vs. bonds, etc. When investing within funds, you will have several basic asset classes to choose from in which to create your diversified portfolio.

A fund's capital gains exposure–This information lets you know how much potential appreciation and gains exist within the fund.

Internal fund asset classes to choose from:

Warning! You may never fully understand every class category or sector. There is just too much information to analyze. Therefore, we need to understand the individual fund, its parameters, and history. You do, however, need to understand the various areas the holdings originated from. Let's take a look:

Cash

Bank Savings & Certificates of Deposits

Money market Funds:

T-Bills, corporate, and municipal short-term debt.

Stocks:

US equities, foreign & global
Developed foreign markets, emerging foreign markets,
Sectors such as oil, gold, utilities, solar, real estate, preferred and commodities
Within these classes, there are several smaller groups of similar securities to refine your allocations. Let's look at some of them:

US Equity Classes:

US large-cap stocks:
US large-cap growth stocks
US large-cap value stocks

US mid-cap stocks:
US mid-cap growth stocks
US mid-cap value stocks

US small-cap stocks:
US small-cap growth stocks
US small-cap value stocks

Foreign Equity Classes:

Foreign Stocks (developed countries):
Foreign large-cap growth stocks
Foreign large-cap value stocks

Foreign small-cap stocks:
Foreign small-cap growth stocks
Foreign small-cap value stocks

Emerging markets stocks:
Emerging markets value stocks
Emerging markets growth stocks

Global real estate (REIT's)
Pacific Rim/Asia stocks
China Region stocks
Japan stocks

Latin America stocks
Europe stocks

Bonds:

Government, Corporate, Municipal, international and emerging markets

Taxable Bonds:

Government bonds
Short-term government bonds
Intermediate-term government bonds
Long term government bonds
Treasury inflation-protected securities (TIPS)
Bank loan
Emerging markets bonds
Non-traditional bonds
Convertible bonds
Corporate bonds
Multisector bond
High yield bonds

Tax-free Bonds:

Municipal Bonds:
Short municipal bonds
Intermediate municipal Bonds
Long-term municipal bonds
National Municipal Bonds
State Specific Municipal Bonds
Florida Municipal Bonds
Massachusetts Municipal Bonds
California Municipal Bonds
Minnesota Municipal Bonds
New Jersey Municipal Bonds
New York Municipal Bonds
Ohio Municipal Bonds
Pennsylvania Municipal Bonds

Commodity Asset Classes:

Broad basket commodities
Agriculture
Precious metals
Energy

(Within these categories are gold, silver, oil, natural gas, wheat, and coffee)

Your portfolio should be diversified among several different asset classes and categories. By diversifying, you will never be gambling on one asset area. Your diversified approach lets you avoid being in the wrong place at the wrong time. Remember, it is better to dilute your return slightly by over-diversifying than concentrating all your assets on one investment, running the risk of the total loss.

By being properly diversified among these classes and categories, there is also the possibility you will have a part of your portfolio in the winner's circle from time to time without taking excessive risk.

Market Sectors—Sectors are pieces of asset classes and investment categories. Sectors are extremely specific areas of the market, in which an investor can concentrate their holdings. Rather than risking money on one stock within a sector, an investor can reduce the risk by purchasing a sector ETF or sector index fund. This fund holds several stocks in that sector. Here, they run the risk of the market turning against them but lessen the risk of a total loss. Investing primarily in sectors is a gambler's game, however. Sectors should be utilized to balance, diversify, and hedge certain risks in the portfolio.

We recommend no more than 5 percent of a portfolio's assets in any one sector. That sector should either offer high income, market hedging, or negative correlation to the other holdings in the portfolio. Okay, you might just feel like gambling a little...Buying contrary to that sector's current pricing might allow you to purchase a share price that might rebound in value; but remember, there is no guarantee. Trying to trade sector funds will give you more diversification than an individual stock, but the price volatility can still be very great.

Here is a list of the various sectors you have available in the market today:

Energy
Natural resources & metals
Health
Biotech
Financials
Technology
Defensive
Cyclical
Utilities
Agriculture
Miscellaneous sector
Multi-alternative
Consumers
Communications
Real estate (REITs)
Currency
Bear market
Leverage
Managed futures
Inverse
Leveraged
Volatility (VIX)
Short equity
Ultra-short bond

More sector ETFs are being developed every day, so be careful and do your homework. Monitor liquidity, spreads, discounts, trading volume, and fund expenses.

Investing in sectors outright is nothing more than speculating, and as we have learned in past markets, very risky. Sectors do, as we have learned, offer the portfolio balance and hedging. For example, gold, commodities, and currency hedging can help a portfolio survive bear markets. They act as insurance.

It's wise when investing, to resist the voices in your head that urge you to "time the market." Remember, the markets are always fairly and efficiently priced. If there is a sector you like, and you think it's a good buy, think again, and determine whether it's priced where it should be in the moment. If, however, you like the fact that your desired sector is down, and you accept the reason it is down, make the purchase. Sectors often drop significantly, and if you understand the risk and decide to be a bottom fisher, you might very well succeed. But remember, it is a big risk and could be a very long-term commitment.

Here are some reasonable gambles with sectors: You want to increase your portfolio's yields, so when Utilities, Preferred Stocks, Oil, REITs, or even certain bond sectors drop significantly, that might be an opportunity to capture higher income for the long term. If your timing is off, at least you have the income and will buy more on the way down, using the reinvestment option. But remember, you are buying yield, not price. If, however, the price does go up, you will have a decision to make. Should you cash in? What if the market of that sector corrects, and the price falls? Just remember, the "consolation prize" is the yield, not the bragging rights!

Thematic Funds—A kind of mutual fund that invests across the sectors related to a common theme. Unlike sector funds, the thematic funds are more diversified since the investments are concentrated in several sectors. These funds are more volatile and riskier than the broad market, but relatively less risky than the sector funds. Some themes might include block-chain technology, digital currency, cannabis, environmental and social consciousness, video gaming, pet stores, etc. New themes and funds are being created every day.

Broad Market Parameters

Positively correlated assets

Positively correlated assets mirror the market, moving up and down almost identically. If you want to track an index, you will look for an index fund with a low tracking error to make sure the fund is following the index.

Negatively correlated assets

Negatively Correlated Assets move in the opposite direction of the overall market. For example, if a security had a correlation coefficient of -1.0 as compared with its index, when the index rises by 5 percent, the security might *fall* by 5 percent.

Negative Correlation is like the term "sheer strength" in the building trade. It gives strength to the left, to the right, upward directions, and downward directions, because its construction and strengths go in different and opposite directions.

So, stocks would have a very great difference or high negative correlation to, say, bonds. If stocks rise, bonds might fall, and vice versa. Owning many different investment funds that hold different indexes or managed securities gives us more downside strength.

Non-correlated assets

non-correlated assets do not correlate with the market. Assets like Gold & Cash have no similarity and move in their own directions, usually opposite to the market. Investors will hold these assets to hedge their other investments.

A country's long-term economic growth potential

When looking at international and foreign funds, we must be aware of the different currencies of various countries. A country's gross domestic product is the total value of goods and services produced in one year. If a country expects production to fall, investors will move their money out of the market, and stocks will fall. If, however, that country is doing so well and its economy is rapidly expanding, its government might tighten the money supply by raising interest rates. This would be done to reduce the chances people spend, buy, and invest too aggressively, causing prices to rise and inflation to increase. This would cause the value of its currency to rise. When the currency rises, other countries' stocks and currencies can fall--a vicious cycle!

Investing in income-producing funds

When interest rates are expected to rise, investments that are known for their high-dividend yields suffer and fall in value. When the resale value drops on a stock or bond, the new buyer gets it for a lower price. Unless the dividend drops, the investor, who bought the asset for a lower price, gets the same amount of cash dividend and is getting a higher yield relative to his or her lower purchase price.

During the early 1980s, interest rates skyrocketed; long-term US government bonds dropped 14 percent in net asset value, but intermediate-term US government bonds dropped 7 percent. If you reinvested your yield (dollar-cost averaging), the damage was minimal because you bought cheap shares and built your portfolio, but if you spent the dividends, your loss was permanent. The opposite is true if rates go down. Thus, when buying income-producing stocks and bonds, you need to hedge your bets with diversification in not only the types of investments but parameters, as well.

Dynamic factors (value vs. growth funds)

Except for the last ten years, value stocks (stocks with low prices compared with their fundamentals) have historically outperformed growth stocks (stocks with high prices relative to their respective fundamentals). In the short term, however, growth stocks can perform very well, comparatively, if, at the time, they are following a trend of popularity and upward momentum. Since trends can be short-lived, we suggest diversification among the different classes of stock funds.

Can the stock market keep going up over time?

People are always asking whether the market can keep going up. Our short answer is yes! Not just a short-lived rebound after a significant drop in the market otherwise referred to as a "dead cat bounce". Over the next 50 years, we are certain of that. But what about the next five years? That's anyone's guess. For the next 50 years, however, if the world's population is expanding, there will be new consumers of the corporations and small businesses' goods and services. Companies will figure out more ways to reduce the cost of production and maximize profits. Thus, stock prices will probably rise.

This all sounds draconian when an expanding economy depends on increases in the population to create more consumers and workers-- not to mention the future drawback to overpopulation. That is a whole different issue.

One tiny little crumb of optimism: investment companies now offer investment funds that specify environmental, social, and governance (ESG) criteria. This is just another way Wall Street is fabricating products for the public. The good news is that we can invest in those funds that invest in causes we believe in, thus making a change for the future.

Remember, stocks are for growth, bonds are for savings, cash is for emergencies. If you were Warren Buffett, you would not need bonds. If you are a retiree who might need to withdraw income or even liquidate for a health emergency, cash and bonds would look very appealing when the stock market crashes, and you need money.

Over the long term, however, a cross-section of stock funds will usually provide a good inflation hedge. As we have mentioned, this is because the stocks in your funds represent the companies whose products and services are going up in price, due to inflation. Short term, however, the stock markets will fall as a result of fears that the Fed will combat inflation by raising interest rates, making the stocks look less attractive.

Decades from now, stocks will likely be up in value, but in the short-term, you'll need to plan your allocations to deal with uncertainties. Index funds tend to be a better choice for the long-term objectives, but managed funds can be developed to outperform on the way down. Thus, the dilemma: index vs. managed.

An index fund or managed fund?

So back to the question: Should I hold an index fund or a managed fund? Well, as we have expressed, if we could put you in a 50-year time machine, you would do much better with an index fund with the lowest expense ratio. This is because of fund expenses matter. However, within the next ten years, we might need the specialization of a managed fund to help reduce the downside of a declining market. A bond-savvy manager provides a critical service by managing the bond maturities in a managed bond fund. This type of manager might also opt to buy interest futures and utilize other management techniques to help protect us on the downside if interest rates go up.

A fund manager who specializes in selecting stocks in emerging countries might be making a safer choice than an index fund because the manager would have the flexibility to go visit the companies. This activity can confirm the company exists and that products are being produced. Simply buying the index might not offer a clear view of the risks involved with that asset class. Also, some managers have been successful in simply selecting the best 50 stocks within an index. This way, they avoid the losers and hold the winners.

Granted, there are admittingly very few managed funds worth their high fees; but if you locate the ones that are, it will be worth your time. Do your homework, and you might find one that does what you want. If you do not believe in management, simply seek out several low-cost index funds, and allocate your portfolio accordingly.

Now that we have such a large selection of exchange-traded funds and index mutual funds, you have the freedom of investing in specific areas of the market while maintaining diversification within the fund.

Semi-managed index funds are being created for this ETF market. They follow a few indexes with a certain allocation--say, four different indexes, each equaling a one-quarter percent of the fund's allocation. When the allocation changes, due to the market change, they promise to manage the fund by rebalancing back to the original percentages.

Although index-mimicking funds are great for long-term passive investors, they have a secret most investors do not consider.

When a publicly-reporting index removes one stock for another stock, the index fund must mimic the index by making the updated allocations. This means getting rid of one stock and buying the new one. By the time the news is out, the stock that will be removed from the index becomes vulnerable to a price decline, for obvious reasons. Thus, your index fund sells the stock at a reduced price. Ultimately, you lose money on the way out, due to falling prices, trading costs, and spreads.

Now the index fund must buy the replacement stock which most likely has risen, all based on the news it will be added to the index. When added to the index, the sheer volume and demand will most likely cause the stock to rise above its previous value. This results in the index fund paying a premium to buy shares, additional trading expenses, and greater spreads. Thus, you lose on the way out and lose on the way in.

One other obscure, off-the-wall analogy regarding an index fund: If everyone just bought index funds for a "buy & hold" objective, the markets would crash! Just kidding but think about it. If everyone bought and held their investments, there would be no buyers or sellers once everyone is fully invested. There would be no prices upon which to calculate your current value, resulting in a lack of liquidity, which would shut down the markets. So, you see, even if we don't trade often, we need others to do so.

In the long run, however, the lower expense ratio and low trading costs will more than make up for this temporary concern. Lower-cost semi-managed index ETF funds are coming. So do your homework! Be aware of the term "closet indexing." This describes a scenario in which a fund charges a high management fee while simply holding index ETFs inside the portfolio. In this case, you would be charged for management when, in fact, the fund manager is simply tracking an index.

Modern portfolio theory

Now that we have learned what to look for when analyzing individual funds, let us start preparing to analyze your old portfolio. We'll need to determine if you should hold your old portfolio as is or re-create a new one. We need to make sure all the parameters line up. Things like allocation of funds, portfolio expenses, historical risk, historical performance, portfolio beta, Sharpe ratio, standard deviation, and alpha need to meet your current needs. We need to know if all these parameters are aligned.

Let's start with portfolio-allocation theories that allow us to allocate your positions with the best assumptions of how good and bad markets might affect you so that you will "survive to retire another day."

Warren Buffett may be our hero when it comes to selecting and holding on to individual stocks--or in his case, buying the whole company. He doesn't like bonds because he has plenty of money, and no matter how bad equities (stocks) get, he'll just wait it out. When you are relying on selling off bits and pieces of your portfolio for retirement-income stability, that is a whole different matter. You must hold non-performing and low-performing investments like cash and bonds. These assets help us stabilize the portfolio and provide a source of assets that can be liquidated with little or no loss.

Harry Markowitz won a Nobel Prize in Economic Sciences. His studies in risk, return, correlation, and diversification are known as the Modern Portfolio Theory or MPT. This is the basis of the "efficient frontier."

The efficient frontier theory shows a portfolio's expected return and the level of risk associated with withholding it. This analysis is an arch which gently slopes upward and drifts to the right. It shows how lower risk provides less long-term returns when compared with higher-risk assets that show the highest return. The objective is to go as high as possible while avoiding the right side--the maximum level of risk--on the chart.

It is all about asset allocation. Unless you want to accept the maximum risk of a stock index, your challenge is to determine which funds to add to your portfolio. Too much cash will bring down the return considerably but will reduce risk. Or, you could add other negatively correlated funds you hope will reduce the downside risk and maybe provide good returns. Be careful, however. In 2008, 2020 investors held real estate stocks (REITs) to offset the overall stock market index. Since real estate has a history of negative correlation to the overall market, it seemed to be a good play. As we found out, though, real estate stocks dropped even more than the overall total market stock index.

So, asset allocation remains a very personal decision. Of course, every person wants to avoid loss in a crash. With this fear, he or she may avoid risk and hold only cash in the future, only to lose to inflation over the long run. That said, investors who gamble with liquidity and lack of diversification could find it very damaging in another crash when they need to sell additional shares to meet their income needs.

When allocating your portfolio, add up all the funds and percentages in the portfolio, run the data through computer analysis, and come up with the historical numbers representing the worst years, best years, historical level of volatility, and all the parameters explained in this book. Past results are no promise or indication of future expectations, but you get the idea.

Asset allocation is a guessing game. You are mixing up a variety of assets. You will most likely never beat an "all in" index since you have different asset classes and categories. With this allocation, however, our goal is to avoid large declines like a single index or area of the market. The old concept of "buy and hold" can evolve into a "HODL" (hold on for dear life) situation if you don't allocate based on your risk tolerance and monitor the status and appropriateness of every fund in the portfolio.

Here are a few examples of allocations:

- Conservative: 20 percent stocks and 80 percent cash and bonds
- Moderately conservative: 40 percent stocks and 60 percent cash and bonds
- Moderate: 60 percent stocks and 40 percent cash and bonds
- Aggressive: 80 percent stocks and 20 percent cash and bonds

This is just an example; your allocation must be determined by completing all the necessary financial diagnostics to determine the needed liquidity, volatility, and risk levels you can tolerate. No investment is going to guarantee everything; therefore, it is up to you or your adviser to attempt to build portfolios that, in theory, meet your needs.

Investing for Investing's Sake!

Trying to time the market seldom works out. Instead, we suggest that you plan out your present and future cash needs. Develop a time frame for when you might need cash and/or income in future years and invest accordingly.

Other parts of your portfolio, however, might be earmarked for inflation protection. This is the risk, and most likely, the probability that things will be more expensive in the future, so what better way to beat the rising costs of goods and services than buying stocks in those companies that control future prices.

Here are the very basics: Hypothetically, let's say you only have cash, bonds, and stocks to invest with, and you can't combine them. Index funds, ETFs, and mutual funds do not exist yet. Where would you place each of these investment vehicles in your plan for short-term liquidity needs, intermediate-term horizons, and long-term investing? Let us look at some examples:

Short term: Cash—In case of an emergency, the funds will be there when you need them, without loss or decline in value.

Intermediate-term: Bonds—Yes, they can fall in value if interest rates rise or the credit quality is called into question. Bond funds, along with their reinvested dividends, may take some" bruising" but will lessen the likelihood of losses, compared with how stocks would perform if liquidated in a down market. They might act as a savings investment to pay off a mortgage or buy a home.

Long term: Stocks--Although they will fluctuate and drop significantly in a bear market, in the long run, the average returns of stocks over time have always beaten the other two investments. Equities, meaning stocks, are the only asset among these three that will give you inflation protection over the long run. This time frame is usually for long-term accumulation for retirement.

Fortunately, you have thousands of funds to choose from that will do the work of choosing and allocating the various stocks, bonds, and cash instruments for you.

Your only concern now is where to place the various funds. You will need to know how to allocate them within your portfolio and how to assess the various parameters.

Investing for Inflation

We have all heard the cries that inflation will erode our future retirement nest egg. When public spending gets out of control, demand increases, and so do prices. When money is easily accessed through consumer loans and home-equity loans, unwise investors borrow money to purchase perishable assets like new cars, vacations, furniture, etc.

A population out of control, along with reasonable employment statistics and excess money lying around, can lead to inflation (uncontrolled price increases). Like an eating binge or alcoholic binge, the party comes to a screeching halt and crashes. To avoid this, the Federal Reserve has the option of raising short-term interest rates that it charges banks on money who in turn lend it to borrowers.

In the long run, however, it's a good idea to own equities (ownership in companies, businesses, real estate, etc.). As populations grow, the demand increases for goods and services. As we have learned, the company, through improved efficiency, can maintain and even increase its profits year over year. With this increase in earnings, investors take note and are willing to pay more for the business through purchasing shares of its stock. So, for the long run investments, investment funds that hold equities help us keep pace with inflation.

The short-term inflation scare is a whole different animal! If the Fed is forced into action and raises interest rates (or the investment community believes it will do so), the markets will be affected. Usually, what will happen is that bonds will immediately drop in value relative to their credit quality and maturity range. The longer the maturity, the greater the decline in inverse value (duration risk), if interest rates rise. Income-producing equities like utility stocks, preferred stocks, blue-chip stocks, and income-producing real estate will all be adversely affected.

So where can you invest in inflation protection? Long term, in stocks, real estate, and businesses; short term in cash and gold. The only pure short-term inflation hedge we have found is high-quality, very short-term Treasury bills. They are safe and will increase in yield over time if rates rise. Other options like oil and gold have gained popularity in times of fear, but over the long term, tend to be very unreliable.

Our advice is to "plan for the worst and enjoy the best of times." Stay with your long-term plan, but have funds in the short-term bucket, since you never know when a correction, bear market, recession, inflationary cycle, or crash will occur. Timing the market is very unwise because no one we know has ever been able to consistently predict where things will be in the future. Therefore, keep inflation in your plans, but stay the course by investing in the short term as well as the long term.

Let's look at the construction of your portfolio by utilizing a combination of prescreened funds.

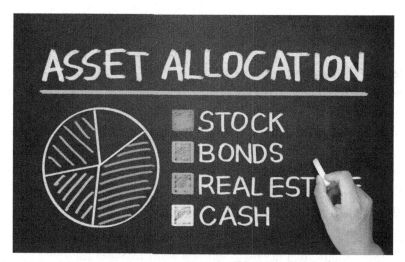

Portfolio Parameters (A combination of all fund's parameters averaged throughout the portfolio)

We need to see how all the funds affect the "sum totals" of the portfolio--the combined expense ratio, number of securities in the portfolio, asset allocations, diversification of individual securities, funds, and companies, etc.

For purposes of analyzing an old, existing, or proposed portfolio, we will need to know all the details. The objective is to monitor the parameters concerning the investor's existing and changing needs for liquidity, income, and risk tolerance. Listed below are the areas you will need to know and monitor. These parameters are with the combined numbers, not for just one fund but a combination of all the funds. We need to know what the averages are to determine if the portfolio stays within your desired ranges.

Asset allocations, sector weightings, and cash balances—It is important to have an idea of how your portfolio is allocated, how much is invested in stocks, bonds, or cash. Most retired investors are looking to create a portfolio that will survive the downturns of the market. Think of this as an "all-weather" portfolio: one that drops less than the market and remains available for income liquidation. It gets much deeper than this. Do you own stocks inside the United States or abroad? Are they concentrated in one area of the market, or are they diversified? What percentage of your holdings are in stocks, bonds, cash, etc.?

Total securities inside the portfolio—The primary purpose of owning investment funds within a portfolio is to reduce the risk of owning too much of any one area of the market. Our plan is not to beat the market on the way up, but to reduce the loss on the way down. The combined amount of stocks, bonds, and cash-related securities among all the various funds in the portfolio is important. One fund might hold up to a hundred securities, but with many different funds, your portfolio should hold thousands.

Think about this: A physician's credo is "do no harm"; ours is "lose no shares." Values will fluctuate, but we want to avoid total loss of the portfolio to bankruptcy because of the risk of individual stocks going into bankruptcy and individual bonds going into default. If the portfolio owns a combined ten thousand stocks and bonds, the bankruptcy of just one stock might not even be noticed.

Equity & fixed-income style-box ratios—It is important to know where your stocks and bonds in the portfolio are from. What percentage of stock holdings are with large companies vs. small? What percentage are dividend stocks, and what percentage are more growth-oriented? With the bonds, what percentage have long-term maturities vs. intermediate-term and short-term? What is the average credit rating of the bonds, etc.?

Historical three-month, one-year, three-year, five-year, and ten-year performances—We need to know how the portfolio has performed during various time frames. How did the portfolio perform compared with the overall stock market and its category? If you hold a balance of stock funds and bond funds, did you perform better in down markets and understandably less in up markets?

Best/worst periods for three months, one year, three years— We must know how your portfolio reacted to down markets as well as up markets. How much more or less were you down when the market was down? Was the level of diversification worth the lower return? We call this "back testing." Even if you have not owned your portfolio for the same time frame analyzed, we can get some idea of the past performance--which is no guarantee for the future, but it's a starting point.

The total number of funds in the portfolio—By listing the number of funds and their names, we will have an idea of how many funds and fund companies we are working with. This is important, to avoid harm if one fund company were to run into trouble. Having several different types of funds can help us avoid having too much allocation in any one stock, index, or management style.

Risk/Reward scatterplot—This chart indicates how the portfolio is placed on a chart compared with the S&P 500. A rectangular box chart showing your portfolio's left-to-right risk level and vertical placement indicating return. As far left and as high as possible is desired.

Historical 3-year, 5-year, and 10-year Standard Deviation—Historical portfolio volatility over the specified time frames.

Modern portfolio statistics of the portfolio for risk metrics (beta, alpha, and R-squared)

Beta— (risk related to the overall market) With a large group of investment funds in the portfolio, we need to know what the combined market-risk level is. With the portfolio's beta level calculation, you can reallocate the proposed portfolio to match the desired levels of risk. We do this by adding or reducing stock funds vs. cash and bond funds.

Alpha—Indicates the portfolio's average performance over time, compared with other portfolios with the same beta levels. We would like to create portfolio holding funds with a history of better performance than other funds with similar beta levels. Alpha can be misunderstood or misrepresented, however; because if a fund inside the portfolio is the same as its index, there could be no alpha--and even negative returns--representing its expense ratio.

So, shopping for alpha means looking for something different, and with a lower expense ratio, than others in its category. Alpha is more about

118

noncorrelation to the index or category, which might be beneficial to the averages and your portfolio's allocations.

R-squared— (R^2) is a statistical measure used for investment analysis and research that investors can use to determine a particular investment's correlation with (similarity to) a given benchmark. R-squared reflects the percentage of a fund's movements that can be explained by movements in its benchmark index.

Valuations using multiples—A process that consists of:

- Identifying comparable assets (the peer group) and obtaining market values for these assets.

- Converting these market values into standardized values relative to a key statistic since the absolute prices cannot be compared. This process of standardizing creates valuation multiples.

- Applying the valuation multiple to the key statistic of the asset being valued, controlling for any differences between asset and the peer group that might affect the multiple.

Geographic average capitalization—Measures the average size of a fund's US and non-US stock holdings

Combined yields—Combines and averages the weighted-dividend cash distributions of all the funds with the total portfolio.

Combined funds' expense ratio–Combining all the funds' expenses and dividing by the number of funds and fund weightings gives us the average portfolio fund expense.

Additional account and planning concerns:

Portfolio account registration–Making sure your portfolio is not only designed to meet your individual needs but is titled in the proper registration. If you have a family trust, the question to ask is whether the investment should be held in the name of the trust, or as an individual, joint tenancy, etc.

Check beneficiary designations—There are various ways to pass the account & portfolio on to beneficiaries. Retirement accounts usually cannot be owned by a trust, so a beneficiary provision is an important feature used to assure the control and direction of the proceeds. For non-retirement accounts, however, a trust can be the owner. Other pass-through provisions can be selected, however. These titles range from "transfer upon death" (TOD), joint tenants with right of survivorship, tenants in common, community property, etc.

Track mandatory retirement plan distribution after age 72 (reserve assets for liquidation, etc.)–When you reach the age of 72, a yearly distribution will be required by your retirement fund. Selling off shares of an asset that is down substantially could cause unnecessary losses. These losses can dramatically shorten the lifespan of an investment intended for future income. Planning and reserving assets in stable funds provide the cash when needed, regardless of market conditions.

Stay in constant contact with your adviser and/or tax adviser- any distributions from retirement plans are taxable and will affect your total taxable income and Medicare premiums. In non-retirement plans, reallocating funds can create capital gains tax if you exchange one fund for another, so plan.

Buying on Margin—Borrowing money to invest in the unknown and unpredictable markets is for gamblers, sophisticated traders, and hedge fund managers. Although one can make a case for leveraging into an investment you believe will rise in the future, it is not something to take lightly, and we do not encourage this level of risk.

Imagine if you purchased a rental property with a bank loan that was not only at a high rate of interest, but the loan might also mature in a year. Also, if the property dropped in value, you would be required to add more money to the loan. Buying on margin with securities is similar. If the value of the security drops beyond certain margin levels, you would be required to deposit more money to protect the lender, since the security is the collateral. If it drops, and you sell at a loss, your losses are multiplied.

Post Diagnostics & Punch List:

After diving into the planning process yourself or meeting with the adviser, you will have assessed your finances. You will also have assessed your estate-planning concerns, insurance needs, tax status, investments, and portfolios, using the diagnostic process. You will need to do a follow-up on all discoveries and recommendations and develop a to-do list; we call this "the punch list."

If doing this process by yourself, you need to dig deep and make sure you do not miss anything. Spend time to watch online videos to get ideas of what you might be missing when making your list. Remember, advice you get online is generic and not intended to apply to you, be careful; you are just looking for ideas.

Below are listed some of the topics that might be provided by an adviser, either verbally or in writing. The punch list provided is simply a list of concerns that might require your immediate attention.

Of course, if you own businesses, employee stock options, and more complex investments, you will not simply receive a list of items. With these and other considerations, a very in-depth review, discovery, and written analysis is required. A fully processed financial plan like that can cost you up to $10,000. If you spot those complicated and advanced concerns, you should go much deeper and most likely bring your CPA, insurance agent, and estate-planning attorney into the conversation. For example: how to deal with the tax concerns of depreciated real estate properties when you plan to sell them; how to obtain favorable tax benefits on employee stock held inside a company retirement plan to mention a few. For some large estates, asset-protection concepts that only a qualified estate-planning attorney can counsel you on will need attention.

For now, however, let's look at your very simple punch list.

Punch list items:

✓ **Increase your cash reserve**: Short-term emergencies occur and will need cash.

✓ **Purchase disability and/or long-term care insurance**: Many investors do not insure for short-term or long-term disability. How will you pay your ongoing bills if you are out of work or if you incur home health care bills of over, say, $10,000 per month?

✓ **Purchase or cancel life insurance as needed**: If you are lacking assets to protect your loved ones, life insurance can be a good short-term solution. If you are older and no longer require the coverage, you might reduce your monthly expenses by dropping the policy. You can even access the cash in the policy to buy long-term-care coverage, in some cases transferring it without taxes. Many retirees simply cash out old life insurance cash value and take the family on vacation to celebrate the fact they never died.

✓ **Purchase umbrella liability policies where needed:** With lawsuits entering the millions of dollars when someone is injured or killed in an auto accident, your maximum liability coverage is critical. Most auto policies only go up to $500,000. An umbrella policy can be purchased to extend that coverage up into the millions on your auto, home, and personal activities.

✓ **Use excess cash reserves for the home inspection and safety repairs:** Retirees frequently retire in the home they have owned for decades. The home is not only humble, but a risk to their safety if the electrical and gas supplies to the home fail. Other risks can be reduced with handrails, eliminating trip hazards, emergency alarms to request help when needed, etc.)

✓ **Review or establish wills, durable power of attorney, trust, etc.**: As time goes by, the need for these documents can increase. You need to review each document and make sure your current wishes and needs are the same as when you originally made them.

✓ **Have your trust and legal document reviewed by an attorney:** Even though you have reviewed your legal documents and trust, we suggest you pay an attorney for a review every decade or so.

✓ **Re-register certain assets in the name of the trust:** We frequently see people who have established a trust document but have not changed the ownership of the appropriate assets to the trust. Thus, if not properly registered, the asset falls back into the "probate" risk.

✓ **Review or change beneficiaries to certain accounts**: You have heard the story of the retiree who had substantial retirement plans and life insurance. When he died, it was discovered that he never changed the beneficiary designation after his divorce decades ago. After his death, his current wife of 20 years had to sit idly by and watch the ex-spouse inherit the assets. Now, she could probably hire an attorney and fight for her share of the retirement funds, but what would that cost her in legal fees? Make the changes while you are alive and save all your loved one's mountains of grief.

✓ **Delete deceased trustee and name a new one when needed**: We usually suggest institutional trustees because they never die and are held to the highest fiduciary standards. So, in your case, what if your trustee dies? Do you have backups, and are they younger than you?

✓ **Maximize retirement plan contributions if still working:** People who are still working should do everything possible to invest in their retirement plans. Roth vs. regular 401k is a question for your tax professional. However, not choosing an employer-supported 401k and contributing to an IRA, instead, could be a big mistake. The reason for this is that the employer is not obligated to match your IRA contributions, whereas they might be with your 401k. Why leave money on the table?

✓ **Reallocate existing retirement plans to appropriate levels:** Your risk tolerances and liquidity needs may change as you approach retirement. If retiring soon, you will no longer be contributing to your retirement plan and will no longer be buying on the way down if the market falls. Thus, reallocating the total amount of funds is critical.

✓ **Replace any high-fee or poorly rated funds or investments:** New lower-cost funds are being offered every day and rating services that are tracking their performance. It is necessary to continue to assess all your investments to make sure you are paying the lowest fees and getting the highest quality.

✓ **Rollover existing plan to a self-directed IRA (SDIRA), if appropriate:** Where appropriate, rolling your existing deferred compensation plan, 401k, or profit-sharing plans might be a good idea. A greater number of funds and companies might be available in your self-directed IRA. More fixed-income fund choices may be needed that are not offered in the old plan.

✓ **Convert a portion of existing IRA/401k to a Roth IRA:** Remember, converting funds from an IRA ends up being taxable, so the timing is everything. If we find that your income is expected to be low this year and higher in later years, converting might be wise. Look, we all want to receive tax-free income at retirement, but at what cost? You must calculate the tax implications of converting now, regarding whatever you think future tax laws might be and whether you will be in a higher tax bracket.

✓ **Set up the proper educational funding plan, 529 plan, etc.:** Whether you are a parent or grandparent, the 529 plan might be a good choice for a long-term, tax-free education-savings plan. You remain in control of the investment decisions and choose the beneficiary. The remaining balance can be used to pay off student loans.

✓ **Pay off or refinance residence and/or rental property:** Everything depends on your situation. Paying off the house could reduce the stress of paying payments and provide more monthly cash flow. However, you give up the cash sitting on the sidelines. To safely pay off the house, you need to make sure it is fully insured and that you plan to die there. This is because if you pay off the mortgage and then develop a need for your cashback, most mortgage companies are not inclined to refinance once you are retired. (Be wary of high-cost reverse mortgages.)

✓ **Replace certain investments found to be flawed:** After analyzing the individual investments, if the risk level, performance, or expense levels are not in acceptable ranges, we would suggest you reposition into another appropriate asset. Any capital appreciation must be considered, however, since even poor investments might have significant gains over the years. For investments outside of retirement plans, the tax implication should be considered. There is a saying in the investment business, however: "You can't go broke taking your profits." So not selling to avoid taxes could be a costly mistake if the market falls in the future.

✓ **Reallocate retirement plans at your workplace, if needed:** employees frequently lose sight of how they are invested in their 401k plans. They allocated to cash or bonds back when the market was in turmoil. They did not determine whether to allocate the assets based on age, risk tolerance, future retirement income needs, etc.

✓ **Visit your accountant to perform a yearly tax estimate:** Your life is ever-changing, and thus your taxes will be as well. Decisions to increase your 401k contributions, pay off your house, or, if already retired, convert to a Roth IRA all need to be contemplated before acting.

✓ **Start your required mandatory retirement distributions:** Calculate when and how much distribution you are required to begin withdrawing.

✓ **Review your intended beneficiaries to your retirement plans:** You will need to make sure the right people are listed, to inherit your assets. We frequently find that the intended beneficiaries are not in line. Someone may have died, or a beneficiary is no longer in a good relationship with the owner, etc.

✓ **Re-evaluate your existing cash reserve:** People tend to have more money in their cash reserve accounts than they need. It's wise to re-evaluate your comfort level. If you have excess cash, we encourage you to either invest in the market for inflation protection, do work on your home, take a vacation, or gift funds to family members or charity.

✓ **Re-evaluate your existing market volatility tolerance:** Knowing how you feel about the market's volatility is important. When the market drops, you need to be confident enough to hold your positions and even buy more. If you become uncomfortable during a downturn in the market, you run the risk of selling out at the bottom. If you are confident with your assets, allocations, and risk tolerance, you are more inclined to hang on and survive in the long term. You need to frequently rethink how you feel about losses. If your risk tolerances change, you will need to reassess your portfolios and reallocate.

✓ **See your Accountant/CPA before selling real estate:** Selling your home or rental should not be done before running the plan past your accountant. Answers will be needed for these questions: Will there be any capital gains on your home sale, beyond your tax exclusion? Will you pay additional capital gains taxes on the depreciation you claimed in prior years on rental property sales, etc.?

✓ **See your Accountant/CPA before converting to Roth IRA:** We mentioned this before, so take the advice this time. The reason for visiting your tax person is to do a tax calculation that determines if a conversion would be wise or whether you should wait until you are in a lower tax bracket. The tax estimate will determine the best course of action.

Considering that every person has different risk tolerances-- liquidity needs, political views, and tax brackets--this list is never-ending in its various issues and concern. So, investigate your life, your future, and plan accordingly.

Post Punch List:

After you develop your to-do list or receive one from an adviser, you will begin your assignment and complete as many items on the list as possible. After all, if you are not properly insured or lack the right legal documents, what is the value in building up your investments? You do not want to hand them over to someone else in a lawsuit, or undesirable relatives after your death. Each of these areas was covered in the diagnostic reviews.

Remember, investing has no value if you ignore the overall financial-planning process. Make sure you complete your "punch list assignment" before focusing solely on your investments.

If you receive recommendations to exchange investments, your adviser will help you do so with your current investment company, if appropriate. However, he or she might recommend that you create a new portfolio to diversify among several well-known investment funds and fund companies. Before selling and repositioning any investment, however, you should check to make sure you are not adversely affected by taxes, early withdrawal penalties, fees, commissions, or cost.

If you wish to work with an adviser, you must meet various requirements. You must be serious about working on and improving your overall financial situation. You must be willing to meet your adviser and provide valuable, and sometimes sensitive information. You must be patient with your investments. All investments beyond guaranteed savings vehicles will fluctuate in value. You must realize that planning and then investing are about reducing losses in bear markets, rather than gambling in bull markets. Therefore, you will never consistently beat the market if you are properly diversified. Well, "never" is a strong word...let us hope to beat the market on the way down. Meaning, most retirement investors are willing to give up some of the upside returns in return for fewer downside losses.

There are no guarantees, but diversifying has proven to reduce the overall risk of a total loss since you are substantially diversified, hopefully, among several securities, funds, and fund companies. You will need to accept the fact that you are slightly diluting their returns in exchange for greater safety from the bankruptcy of stocks and defaults from bonds.

It's important that you understand the process detailed in this book; that you understand it does not end when the diagnostics are complete, and the new investments are made. You must understand the areas and level of risk that comes along with investing. We will continue to educate you in the construction of your portfolios and help you appreciate the downside risk planning, as well as the upside growth potential, all the while keeping an eye on your financial plan.

It's also important you have a clear understanding of the value the financial adviser's administrative staff brings to the table. You'll hopefully understand the extensive efforts they'll do to assist you while setting up your plan.

Although you could simply buy the investments we recommend on your own, we hope you'll understand the value an adviser can bring to the planning process, diagnostic reviews, investor suitability, asset research, and portfolio allocations--just to list just a few.

If, after learning all the steps required before and after investing, you do not see the value of hiring an adviser, we advise you to do the process yourself and save the adviser fee. You have the tools available, both in this book and others.

Most investment companies will be glad to assist you in placing your investments. If you can do the financial planning, insurance, estate planning, and tax planning, as well as understanding the investment and asset-allocation process, you are all set!

If, on the other hand, you want to enjoy your retirement and concentrate on your future activities, not bogged down trying to do your financial planning and monitoring, then having an adviser may be for you. This book will help you know what to expect before, during-- and especially after--the investment process.

To bring you this extensive lineup of services, the adviser incurs substantial expenses for continuing education, certifications, and other expenses, all supported by the fee they charge. These expenses and other costs of doing business while serving you, such as employee salaries, rent, insurances, licenses, all require that the adviser carefully manages his or her time and resources. Your adviser fee should cover asset allocations, financial- and estate planning, trading costs, IRA fees, investment holding platform fees, and ongoing service expenses, etc.

If you decide to hire an adviser:

After completing the required prospective client and adviser reviews, various diagnostics--either verbally or in writing--the adviser is now ready to develop a relationship with you. You will have received either a full financial plan or a "punch list" of those tasks you need to complete along the way. If everything has been reviewed, your adviser will create a new portfolio(s) for your investments. They will make suggestions of various funds and portfolios in which to hold them. After all is done, the relationship begins to take on a new status, one of monitoring your finances and growing your friendship.

If you are an existing adviser:

We suggest you follow this well-thought-out, strategized, and organized process that will help you create and establish a simple financial direction to assist you in organizing and managing your practice. By following and utilizing our process, you will have the ability to "add value" to your clients, not only in the planning process but after the portfolios have been created. Ongoing monitoring, administration of, and supervision of your client's finances will prove your integrity and ongoing value, which any client could appreciate.

Phase II Portfolio Construction

(Reconstructing the Present)

New Portfolio Construction Process:

Reviewing the previous diagnostic analyses, you will have a better idea of your overall risk tolerance, income, and liquidity needs, for now, and for the future. If you use an adviser, he or she will explore your investment philosophy and how you reacted to previous market corrections, bear markets, and expectations of your future investing.

You will learn all the weak spots of your financial situation and have time to correct them. You will have been given time to update your estate-planning documents, correct all investment registrations, beneficiary listings, add or delete the appropriate insurance coverages, etc. You will have analyzed your past investments and determined which ones to hold and which ones should be sold. Now it's time to develop a new portfolio.

Developing that new portfolio is a very serious endeavor. You or your adviser will have the ability to manage and allocate your portfolio but only based on strict criteria. It can be a big mistake to charge forward and just sell everything and start over. This is what many commission-based brokers, insurance salespeople, and even some fee-based advisers will want to do.

Many fee-based advisers will want to liquidate everything and drop your cash into their one-size-fits-all portfolio. Your money buys into a pre-allocated portfolio that every other client with the same risk tolerance will be offered. So, to "fit you in," you'll need to sell all your existing positions to provide the cash to buy all their recommended investments. In an IRA, this creates no tax threat, but doing so may cost you losses as a result of spreads widening from lack of liquidity.

Outside of retirement plans, referred to as "non-qualified" plans, capital gains taxes become a concern. If you have accumulated gains--even if your funds are not that good--exchanging or selling them will still create capital gains, regardless of how great the new funds you want to buy might be. This is also a reason to be wary of the "automatic rebalancing" services.

As we have learned, an individualized investment plan is critical. This is because the one-size-fits-all portfolio could harm you by triggering substantial capital gains taxes, excess trading losses, or early withdrawal penalties. This can happen when your new well-meaning adviser hires an outside portfolio manager. These managers may never even have met you. They allocate the new portfolio based on one overall portfolio that represents your new allocations and everyone else's. They sell everything (triggering your capital gains taxes all in one year) and drop you into a "bucket" portfolio.

Next, as their "outside portfolio manager" determines, they will input a computer buy, sell or exchange order for the portfolio you are in, and instantly, you and everyone else will be magically reallocated into other funds. This is touted as a great service; however, the problem is that it's based on a group trade, not on your situation. As we stated earlier, this can end up triggering taxes, trading losses, and spreads among individual securities. Rebalancing is an individualized process to take place when needed or when needs change, not one size (or trade) fits all.

A thorough review of your liquidity needs and risk tolerance must be revisited throughout the process. You need to make sure you have a generous level of cash reserves that can withstand an emergency of any level and for a long time. What would you do if you were disabled and could not work? What if you got injured and needed home care while recovering? What if a worldwide pandemic caused massive layoffs and unemployment? When you create a portfolio, you are, in effect, creating a financial plan. For example, a young person might start off contributing to their 401k in conservative funds until they build up several funds that could be used in the event of a layoff (significant taxes and penalties would apply if withdrawn), a disability, death, etc.

After accumulating a minimum emergency fund inside of the 401k, this young person now kicks into second gear and starts investing every month in volatile growth funds. These funds are very volatile in the short term, but they can be bought each month while averaging the overall cost. In the long run, however, the growth over time can be incredibly significant.

Remember, if we could place you in a time machine and have you wake up in 50 years, you could invest 100 percent in stocks and probably do just fine. Cash and bonds should only be used to dilute the risk of the portfolio, be used as current income, or be held aside for future investment when the markets are down.

A person depending on withdrawing money from his or her old 401k as his or her only source of income would be overly cautious and nervous about market fluctuations. Many 401k plans lack the variety of conservative funds you might need. For this person, a more diversified portfolio, using cash and bonds to buffer the stock funds, is wise. Also, a staged liquidation plan, using cash in the early years of distribution, then bond funds for the next several years, and stock funds for the long run, can more easily be constructed outside the traditional 401k plan when transferred to a rollover IRA. That is a very crude but good example of how to safely withdraw income from a plan that also needs to invest for growth. Let's break it down even more specifically.

Where to invest your funds up to and through retirement

Each stage is designed to be spent in the time frames indicated. The hope is that the earlier liquidations will avoid losses, and the later stages will have time to grow before they are used for income. This spend-down staging process is used for immediate income needs that will last over time.

Where to invest for future years' distribution needs

- **Year 1** monthly income-distributions allocation might be in a low-yielding cash account and short-term CDs

- **Years 2-3** might be allocated into long-term CDs and money market funds

- **Years 3-5** might be allocated among short-term bonds, floating-rate, and short-term high-yield funds.

- **Years 5-7** might be allocated among intermediate-term bond funds, balanced funds, etc.

- **Years 7-10** might be allocated among equity income funds and total return funds, etc.

- **Year 10-15** might be allocated among all stock-related funds, like growth funds, international funds, other categories, and sectors, rental real estate, etc.

Spend-down process: As long-term needs evolve into short-term needs such as lump-sum liquidations for college, the pay-off of a mortgage, long-term care, etc., allocations must also evolve.

We like to visualize this concept using the analogy of airplane turbulence. When you are high up in the air, the weather is not much of an issue, because the pilot can adjust for the turbulence and stay on track. However, the closer you get to the ground, as you make your descent, turbulence begins to pose more of a risk, since veering off course could mean crashing into the ground! You wouldn't want *any* turbulence while the plane was touching its wheels to the ground!

We will consider the *standard deviation* to be the "turbulence" in our investment scenario. Call it our "glide path." The further away you are from retirement, which would be "landing," the more risk you can take because you can reevaluate and get yourself back on course with time. However, as you approach landing into retirement, you do not want to take the excess risk that could reduce your portfolio value when it comes time to liquidate or begin to take income.

For purposes of an example, let us assume you were only choosing from individual funds...

Airplane Turbulence. Landings and liquidations:
The Farther from Ground, the Less Worrying

more volatile

Aggressive growth (small-cap stocks)

Growth (mid- to large-cap stocks)

Growth and income (income stocks)

Balanced (stocks and bonds)

Income (bonds)

Money market (cash)

less volatile

There are several other classes of funds that we have not listed here, but this will give you a general idea. The landing represents the moment you plan to begin spending those funds for things such as children's college tuition, buying or paying off a home, and so on. If the investment is planned for retirement, and subsequently for income, we suggest that you accept some degree of volatility while drawing income from these assets. The classification of funds used during the spend-down phase would be balanced. Investing up to retirement is less demanding than investing through retirement. The need for your investment portfolio to pay out income and last as long as possible is important. Losses become more sensitive than during the accumulation stage.

Diversification among various funds would be wise, with the types of funds becoming more conservative as you get closer to spending down the principal. A retiree would end up in a balanced portfolio because they might live a long-life span, whereas a college student, who will spend the entire principal for school expenses, will reallocate fully to cash. The specific funds and allocations should be created based on your future cash needs and risk tolerances.

The best approach is always personal financial planning and the allocation of investments that meet your individual needs. Primary elements like diversification, income, and overall expenses are our starting place when creating your portfolio. The need for reducing risk and increasing income is a constant concern as you get older. You will continue to learn the various factors, variables, and parameters required in designing your precious nest egg.

We will practice a value-driven approach to selecting investment funds. This means investing in funds that hold underpriced assets with higher dividend yields and expectations for future growth. If the timing is off and the market drops, we will have the dividends available to purchase additional shares by reinvesting at lower prices.

Buying underpriced assets builds in a margin of safety to every investment, with more room to grow and less room to fall. These funds are less momentum-driven, meaning they do not follow trends like tech stocks or specific sectors might. The value vs. growth stocks-- or in our case, funds--will always be a debate about which one is best.

Value stocks represent companies that might be currently down in price or that use leverage to increase future gains. So, value stocks expect returns on their low price. However, no one knows that this will be true in the future. Have Amazon, Netflix, Google, and Apple changed the paradigm forever? Who knows? For the long term, value funds have a history of outperforming growth. That is not to say you should not own growth funds; you will by default anyway. Most diversified funds have a mixture of both categories, especially total market index funds.

You need to have an understanding and confidence that your funds and portfolio have long-term value. This way, when, not if the next market crash occurs, you have a Plan B, meaning you hold income-producing funds that add value even when their share price and marketability has declined. Investor emotions are the bane of investor success. Getting in at the top and out at the bottom will not allow for success.

Thinking that the market will go up because it has been doing so in the past is a bad bet. Likewise, thinking it will continue to fall when it has been falling is an even bigger mistake. We must have a plan to deal with our emotions in both scenarios.

Following the crowd up the mountain and then off the cliff will never be beneficial to your long-term success. Falling off the cliff in a declining market is much easier than regaining the high ground, i.e. regaining your investment's original value. For example, if your original share price is $100, and it then drops 50 percent, to $50, you would need to make a hundred percent gain to get back to your original price.

Therefore, you want to buy quality lower-cost funds with a plan to diversify and the ability to stay invested no matter how bad the market gets. Remember, you were not planning to sell your shares anyway, so why give them up if the price declines? The only action you must take is holding, reinvesting, and if possible, buying more. Remember our credo, "Lose no shares." They may go up and down, but if we own funds and stay diversified across the market, no one stock or bond in the portfolio can bring us down.

Value investors and fund managers both seek underpriced securities with solid fundamentals. These companies are not always in the news as the "next big thing" but have good fundamentals with price and income. Buy quality, good fundamentals, diversify, and avoid trying to time the market.

A portfolio is like an estuary in nature; it has taken much time-evolving and should be held with great care and respect. Knowing the portfolio's purpose, need, and time frame is critical. Monitoring the portfolio parameters is a given, but the portfolio should be "held, not stirred," meaning once the allocations are made, they shouldn't be disturbed until your needs change. Occasional fund replacement and reallocation is appropriate if your needs and desires change or substantial market conditions evolve. Opportunity trades can also pop up only if a need to allocate occurs, and certain sectors are depressed in price. There is no guarantee the price is a "good deal," just an opportunity.

Managing your old appreciated funds and buying new ones:

Before you can construct a new portfolio, you need to know whether you have full flexibility to sell or rollover previous retirement funds without hurting your tax bill. For non-retirement portfolios, deferred capital gains can cause significant pain if positions with gains are sold. Determining the cost basis of funds be sold or exchanged is critical.

If taxes will be due, you or the adviser should consider this. You should work to develop an acceptable plan to move from the previous retirement funds to the new funds with the least amount of taxes due in any one year. For funds held inside and outside retirement plans, early-withdrawal penalties and other fees should be researched before old securities are sold or exchanged. Selling in installments over the next few years may reduce the overall tax liability; it could, however, prove to be a mistake if you held on too long, and the share price drops.

Planning is important. You will need to answer questions like, do you sell everything? Do you lock in the gains and pay the maximum taxes while avoiding future market declines? Or should you hold on to those appreciated positions and risk a future market correction? It all depends on your life and situation. There are several reasons for you to sell and several for you to hang on. This is the planning process.

It is easy for Warren Buffett to hold only stocks since he doesn't need the income or cash. You, on the other hand, need to be careful, wise, and optimistic.

The best way to know what the tax liability might be is to contact your tax preparer and perform a tax estimate. You might get good news, that you won't owe any capital gains taxes. On the other hand, a complete sale of all shares might move you up into uncharted tax territory. Therefore, the opinion of a tax expert with no ax to grind is the person to consult to get the recommendation.

When selling shares of funds:

To lessen the risk of selling all at once and then watching the fund share go up, you can sell more than once a year. You can do" reverse dollar-cost averaging." Here, you sell so many shares or a dollar amount per month over time, thus averaging out the share prices at the time they are sold. This is where ETFs can be helpful since you can buy and sell them at the market instantaneously unlike the delayed process of a mutual fund that settles in a few days.

If taxes are not a problem, you can sell all at once (or over a few days) and buy a similar, but better, fund, and not miss out if the market goes up. When buying into the market, there are many different options. Let us review a few.

Choose from several buy-in methods:

*The old saying "buy low and sell high" is but a myth–*Let's look at some buy-in methods that, at the very least, might settle your nervous stomach when buying into the market. These plans allow you to ease into the market at the level you are comfortable with.

- A lump sum into one or more investments for conservative accumulation through dividend compounding, with CDs, bonds, and so on.

- A lump sum into income-producing fixed assets like CDs, bonds, or fixed annuities, with the interest reinvested into growth-oriented investments such as stocks or stock mutual funds.

- A lump sum into income-producing fixed assets with earnings and partial principal reinvested into stocks and/or mutual funds over a predetermined time frame.

- A lump sum with 50 percent invested into a fixed account (cash and bonds), 50 percent into a growth-oriented mutual fund, and consideration of annual rebalancing back to a 50/50 allocation.

- A lump sum into a diversified asset-allocation model (75 percent stocks, 25 percent fixed income), and quarterly rebalancing back into the original allocation percentages. Rebalance until your financial goals are on track.

- Investing a lump sum of dollars into desired investment allocations, while reinvesting dividends with no other investment reallocations. A dividend reinvestment plan (DRIP) simply means letting the dividend re-invest by buying more shares. This technique is usually a given; letting the stock funds reinvest dividends is incredibly wise. You are buying new shares as the old ones decline or increase in price. There is no guarantee of gaining the best price, but if you are a long-term investor committed to a stock or fund, we recommend reinvesting the dividends and averaging out the purchase prices. Rebalancing is not performed.

Now it's time to construct the new portfolio

The "new portfolio" will contain only no-load funds from well-known investment companies and lesser-known companies that have been vetted and monitored. You will establish what is referred to as a "brokerage account" with a well-known brokerage company. You will manage the account and fund allocations yourself, or if you hire an adviser, he or she will be given a limited power of attorney by you. This is also referred to as a "discretionary account," where the adviser can trade within your account for your best interest. They must follow specific standards of care to do what is right for *you* with no conflict of interest that would harm you.

For example, you should never borrow money from, or lend money to, your financial adviser. Do not invest in a private investment created and sponsored by your adviser. Be careful if your adviser is also your accountant and tax adviser, insurance agent, or attorney. This gives them an unfair advantage over you by limiting your access to outside advisers for purposes of "checks and balances" and second options.

Listed below are just a few of the concepts we will take into consideration while constructing your personalized custom portfolio. We do not recommend combining your portfolio allocation plan with other investors. Where other companies may program computers to determine how to reallocate your funds, we strongly suggest that you or your adviser personally manage your money. Our objective is not to *beat* the market but to *survive* it and provide a risk/return ratio appropriate for you alone.

Holding several different investment funds ranging from ETFs, index funds, and managed funds, you'll need to decide what percentage of each of these funds you will choose. Some investors are committed to only one of these different types of funds. For example, people who only want the lowest cost (expense ratio) will look to funds such as ETFs or index funds. Other investors believe managed funds are superior.

As you will see, our philosophy is to use the lowest-cost funds where appropriate and use managed funds where needed. For example, an index fund is like the dock on the ocean's shoreline. If a big wave comes by, it will be submerged, with no capability of getting out of the way. The managed fund, however, can allocate in different areas than the index and invest with certain defensive techniques which might prevent losses when the overall market is falling. The passive index equity portfolio manager attempts to replicate the performance of a benchmark, only acting when it is necessary. The active manager, however, seeks different holding techniques and management techniques, in hopes of outperforming the benchmark.

We agree with the statisticians that over decades, the index fund is hard to beat; but in the short-term, managed funds provide different holdings--and sometimes better defensive moves that might just avoid the full loss of an index when the market crashes. Case in point: You can buy a low-cost preferred stock index fund in the form of an exchange-traded fund. This fund, however, like long-term bonds, is very susceptible to rising interest rates. When compared with a popular managed preferred stock fund that held variable-rate preferred stocks and interest-rate futures, the downside results were better than the ETF preferred stock index fund in times where the interest rate had risen. They also proved valuable during the 2020 downturn.

Now, in the long run, the high management fee of the managed fund might reduce that edge. But most of us are concerned about the downside over the next five or ten years when we might need to use the money. Therefore, consider a managed fund if it provides a unique management style you agree with. New funds are coming out every day. Passively managed ETFs might even provide the defensive strategies you desire, thus reducing the dreaded "fund expense ratio."

Another consideration is taxes. Equity index (stock) funds and similar ETF index funds are better held outside of the retirement plans if all you are concerned with are taxes. These funds are the most tax-efficient funds available since they buy and hold the internal securities. ETFs are even more tax-efficient than an index fund from a fund company. The index fund must retain cash available for liquidations, where the ETF does not.

High turnover funds, income-producing equity stock funds, cash, and income-producing bond funds should be held inside the retirement plan. The income produced by these funds is tax-deferred inside the retirement plan until withdrawn, and it is taxed the same as all profits coming out of the plan, as ordinary income. If you are in a high tax bracket and need to buy into bonds outside of your tax-deferred retirement fund, you have tax-free municipal bond funds available in the index fund, ETF, and managed fund categories.

New portfolio investment concepts
Rule number one: You should diversify among several investment fund companies, among several different funds, and among thousands of different securities inside the funds and in the portfolio.

This concept reduces risk from:
- Single Fund Companies—too big to fail, hack or pandemic
- Individual funds—redundancy of holdings and management style
- Group of Portfolio's Securities–bankruptcy & default

We do this by diversifying laterally and vertically to build a stronger, multidimensional diversification model. We want to strengthen the total portfolio from all angles. Holding individual securities and "not trading" is trading, because a single stock could be devastated overnight simply because of bad news. By diversifying among several internal securities, different funds, and different fund companies, you are strengthening the total portfolio.

Lateral and Vertical integration construction concepts

Lateral integration
(time frame investing)

This is an investment staging program for all occasions. Like the staging concept, we discussed previously, here, the concept of time and need for liquidity (cash availability) is imperative when constructing an investment portfolio for the future. A plan for when you might need to withdraw funds and decide which securities should be sold, it is imperative. This provides the opportunity to leave some of the securities untouched for a longer life span and to allow time for growth while, at the same time, maintaining available cash to withdraw without concerns about market conditions.

When creating a new portfolio, we must not only invest for tax efficiency and inflation, but we must also create a hypothetical emergency plan. We must think about which area of the portfolio would be sold off if a need developed for cash. With this concern in mind, we break the portfolio into three distinct phases, or "stages," as we will call them. These stages need not be equal in the allocation and only represent a hypothetical image of amounts of money and time frames of when the investment might be needed.

Stage 1 funds are those that can be liquidated immediately, with little or no loss. Stage 2 funds would be those that would suffer acceptable levels of losses--as indicated, but not guaranteed, from historical data--if liquidated in a down market. And finally, Stage 3 would involve funds held for long-term objectives and never liquidated in down markets.

The above method of staging separates your investment portfolio into three different segments that independently meet certain criteria and needs. By staging the investments properly, you will give your investments the room to roam during the market's ups and downs. Doing so helps avoid panicking and pulling the plug on the investment process. Given the chance, your investments will achieve successful results. A plan allows you to keep your long-term commitment without bending to outside pressures that may force unfortunate decision-making. We can never predict the future and know when we might need emergency money--or how much. Let us explore our plan.

Detailed investment options to fit each stage:

Stage 1 lateral integration (0 to 5 years)
This stage deals with the need to always have immediate cash on hand for emergencies or opportunities. This is the cash you stash away for a rainy day. That rainy day can cause the house of cards to come tumbling down if you are not prepared with a quick infusion of cash. An emergency might be the car breaking down, a temporary work layoff, your pet becoming ill, the roof needing to be replaced, or some forgotten bill landing on your doorstep. We are sure you can help us out with the list of unforeseen contingencies that can upset the best-managed finances. Stage 1 addresses these concerns with investments that are safe and liquid.

The following are investments that meet Stage 1 criteria:

Certificate of Deposit—your brokerage account can purchase various maturities of CDs to meet your liquidity needs

Money market mutual funds—These investments are a collection of short-term assets, usually with maturities from days to months; they can earn higher yields than bank checking or saving accounts. Some of these funds are composed of bank certificates of deposit (CDs), which typically have a higher yield than a savings account. There are many securities continually maturing in the fund, and therefore, your cash is always available to you.

These funds provide a superb vehicle for the investor who also is invested in fixed-income mutual funds and equity mutual funds. If you hold the funds at the fund company itself, not a brokerage account, the money can be transferred from the mutual funds to the money fund with a phone call. Any cash not needed can simply be transferred back to the original fund. This makes gaining access to your money and investing back into the market a relatively painless process.

You can, of course, use other short-term cash-equivalent investments to meet the needs of Stage 1, but we recommend money market mutual funds and adjustable-rate funds which can be liquidated with very little, if any, volatility in the share price. For the more aggressive investor, this Stage 1 can utilize higher-yielding investment funds, such as floating-rate funds (short-term low-rated corporate debt.), etc.

Stage 2 lateral integration (5 to 10 years)
Here, we establish a position of investing that many investors fail to appreciate. We have discussed the importance of maintaining a cash reserve for emergencies. Stage 2 also provides liquidity, as in Stage 1. However, if the funds are not utilized, they are positioned for potential accumulation in value. This is an interim investment that is available for short-term needs as well as long-term growth potential.

This investment stage provides liquidity but carries the risk of price fluctuation. You might want to consider your risk-tolerance level for intermediate-term loss, holding those investments that have provided historically lower volatility.

As an investor, it is wise to remember the concept of "standard deviation." Standard deviation tells us how much volatility an investment has experienced historically. Another statistic to become familiar with is "total return." The total return is the yield and share appreciation of an investment over the past several years. Total return figures, combined with the standard deviation, can assist you in determining if an investment is appropriate to be placed in this stage. Funds like index, ETF, or managed intermediate-term bond funds, balanced funds, and total return funds could be used if the investor is comfortable with their historical volatility. This is important because the funds might be called upon for liquidation in an emergency if Stage 1 is used up.

For the more aggressive investor, a variety of stocks and growth-oriented mutual funds might fit Stage 2 needs. These assets can fluctuate greatly in changing markets, and investors should be patient and willing to take a substantial loss if they need to liquidate when the market is down. Stage 2 is primarily for liquidity with risk levels you are comfortable with.

Stage 3 lateral integration (10 years and beyond)

This is the area of investing that most people become involved in. Over the long run, growth-oriented investments, which belong in this category, are among the most profitable investment assets. Unfortunately, many investors enter the market without the necessary planning and experience.

It is usually inexperienced investors who get burned because they cannot stand the heat. They tend to enter the market when things are going great and leave it when things are not doing as well (buying high, selling low). They are the investors that the rest of us make money on. When the market hiccups, they sell at a great discount to people like you. We do not take great pleasure in saying that, but it's true. In Stage 3, investors must be committed for the long term, or they may get burned.

The investments utilized in Stage 3 are the most volatile and require the most time to grow. You may find yourself needing to add capital to an ailing investment, which can be tough if you have not prepared yourself psychologically for the commitment required. Remember, if an investment is legitimate, hold it in the long run, and when the market drops, buy more. Use dollar-cost averaging (DCA), which is the practice of making regular, periodic purchases to average out the share price through the market's ups and downs.

Beating the market simply means taking advantage of bad times. Buying while the market is declining ultimately benefits the long-term investor. Of course, we would not buy any investment if we knew ahead of time that it was going to decline in value. We would simply wait until it dropped and then buy. Because no one knows what the market will do ahead of time, we need a strategy that will make up for buying at the top of any market. This strategy is important mainly for keeping investors investing. If the market dropped nearly every time you invested a lump sum, who would want to invest in anything? This three-stage program is designed for the lump-sum investor and the periodic investor.

This third stage of investing takes into consideration all kinds of growth-oriented investments. This stage does not require the asset to be liquid. That is a great advantage because it allows for long-term goals to be met and short-term market declines to be tolerated and taken advantage of by adding money.

Let us look at some possible investments and programs that one might select for the third stage:

- Individual long-term bonds (higher yield, higher volatility)
- Individual stocks
- Managed Mutual funds, index mutual funds, and exchange-traded funds (usually growth-oriented, aggressive growth, and foreign funds)
- Limited partnerships
- Real estate
- Businesses
- Employee retirement plans (401(k)s, IRAs, pensions, etc.)
- Collectibles

Of course, investor risk tolerances and the level at which an investor is willing to be personally involved are important in determining which investments to choose. Although this book addresses the construction of an investment portfolio, some people also invest in outside ventures such as real estate.

Remember that saying we keep repeating, *"It's not what you invest in; it's how you invest that matters!"* Any of the investments we listed could be a potential disaster. What we should avoid is buying an improper investment for a stated goal. Say you bought a new home, and the market dropped right after you purchased it. That might be a blow to your ego; however, your payments are still the same, and you still live on the property. If, on the other hand, you bought with the expectation or the need to sell a short time later, expecting to make a profit, then you do have a serious problem.

So, was this real estate purchase a foolish investment? Well, let's see:

Yes- it was a foolish investment:

— if you the investor expected to profit within a short time.

— if you can't afford the monthly payments.

— if you can't hold on long-term.

No- it was a wise investment:

— if you can afford the payments and upkeep costs.

— if you paid cash for the property.

— if you plan to live in the house long-term.

— if you did the research and bought correctly in the first place.

— if you love the house.

Someone once said: *"It's not having what you want that counts, it's wanting what you have!"* Real Estate, collectibles, and tangible investments require a long-term commitment.

Let's Recap:

Stage 1 must provide instant cash and stability of assets. This stage is where you hold cash for emergencies. Yield is not the objective of this stage; safe and immediate access is.

In Stage 2, these investments are designed for intermediate-term savings periods, and although these investments can appreciate, they should have historical volatility levels you are comfortable with. These investments must be liquid within ten days, if needed, and can fluctuate in value.

Finally, in Stage 3, we have investments that can be held long-term and will most likely produce some losses along the way while striving for long-term growth.

The following are examples of each of the three stages for the three different types of investors: the very conservative investor, the conservative growth investor, and the aggressive investor.

Very Conservative Investor

Stage 1

US government securities, money market mutual funds, insured certificates of deposit, and government adjustable-rate mortgage funds—The money market investment vehicle provides check-writing privileges while remaining stable in price per share when purchased directly through the fund company. Also, the US Treasury indirectly backs the asset because it holds a large variety of US Treasury bills. The certificates of deposit are usually insured and have different time frames to choose from, and the adjustable US government securities can fluctuate in value.

Stage 2

Short- or intermediate-term US government securities, mutual funds, index funds, and exchange-traded funds—These Index, ETFs, and managed funds provide fast access to your cash and are some of the least volatile securities due to their short-term internal maturities. The yields are usually 1 percent to 2 percent higher than money market funds, and any short-term fluctuation in share price might be made up in income if held long enough. Also, the federal government indirectly protects its government-issued investments in the fund from the default, although it does not protect against share-price fluctuation.

Stage 3

Intermediate- to long-term US government securities--These funds can produce some of the highest yields in the conservative-investment arena. Many different types of US government securities mutual funds exist. They do run the risk of share-price decline if overall interest rates rise after you invest. The long-term conservative investor who lets the dividends reinvest, or who appreciates the fact they are usually earning several percentage points more interest than other assets, may be pleased.

Again, because many of the assets in the fund are, in one way or another, backed or guaranteed by the federal government, investors can sleep at night knowing they are protected against default. While these funds are prone to decline in price with rising interest rates, the risk can be reduced if held long-term and you reinvest the dividends. Individual bonds can be held to maturity, eliminating the risk of the price decline one might experience within a mutual fund.

High-grade corporate bond mutual funds, index funds, and ETFs—The bonds are backed by the corporation issuing them. In a mutual fund, you are a small investor who benefits from other people's money through the pooling of all investments into the fund. These funds usually provide high rates of return, like the US government securities mutual fund. So, why buy them if the yield is not that much more? Diversification, that's why!

Please Note: *For non-retirement accounts, you can replace taxable-bond mutual funds with municipal tax-free bond funds if your income-tax bracket is high.*

This example of investment strategies was designed for the extremely cautious investor who is not willing to accept much risk and is only interested in earning income. Growth is not even a consideration here. There are many more assets to choose from out there, so do your homework.

In addition to this model: If you have the money with one fund company, you can practice a multiple-dividend reinvestment plan. By investing in a money market fund, a short-term bond fund, an intermediate-term bond fund, and a long-term bond fund, you can reduce the risk of interest rates rising by redirecting the dividends from all four funds back into the long-term bond fund. If the shares of this long-term bond fund drop in value, you would be quadrupling the "dollar-cost averaging" share-purchasing plan. You'll turn a negative into a positive by buying shares of the long-term bond fund at a discount while, at the same time, the yields of the money market fund and short bond funds are rising.

Conservative Growth Investor

Stage 1

Money market mutual funds, adjustable-rate US government securities fund, short-term government securities index funds, managed funds, and ETFs—Same thing here; these assets can be liquidated with little or no loss.

Stage 2

Short-, intermediate- and long-term bond mutual funds, index funds, and ETFs—All of these funds produce higher income for reinvestment and can be purchased as taxable or tax-free funds.

Income-producing utility and preferred stock managed mutual funds, index funds, and ETFs—These hold income-producing utility stocks and bonds. These securities have the potential for capital appreciation, as well as dividends that can be reinvested. They can be volatile in the market, but because of their high dividend earnings, most investors stay with them through the ups and downs.

Balanced managed mutual funds, index funds, and ETFs–While holding a mix of stocks and bonds, these funds provide some growth potential, as well as income available for reinvestment of shares. These funds are great for buy-and-hold positions because of their diversification. If reducing taxable income is a concern, consider investing 50 percent in municipal bond funds and 50 percent in tax-managed growth-oriented funds or index funds.

Stage 3

Private business—Not only a current source of income for business owners but if held long-term, the private business can provide future sales profits.

Personal residence—Although real estate is a somewhat volatile commodity, if held long-term, the results are generally favorable. There are also substantial tax benefits other than the mortgage loan interest. This asset, although somewhat restrictive, since you live in it, will act as an inflation hedge.

Variety of growth-oriented mutual funds, index funds, and ETFs—Investing in a wide range of growth-oriented funds will provide the potential for long-term growth as well as diversification. If a US stock fund is purchased, you should consider buying another fund that holds foreign stocks to balance and offset the portfolio.

Aggressive Investor

Stage 1

Adjustable-rate government securities, floating-rate securities, short-term high-yield managed funds, index funds, and ETFs—Slight volatility is not a concern here and reinvesting the dividends will help to maintain the principal account value.

Stage 2

Growth-oriented Mutual Funds, index funds, and ETFs—Utilizing a wide variety of growth-oriented and aggressive growth mutual funds maintains the needed liquidity in the portfolio. Although the market prices of the funds can fluctuate greatly, the long-term benefits can be rewarding. For the aggressive investor, risk and volatility are not a concern.

Stage 3

Aggressive growth-oriented mutual funds, index funds, and ETFs—There are several growth opportunities available, including foreign and domestic stocks. Tax-managed mutual funds, index funds, and ETFs should be considered for tax reduction outside of a retirement plan.

Individual Stock—Diversify your holdings with various stocks from various investment sectors. Holding large quantities of a single stock can put you in a very high-risk position. You can increase or decrease your risk by the number and quality of the stocks you hold. The market share price is referred to as the stock's "handle".

Rental Real Estate—Provides terrific tax benefits as well as capital appreciation and possible rental income. Real estate inside retirement plans is not recommended, however. The reason is that you lose various tax deductions and must pay for taxes and repair with funds within the plan.

Limited Partnerships—Limited partnerships are not for every investor, due to the long-term commitment requirements and volatility. If the partnership is legitimate and charges low expenses and fees, you will have opportunities in real estate, oil, leasing, solar, art, etc. Be incredibly careful with this one.

Private Business—Owning your own business can present the highest risk of all but can potentially bring you the greatest return. Income, tax deductions, and future business sales value can be substantial.

Collectibles—If you are savvy in any collecting field, such as art, metals, coins, or antiques, this can be a very profitable avenue, but it's not recommended for most investors.

When designing your own three stages within the investment plan, make sure you stick to the basics: Stage 1 requires liquidity; Stage 2 provides for semi-liquidity, and Stage 3 is illiquid but provides substantial potential long-term growth. Keep in mind that the entire system is designed to allow your long-term investments to be left alone to maximize growth.

You are the only person who can determine the level of risk and volatility any stage will assume. Don't just focus on being overly conservative. Future growth is needed to fight inflation.

It's important to remember that each investment has its benefits and shortcomings. Cash is stable, and stocks provide growth, but neither meets all our needs.

Reverse lateral integration plan

Managing risk and loss is foremost. Reducing loss is more important than managing gain. For example, if you have a balanced portfolio outside a retirement plan and need a couple of lump-sum withdrawals-

- one this month and another in a few months--how would you go about taking money out? This is a typical example: If you are building a house, you pull money out over stages as the building process develops.

So how should you pull money out of your balanced portfolio? Should you:

Pull all the money out at once, equally, from all funds?
Sell and withdraw the bond funds' proceeds?
Sell and withdraw the stock funds' proceeds?
Sell half the bond funds and half the stock funds?

In our three stages of investing, the "lateral integration" plan works in all markets for the reasons we discussed. Once you have used your emergency plan assets, however, you'll need to reallocate back to the original model to be prepared for the next emergency or opportunity.

In this example, we have time to plan out our liquidations but still need to be careful. Once we sell something, the market could go straight up or straight down. Until you can rebalance, what should you sell first?

Well, we like to practice that old saying, "Plan for the worst of times and enjoy the best of times." Therefore, we would recommend, in a stable market, that you go ahead and sell your equities (stock funds) for the first round of liquidations because potentially, they are the most volatile. Save the fixed assets (bond funds), which are relatively more stable, for the second round of liquidation. If needed, the third unexpected liquidation would be from the money market funds and any cash reserves. This way, if the stock market crashes right after the first round of liquidations, you will have sold at a higher point in the market, and you will have thus avoided losses. We refer to this as a "reverse lateral integration plan."

If the market is down at the time of liquidation, the original lateral integration plan would be used. You would withdraw from Stage 1 first and, if needed, Stage 2, and so on, leaving Stage 3 for later.

We will discuss proper asset allocation within these stages in future pages as they will relate to the portfolio design.

Next is the determination of which types of funds to use and where to place them. Remember, a diversified portfolio is a stronger portfolio. When properly diversified, you are never "all in." You will never have bragging rights to say you gambled everything on one stock, fund, or index. The tradeoff is you are seldom "in the wrong place at the wrong time."

These three stages of the program can be practiced by creating three different portfolios or just one with three different levels in mind.

Vertical Integration
(bottom-up allocations)

There are three levels of portfolio assets utilizing distinctly different types of no-load investment funds. Imagine a pyramid in three equal horizontal levels. In creating this pyramid, our objective is to provide the maximum level of diversification among not only the individual securities inside the fund (cash, bonds, and/or stocks) but among different funds by their objectives, indexes, and managers, to avoid redundancy. Finally, we want to diversify among different fund companies to avoid a "too big to fail" concern--or nowadays, "too big to hack, or centrally located bio/pandemic hazards affecting a company's home office.

For example, on May 7, 2018, Equifax revealed that as many as 143 million people's names, social security numbers, and dates of birth were leaked. On top of that, approximately 209,000 individual's credit card numbers were leaked as well. No matter how large a company is, there is always the risk of security being breached. Fortunately for Equifax, they were able to remain in business, but other companies may not be so lucky if they encounter a similar problem. Of course, we all remember the 2020 Coronavirus.

When creating your complete portfolio, we have talked about the importance of diversification, diversification among all areas! You will not get the highest return, however. In fact, the greater you diversify, the more "diluted" your return becomes. Most investors would, however, be willing to give up some of those gains to reduce the losses due to bankruptcy, default, or market crashes. Thus, in doing so, diversifying among all categories, indexes, passive and active management philosophies, and countless "investment factors" must be managed to create the ultimate portfolio.

If you recall, in 2008, the S&P took nearly five years to recover, and that was after trillions of bail-out dollars and by artificially reducing interest rates.

Strategic allocations within the funds and the portfolio allow for a more balanced approach. This strategy allows the investor to plan for the long term but survive the short term by proper asset allocation and investment time management.

Let's look at the various levels of categorizing the different funds you might use in a portfolio:

We diversify not only Stocks vs. Bonds, US vs. International, Small vs. Large, but managed vs. non-managed as well. Although we believe a fund with lower expense ratios provides more room for the fund's profits, investing in "just an index" limits your ability to customize your portfolio. Why own just the index, which, in 2008, might have been down as much as 65 percent at its lowest point, when you can allocate your overall portfolio in funds with less historical volatility?

Here are the various levels of funds selection available for your overall portfolio. Our pyramid concept allows us to visualize three different levels, amounts, and types of funds to fill those levels.

Imagine a three-layer pyramid:

Level One, the base of the pyramid–the largest portion at the bottom of the pyramid. We choose a variety of low-cost index funds from many different well-known investment fund companies. An example of a fund in this level is known as a "total market index fund" for both bond indexes, stock indexes, international, global, etc. Total market and broad market index funds give you the largest number of internal securities spread across a broad base. They also have some of the lowest expense ratios in the market.

These index funds are specifically designed to give you a broad mix of bonds or stocks that represent the total market. With these funds, the objective is to maximize diversification among all types of securities, rather than to try and pick which index will be up tomorrow; you could include the S&P 500 if you want to, although it is not as well spread out as the total market. The S&P holds 500 stocks; most total market index funds would hold 2000-plus.

If you choose total market index funds from large well-known companies like Vanguard, Schwab, SPDR, iShares, or Fidelity, chances are you will find some of the lowest fund expenses in the industry. Since an index fund is "non-managed," its size does not otherwise hinder the manager's ability to buy, sell, and move around. Bill's firm buys into the total market index fund to avoid mistakes a manager might make. As the total market index fund grows and gets larger, it can reduce the overall fund expense.

You need to invest in funds that can at least be held for a few years. With a bond total market index fund, you will be owning a cross-section of short-term, intermediate-term, and long-term bonds. If you are trying to avoid interest-rate risk, you would avoid this index in favor of a short-term bond index fund used in Level Two, the more specific or custom level of the portfolio.

In the total market index, which is "buying one of everything," this is helpful when the fund wants to add or eliminate a position. In smaller indexes, as we know, if the word gets out that a stock will be added to the index, its price can shoot up considerably, causing your index--and ultimately you--to pay more for the shares purchased.

The opposite is true for the stock the index is getting rid of; its price drops before the index sells it to make room for the other higher-priced stock. The very large total market index suffers less, simply because of the greater number of positions in the fund. So, in this type of index, you are buying low-to-no turnover, greater overall diversification, and substantially fewer fund expenses--not to mention, in the ETF category, better liquidity. For those who don't believe in fund management or adviser-directed allocations, this is perfect for the "invest and forget" investment.

Level Two, the midsection of the pyramid—This middle section is reserved for more specific categories of low-cost index funds and exchange-traded funds.

These categories narrow down the objective of the fund into more specific indexes, categories, or sectors of the market.

Index stock funds that mirror specialized indexes, such as:

- Large-cap companies (Market capitalization up to around 5 billion)
- Large-cap value stocks
- Large-cap growth stocks
- Mid-cap companies (Market capitalization up to around 3 billion)
- Mid-cap value stocks
- Mid-cap growth stocks
- Small-cap companies (Market capitalization under 2 billion)
- Small-cap company value stocks
- Small-cap company growth stocks
- Large-cap, mid-cap, and small-cap international, global, and emerging markets index funds, etc.

More specific market indexes and categories sometimes referred to as "sectors":

- Industrials
- Consumer discretionary
- Consumer staples
- Real estate
- Energy
- Financials
- Health care
- Technology
- Telecommunications
- Utilities

Index bond funds, mirror bond indexes

(Short-term, intermediate-term, long-term listed below):

- US Treasuries
- Mortgage Securities

- Corporate Debt.
- TIPs
- Municipal Securities
- Floating-Rate
- International
- Emerging Markets

Exchange-traded funds:

Today, not all ETFs are index funds. They have evolved into various combinations, ranging from the traditional index fund to the passively managed index fund, and finally, to the fully actively managed ETF.

Oh, and we cannot forget the leveraged and inverse leveraged funds. **WARNING!** Stay away from those funds! They are extremely dangerous and can cause you to lose everything. Do your homework and avoid losses you will not be able to make up by waiting for the market to recover. Just stay away! We never use these speculative funds.

Here are some choices among the passive and passively managed ETF universe.

Passive Index and Exchange Traded Index funds:

These funds will hold a specific selection of securities matching various stock indexes and bond indexes as previously described. There are tens of thousands of indexes available for the industry to follow. Be selective when looking at what index or category the fund is being compared with. The idea of the index is to follow an average of its index or category, but that is just a beginning point.

Managers of index funds have the job of tracking an index as closely as possible, reducing tracking error. To gain "the average of the index," a fund must hold the same securities and allocate them exactly in the same weightings. Some index funds, however, refer to the name of the index it follows in its name but might allocate the internal securities differently; some leave out the smallest weightings of stocks in the index to save on trading time and costs. Following the averages, however, is no guarantee of average returns. As the saying goes, *"Head in the oven, feet in the freezer, your temperature should be about average!"* Not true! So do your research.

Some examples of indexes might be the DOW index, S&P index, small-cap index, mid-cap index, large-cap index, utilities, preferred real estate, etc....you get the idea. If your index fund follows an index, then its "standard deviation" should be the same. The performance will be less by the amount of the management fee and any internal trading costs.

More examples of funds for Level two

Passively managed ETFs also referred to as "factor funds":

These involve an investment process that is repeatable, observable, and predictable. Listed below are categories of these types of funds:

ESG funds:

Relatively new to the scene, these environmental, social, and governance funds are designed to exclude undesirable securities within the fund. Stocks in guns, oil, tobacco, and other investments that investors would object to owning are excluded. Stocks with desirable social-impact practices might be selected. Companies that practice environmentally sustainable practices and policies would be selected over others. Greenwashing, some funds claim to be investing in securities that are environmentally, socially, and governance compliant; however, they fail to meet the claims made about them and thus mislead investors.

Smart beta:

Objectives are active, but management is passive. Passively-managed index funds--i.e., smart beta (also known as "Factor" or rules-based investing)--simply try to reduce the funds' beta (risk compared with the overall market) below the overall market by weighting the internal positions to more conservative assets. William Sharpe made up the name "beta" as he developed the Capital Asset Pricing Model (CAPM), which came from the Modern Portfolio Theory (MPT). It refers to a portfolio's sensitivity to movement in the overall market.

These funds remove an element of idiosyncratic risk, specifically manager risk. The fund is designed to be strategically allocated among a few different indexes or categories in the market. This strategy is designed to reduce short-term risk and produce long-term gains. Some factors associated with higher returns and lower risks are value, small-cap stocks, momentum, low volatility, quality, and yield. The title "smart beta" is just a marketing term. If the allocation within the fund meets your needs, just accept the fund as appropriately allocated, not as some miracle investment. It's simply a way to avoid the top over-priced stocks at the top of an index.

These categories are rebalanced on a regular schedule maintaining the original allocations and hopefully a lower beta.

Strategic beta:

Nearly the same as "rules-based investing," smart beta. We prefer the term "strategic beta"; they both do the same thing, but the term "smart beta" infers some level of superiority and is misleading. These funds steer away from traditional market capitalizations in favor or one or more factor characteristics within an index; equally weighted vs. cap-weighted, rebalanced quarterly. The higher the beta, the higher the expected return, referred to as "risk premium."

Multifactor:
Multifactor ETFs blend several factors to ideally minimize the risk of any one factor and to provide a more diversified ETF product to investors. Six main factors deserve investors' attention: value, momentum, size, quality, volatility, and dividends. Each of these factors has been researched by multiple scholars and/or professional investors. Many are present across asset classes and in different markets around the world. The hope is that, if used correctly, the single and multifactor investing may produce a better risk-managed return.

Minimum Volatility:

A "min vol ETF" attempts to reduce exposure to volatility by tracking indices that aim to provide lower-risk alternatives. They will do this with limited but timely reallocations of internal investments of the index being followed. For example, a min vol ETF might show less risk during market turbulence, compared with a broadly diversified index, by avoiding the top momentum and higher-risk stock that the overall market might invest in. Some min vol ETFs can do this by purchasing securities that exhibit relatively low volatility and concentration risk.

Low Volatility:

Low-volatility ETF portfolios are much more extreme in seeking less volatility. They tend to offer above-average downside protection in exchange for below-average upside participation. Over the long term, this should translate to better risk-adjusted returns for investors with low-risk tolerances.

Many of the stocks in the fund belong to old and established companies that have long since passed their "heydays" of popularity. These securities are from large, high-income-producing companies. Given their history of low highs and low lows, investors like these stocks, and thus they like the fund's high dividends and lower volatility. If earning is in question however as they were in the 2020 Corona Virus outbreak their share prices dropped more than most growth funds. This is because if the earning of a company is called in to question, the share price will drop immediately.

Minimum-volatility funds hold stocks of an index, but in different proportions; whereas low-volatility funds aggressively select stocks with exceptionally low volatility, whether they are in the broad market index or not. With these stocks, although they exhibit less historical volatility and pay high dividends, risk can appear through interest-rate risk. Do not think this is a magical way to invest in stocks without risk.

Buffer ETFs:

A new concept, these funds are designed to track a popular index; however, they offer limited upside gains and downside protection. They provide limited upside, but protect against, say, the first 9 percent of loss; so, the investor does not lose any money unless the index declines more than that 9 percent. Another fund might guarantee against losses of the first 15 percent of the decline in the market, and yet another might protect against the first 35 percent of the loss. Each fund holds a portfolio of custom exchange-traded FLEX options that have varying strike prices (the price at which the option purchaser may buy or sell the security, at the expiration date), and the same expiration date (approximately one year). The layering of these FLEX options with varying strike prices provides the mechanism for producing a fund's desired outcome. Higher expenses can be expected for this strategy.

Thematic ETFs:

Categories of investments that focus on a theme, philosophy, or belief system, such as cybersecurity, digital currency, bitcoin, cannabis, pet supplies, gaming, etc.

Other factors: when looking for ETF funds, include size, value vs. growth, momentum, geography, inflation, yield, etc.

As investors are leaving the higher-cost managed mutual funds and migrating to this lower-cost, more transparent, tax-efficient ETFs, one must be incredibly careful to analyze what they are buying.

For the lowest expense ratio, the index ETFs provide the same low cost and massive diversification that the index mutual fund provides. The difference for the ETF is the hour-by-hour ability to sell your shares in the open market, for better or worse. For this reason, we need to ensure the ETF you are either buying or intend to sell has enough trading volume to provide the liquidity you seek. When trading ETF shares, you absorb the cost of the spreads. Alternatively, when buying or selling non-ETF mutual funds, which are bought or sold at the end of the trading day, the spreads are absorbed by the fund company and shareholders of the fund.

Level Two of our pyramid goes beyond Level One, where we just buy the index and hold funds for the portfolio. Level Two takes on more strategic positioning of securities of each exchange-traded or index mutual fund, then positioning those funds and allocations to create the desired portfolio.

Level Three, the top of the pyramid—The top and the smallest part of the portfolio is a handful of well-managed funds chosen based on their historical performance, or history of lower volatility, history of superior management, etc. These funds usually have higher management fees than the index funds; however, they might offer defensive management techniques. Simply by holding different positions than the index, managed funds might avoid severe declines.

These managed funds are suggested more for downside measures than beating any one index. Unlike the total market index funds that benefit from size for expense reduction, the managed fund usually benefits from being smaller and more agile. The bigger the fund gets, the less agile it becomes. Being required to buy more possibly overpriced securities at the top of the market might cause the old shareholders to become diluted and share their prior gain with new buyers.

This is one reason you will occasionally see a successful fund closed to new investors. They want to avoid dilutions with new investor dollars pouring into the fund. For managed mutual funds, bigger is not always better.

When searching for managed funds, one needs to look at the history of activity and performance. For example, a utility index fund will hold all the utility stocks in the index. When those internal stocks representing the index experience decline, the fund will drop in synchronicity. In a managed fund, however, where the managers allocate the portfolio into less volatile utility stocks and buy interest-rate futures, they can hopefully reduce share-price losses due to rising interest rates.

Other reasons to manage a fund might be to selectively extract many of the underperforming stocks in an index and attempt to create a fund by only holding the best and most promising stocks from that index. Considering the S&P 500, a managed fund manager might closely analyze and track the most promising 50 stocks in the index and exclude the other 450. If successful, the managed fund might create very desirable returns which would outweigh the fund's higher management fee.

Other reasons investors might choose a managed fund might be in a situation where the securities the fund purchases represent very volatile or sensitive sectors. For example, emerging markets securities might concern the investor who wants more of a hands-on method of selecting and monitoring the securities in the fund. Rather than trusting a group of stocks that some index selects; investors of managed funds have faith that the manager is looking out for their best interests.

The average returns have not born this out, if you compile all the managed funds compared with their respective indexes, however. This is primarily due to overpopulation of commission funds sold by retail mutual fund companies, banks selling mutual funds, and insurance companies creating and selling their mutual funds. These funds were designed for income to be earned by the broker, his/her brokerage company, and those who managed the fund. So, work hard to find the exceptions.

Investors can avoid those "bloated" funds and possibly witness their demise as competition and fee compression occurs. You will learn how to find the best-managed funds by carefully selecting the fund based on the historical parameters you have learned with this book.

You will only select the most successfully managed funds, those that have a history of meeting the fund's objective. Whether the objective is beating its index on the way up, or strategically beating it on the way down, there are exceptionally good managed funds out there that still add value.

These managed funds are the best of the best. Their performance compared to its category is superior. Their downside performance has been less risky, and their performance after fund fees is greater than their index. So, happy fund-hunting!

It's no surprise, though, that some of the best-performing managed funds also charge lower fund expenses. Yes, expenses do matter, but the primary concern is the structure, method of asset selection, philosophy of the manager, asset monitoring, and general guidance of the fund. A managed fund gives you more flexibility to invest in the best securities the fund manager can select. The fund manager, however, could also make some big mistakes and take the fund down with him or her. Therefore, you should choose funds with a long history with the managers and ones that have survived market corrections. Many ETFs coming out now are also managed. If they provide a strategy you cannot get with other index funds or ETF funds, that is fine, but be careful of fads. High-cost managed funds are showing up in the so-called "low-cost" ETF world.

Managed funds have been the ones to offer a greater choice of fund structures. They offer every investment strategy you can think of. They do so mainly to compete for your business, in hopes that their investment philosophy will appeal to you. They create many gimmicks to attract investors looking for the next strategy to beat the market. We, however, prefer to recommend managed funds to reduce risk exposure. This makes sense in areas that require ongoing management.

For example, using index bond funds is great to reduce the fund expenses, thus increasing the net yield. If, however, interest rates are expected to rise in the future, one can go to cash and earn much less. Or simply invest in a managed fund and let a bond fund manager deal with the risk and liquidity. If interest rates never rise, you are earning higher yields than going to cash. If rates do rise, hopefully, the manager provided investment methods and strategies to reduce the downside losses where an index fund would not. Either way, if chosen correctly, both the index fund and the managed funds can add value. By default, however, managed funds have tended to lose less on the downside simply because they are not comprised of the index. They hold other securities that are not in the headlines.

Buying a managed fund is a little like buying a new car with extras or options. If you will be paying more for them, make sure you need what they are offering. Make sure you believe in their investment strategies and philosophies. Remember, if we do our job correctly, you will never beat the index. This is simply because you diversified away from any one index. A retirement portfolio needs to be designed for cash emergencies, with income and long-term growth to offset inflation and taxes. Having a little bit of everything is wise but is never going to be the most profitable.

Our takeaway

When creating your ultimate diversified portfolio using these strategies, not only are you diversified among the different securities within the funds, but you will hold different funds, preventing redundancy of indexes and fund strategies. You also diversify among managers and fund companies.

Taking diversification further, our vertical integration model allows for investment philosophy diversification. We do this by using the non-managed total market index funds (super-low expense ratios), passively-managed strategic beta ETFs (low expense ratios with investment monitoring and rebalancing), and a few prima donna top-performing managed funds providing investment strategies that require intensive management activities. We gain from each perspective.

More rules-based investing

New Portfolio Design and Structure:
Using the lateral and vertical integration concept, you will use ten to twenty different funds from the areas discussed. You will be - combining no-load, passive index, exchange-traded, and actively managed funds. The portfolio will achieve the needed diversification necessary to reduce individual risks that one investment security would pose. You are maintaining a balance of fixed-income securities (bonds) and equity positions (stocks), inside different types of funds and different fund companies.

We suggest following maximum fund-allocation limits for fund allocation, to avoid overconcentration in one fund. As detailed in the investment- and portfolio-diagnostic process, the investor's need for personal risk levels, liquidity, and suitability are all considered. This is accomplished by using sophisticated programs designed to combine all the funds in a portfolio to determine the combined characteristics of the portfolio. A historical picture of the funds and portfolio's prior performances (past results are no indication or assurance of future performance) is reviewed to confirm and maintain the desired portfolio results.

Each portfolio will have different allocations of cash, bonds, and stocks inside the various funds. But remember to be aware of the parameters for each fund as they relate to the portfolio(s).

Many retirees choose these parameters to construct a balanced portfolio; yours might be quite different:

- Diversity among securities, funds, and fund companies
- Appropriate allocation percentages among funds
- Low standard deviation (historical volatility)
- Low beta (overall risk level compared with an index)
- High alpha (performance compared to similar portfolios)
- High Sharpe ratio (risk vs. reward)
- Moderate to highly rated bonds (credit rating of bonds)
- Low bond duration (reduces bond risk during rising interest rates)
- High yields (relative to the risk taken)
- Low average combined expense ratios
- Marketability and liquidity of funds in the portfolio
- Tax-free and tax-efficient funds for taxable accounts

For example, let's look at what a balance portfolio's parameters might look like. These numbers were generated from a generic Morningstar fund report. Your portfolio will be designed to meet your personal needs and preferences and would be current, compared with this *hypothetical* example:

Combined funds internal allocations: 2.62 percent in cash; 52.40 percent in bonds; 7.62 percent other, preferred stocks, convertible bonds, gold, etc;

34.70 percent in US stocks; 2.66 percent in non-US stocks

Up to ten different funds and ETF fund companies: Vanguard, Charles Schwab, Fidelity, T. Rowe Price, iShares, Wisdom Tree, Invesco, etc.

Up to twenty different funds: various index funds, various exchange-traded funds, and various managed funds

Total portfolio internal securities held inside and among all funds in the portfolio: Equities (stocks) 3,611; Fixed (bonds) 20,158, there are many more bonds issued every year than stocks.

Approximate vertical integration allocations:

45 percent, base of the pyramid with total market index funds

40 percent, middle pyramid with sector, index & factor ETFs

15 percent, top of the pyramid with managed funds

Combined portfolio's past ten years' risk metrics and parameters

(Hypothetical portfolio of funds; historical results listed below are not current. Past performance is no indication of future results):

Worst year performance: February 2008 to March 2008 was -17.03 percent, compared with the S&P loss of over 50 percent.

Last twelve-month yield net of fund expenses: 2.2 percent

Ten-year standard deviation: 7.5 percent

Ten-year Sharpe ratio: 1.45

Ten-year beta: 0.38

R-squared: 90

Minimum average bond credit rating: BBB

Average bond duration: 3.3 years

Average portfolio-expense ratio: .19 percent

If it turned out that you didn't need the asset for income during later retirement and you intend to leave the account to younger generations, you might go out further on the risk curve and reallocate to more equities (stocks).

Strategic asset allocation is used to determine the long-term policies and asset weighting in a portfolio. These techniques determine desired asset allocations among stocks and bonds inside the funds and portfolio. If the market changes significantly, the allocation is rebalanced back to the original percentage allocations.

In a 50-50 portfolio, if stocks rise significantly to, say, 60 percent of the portfolio, they get reduced to the original 50-percent allocation. This, although extremely basic, keeps the desired risk level the same over time. A more strategic method of rebalancing is to return to the original standard deviation, beta, and Sharpe ratios, rather than just stocks vs. bonds.

Our philosophy is that the adviser should regularly check in with the investor to determine if this way of thinking is still in line with the desired needs and comfort levels. Why? Because things can change, which might result in the investor opting to stay invested in the overweighting of stocks if the market has risen.

Some examples of what can change:

> The client started drawing Social Security. That is like adding a million dollars' worth of bonds to the portfolio and using the interest earned. This income may add confidence and allow for more volatile investments in the portfolio.

> Maybe the client just inherited money and has more confidence and less fear.

The client has developed a desire to leave the portfolio to his or her beneficiaries, who are much younger and thus need to be invested in more equities (stocks).

Letting a computer perform automatic rebalancing without checking in with the investor is not wise. This is not to mention the tax liability that can occur in non-retirement portfolios if the computer sells appreciated shares to buy non-appreciated shares.

Tactical asset allocation (TAA) also makes changes to the portfolio's allocations, in hopes of being in a different place when the market drops. This strategy is like investing as a contrarian. If you believe interest rates will rise, you will get out of long-term bonds and buy short-term. If you think that interest rates have met a peak, you might buy long-term bonds, in hopes that rates will decline, and the bond will rise in value. As you try and time the market, please remember, timing can be dangerous without proper diversification and a long-term commitment.

Remember our core belief: Be diversified to a fault! Yes, you will dilute your return a little on the way up, but you might be pleasantly surprised on the way down.

Beating the market is not the concern; surviving it is! Remember that analogy about putting you in a 50-year time capsule and waking you up in the future. In this scenario, yes, a total stock market index fund will probably do better than the managed funds and different asset classes such as cash, bonds, real estate, etc. That's because you would have no concern for the short- or moderate-term time frame. You would be asleep, not needing to access your stock index fund. With the broad diversification among the stocks in the index, the low cost of the fund, and dividend reinvestment, you would come out smelling like a rose.

However, as we have mentioned many times, most retirement investors do not have 50 years to wait. If the total market index crashes, as it did in 2008 and 2020, they would be withdrawing funds to meet their cash-flow needs. Pulling your required minimum distributions from shares that just dropped in half would severely reduce the life of your retirement portfolio.

It is a good practice to look at money market funds and bond funds as assets to have on hand for future emergencies. They will act as a seat belt and an airbag, available in an emergency in case the overall market is down when you need to liquidate assets.

You have heard of the terms "puts & calls." If you own a put option, you make money if the targeted stock falls in value; if you own a call option, you make money if the stock goes up. Well, a simpler way of investing is to consider the fund approach. Think of the bond fund acting like a put: if the stock market drops, chances are your bond fund might go up in demand and hence in value. If the stock market goes up, it's like owning a call; you make money on the way up with your stock funds. Remember, options expire but a diversified portfolio will live on forever!

Bonds should not be looked at as good investments but rather as good savings vehicles, instead. They can also be held while earning interest, while also waiting for the stock market to decline, exposing good buying opportunities. If used for income only, bonds can be laddered to provide liquidity with short-term bonds, intermediate-term bonds, and higher-yielding long-term bonds. More diversified options can be constructed using certain short-term, intermediate-term, and long-term bond index, managed, and ETF funds. If a fund doesn't satisfy the concern that they never mature like an actual bond, there are now bond ETFs that hold bonds until they do.

Other methods investors might utilize are derivatives and hedging instruments. These investments can assist an investor like insurance can protect a homeowner. The problem is that the investments, like options contracts, expire in the short run, and unless you are right about your bet, you lose the premium (investment) when it expires.

Although these options and derivative instruments have helped a few investors in the short run, we do not recommend them for the long run. We advise the individual investor to either stay away from them or become an expert, in hopes of protecting yourself from what could develop into a "gambler's" mentality.

Consider that if you could buy fire insurance on your neighbor's house (as indicated in the movie *The Big Short*), the house would have had to caught fire within the option's life span, which can be as short as four months. So, if you like to predict the future by investing in options, you will have lots of fun. On the other hand, if you grow weary of losing your option money on bets that never came true, we recommend a responsible asset allocation that represents your personal investment needs and risk tolerances.

Stay diversified among the following categories (revisited):

Among fund-sponsoring companies—Avoid those that are too big to fail, too big to hack, or suffer from a centrally located biohazard. You should recognize many of the fund companies from your old 401k statement, and others from advertisements. No matter how much you love a fund company, it is not worth concentrating all your wealth with a company that might develop problems we cannot even comprehend right now.

At least half of your portfolio might be structured with some of the biggest and well-known fund companies, such as Vanguard, Fidelity, Schwab, iShares, SPDRs, etc. The other half of the portfolio might utilize many of the less well-known funds available in the market. New ETFs are coming out every day, so your choices will expand, but be careful to pick funds that meet your needs and can be sold without a large spread between what you want to sell for and what the buyer will pay you.

Among portfolios' internal funds—Avoid redundancy among holdings. Even if you only believe in low-cost index funds, why hold one index and watch your funds fall 50 percent in a crash, as some did in 2008 and 2020.

Many different low-cost index funds/ETFs follow low-correlating indexes which might reduce your downside in the next crash. Examples would be a total bond market index fund vs. total stock market index fund--same index structure and low cost, but different holdings.

One index fund might hold large-cap value securities, whereas the other might hold large-cap growth securities. Even if you are an "indexer" (an investor who invests only in particular indexes and index funds), we recommend diversifying among the different indexes. Other investors like to diversify among managed funds. Still, others like to use the strategy of diversifying among non-managed, passively managed and fully managed funds and ETFs.

If any of your funds are managed, it's good to avoid using the same manager to manage all your different funds. If you have many funds with one company, the same manager may be managing several of your funds; hence you might have too much overlap of stocks among your different funds. Using index funds, smart-beta funds, strategic beta funds, and multifactor funds will assist you in reducing the redundancy of individual securities.

Factors are quantitative characteristics of securities you invest with. They help investors focus on areas of the market that are more specific to desired risk exposures and historic return premiums. The harvesting of certain factors allows for more concentration of desired elements and characteristics, such as risk or expected investor-behavior patterns. Unlike index funds that hold a predetermined pattern of securities, factor investing allows for concentration within desired segments of the overall market index.

Factor investing allows you to "stack the blocks" as needed. Multifactor investing takes the desired factors and mixes them like mixing multiple colors of paint on a canvas.

When creating your portfolio, you or your adviser have opinions regarding allocation levels among the internal funds. Here are a few parameters for maximum allocation for a portfolio's fund allocations.

Portfolio allocation guideline using various funds:

- No more than 3 percent in any single emerging markets fund
- No more than 5 percent in any single high-yield bond fund
- No more than 5 percent in any single sector fund
- No more than 10 percent in any single equity fund
- No more than 10 percent in any international or global fund

- No more than 12 percent in any single balanced fund
- No more than 15 percent in any single investment-grade bond fund

The overall allocation percentages among the general areas of the market have their minimums and maximums as well. For example, no more than "X" in bond funds, "X" in stock funds, "X" in international funds, "X" in sector funds, etc. This example will, however, let you know how we would diversify among funds to avoid anyone fund harming the overall portfolio; your preferences will vary. So, choose wisely.

Internal securities holdings inside individual funds that make up the portfolio—Many individual securities within the funds in the portfolio, reduce the risk of individual bankruptcies or individual defaults.

You will be holding ten to twenty different funds that individually hold anywhere from one hundred to a thousand internal stocks, bonds, or cash investments. Your total securities among all the funds might exceed 5 thousand to 10 thousand. If one internal stock or bond goes bankrupt, you might not even notice it! Remember, we are not trying to beat any index. We are creating our index-like portfolio that considers a substantial number of investment factors. We just go further by considering different companies, managers, indexes, and portfolio-construction strategies.

We frequently hear from our friends about how they picked a stock that is now worth many times what they paid for it. What we seldom hear about, however, is when the stock they purchased dropped like a rock--or went bankrupt. Placing all our hopes on one stock or bond when we now have so many diversified options is unwise. Why take the risk? Now, if you want to gamble and can write off your losses over time, enjoy the ride! Who knows, you might be right from time to time; but gambling is not for most investors.

Rebalancing the Portfolio

Rebalancing provides liquidity. It forces asset owners to buy at low prices when others want to sell. Conversely, rebalancing automatically sheds assets at high prices, transferring them to investors who want to buy at elevated prices. Thus, rebalancing a portfolio is counter-cyclical, supplying liquidity.

Rebalancing is an asset-management strategy. This technique is not necessarily designed to "beat" the market. It ensures that you maintain a relative balance of positions and risk levels, such as when the stock market is up, and you rebalance to bonds. What if the stock market kept going up? Did you make a mistake buying more bonds?

Rebalancing is an "autopilot" mechanism designed to maintain risk levels, not to generate more profits. If you reassess your risk tolerance, income, and liquidity need, your allocation needs will become apparent. As we previously detailed, say you started Social Security Income at retirement: that extra 20,000 or 30,000 dollars a year might be equivalent to owning a million-dollar T-bill or CD. With that in mind, rebalancing to bonds might no longer be desired. Maybe you want to let your stock position build-up, even if that increases the risk level to the portfolio. So you see, proper rebalancing is a personal re-evaluation and reallocation assessment, not a computer program.

Let's look at what most institutional portfolio managers do when creating asset-allocation portfolios. Your portfolio may use some or all the following actions:

Develop an investment Methodology
- Develop a clear outline of investment objectives
- Develop and document investment-management philosophy
- Create and stay with a disciplined investment process
- Determined allowed asset classes, sectors, and indexes
- Document investment approaches and reasons for processes
- Document all portfolio-development methodologies
- Establish a small exposure to contrary investing

Ongoing Research
- Monitor existing positions to verify original investing thesis
- Maintain quantitative data for future evaluation of investment performance, risk, expenses, and characteristics
- Maintain research and knowledge of current ETF offerings
- Maintain research on new allocations and ETF strategies

- Research ongoing investment methodologies and benchmarks

Create investment-fund analysis and selection process
- Identify allowable asset classes and vehicles
- Develop quantitative fund selection criteria, such as
  - Level of risk
  - Expected performance
  - Time frame
  - Liquidity needs
- Evaluate appropriate benchmarks for each portfolio
- Develop historical stress test for each portfolio

<u>Documentation</u>
- Regularly monitor selected investments and process
- Document changes and rationale for new positions
- Document conversations with the client regarding portfolio
- Document rationale for each trade processed
- Document rationale for no trade or reallocation

Overwhelming, wouldn't you say? Fortunately for you, the process in this book will assist you or your adviser with a simpler way of creating your portfolio.

Let's recap:

When constructing a portfolio, remember all the parameters we learned.

1) Select a group of indexes, exchange-traded, and managed funds. (Objectives, size, expenses, ranking, performance, trading volume, etc.)
2) Enter the funds into a portfolio program on an equally weighted basis; (we will rebalance once they are all entered)
3) Review the combined group of funds in the portfolio, its combined historical parameters, and risk metrics.

Examples:

- Portfolio Allocations
- Historical standard deviation

- Best- and worst-performing time frames
- Historical beta
- Sharp ratios
- Historical alpha
- R-squared comparison to the market
- Average bond credit ratings & duration risks
- Portfolio yield
- Portfolio's historical performance
- Portfolio's combined expense ratio

These and many other selected status points will show up on your program's portfolio reports. After allocating the funds equally, you now have a starting point for which to allocate; then reallocate until you get the numbers in the desired parameters to match your desired levels. If the standard deviation numbers are too high, you can reallocate more money to money markets, bond funds, and low-volatility stock funds.

If you enter the portfolio-construction process with desired levels of these parameters in mind, this is your chance to move the numbers around until you create the ultimate investment portfolio. Remember, past results and statistics are no indication of future performance or risk.

Market Value	Unrealized P/L	%Unrealized P/L	Realized P/L				
116,000.00	+14,324.44	+14.09	0.00	46,200.00		85,500.00
216,700.00	-1,430.53	-6.46	0.00	85,500	31,873.33	278,250.00
46,200.00	+5,309.28	+12.98	0.00	278	40,890.72	65,000.00
85,500.00				116,000.00	72,477.08	231,630.33
278,250.00					85,500.00	
807,650.00	0.00	+0.83	801,000.44	807,650.00	+6,649.56	+0.83	0.00

Phase III

Portfolio Monitoring

Monitoring process for portfolio, investments, and estate-planning

Now that we have addressed analyzing your financial plan, as well as insurance, taxes, previous investments, and your estate plan, we can move on to monitoring the investments for your future. These investments will now take priority with constant monitoring for risk, liquidity, performance, and allocations.

When constructing the portfolio, you will have already established what is referred to as a "brokerage account." This account might be registered as a Rollover IRA account, a regular IRA, a Roth IRA, or a "non-qualified" account. This non-qualified account (i.e., regular account) will be registered as one of the following: in your name as an individual; as joint owners with another person; a transfer upon death (TOD) for beneficiaries; a living trust; etc.

As we have mentioned, we want to highlight the benefits and constraints of diversification. We have discussed layering your portfolio(s) with funds with different timelines to provide liquidity, less bruising in a down market, and long-term objectives with growth funds for future inflation protection.

Throughout the process, your needs and circumstances will change. Therefore, you need to be personally involved with your investment portfolios. If you have an adviser, he or she needs to check in with you from time to time to make the necessary personal adjustments you need. You might need to be more aggressive when others need to be more conservative, or vice versa. Something in your life may have created a seismic change in your needs and desires. This is where it becomes painfully clear that some Robo-adviser or large investment-bank adviser is not going to "make the cut" when it comes to your personal needs.

The larger investment companies put their investors into predetermined investment portfolios and models. These models are managed by computers or investment managers who know nothing about you and your life. It is important to stay on top of your needs and feelings about risk. If you have an adviser, he or she should always be happy to meet with you to calm your fears in a bear market or encourage you to expand your planning and considerations about risk.

Dangerous expectations: Remember, if you are looking to demand performance compared to the market, you are setting yourself up for disappointment. Our experience has been that a managed fund might tend to hold up in a down market only because it is not **invested** in the same holdings as the overall stock market that people follow. In some cases, it might beat the index on the way up if the managers were lucky when they bet on a handful of stocks. But if they are down, they could be down in a big way.

A managed fund, however, can provide a good downside allocation because of its negative correlation to the market or other risk-management strategies. What do you want to accomplish? Do you want to beat the market on the way up? Be prepared to gamble. Beat the market on the way down? Then accept the fact that if the market is up 10 percent, you might only be up 4 or 5 percent.

This is because if you are retired, your portfolio might not only be negatively correlated to the index, but the portfolio might hold as much as 50-to-70 percent in cash and bond funds. There is no way you can expect stock market returns with your balanced portfolio, even if you had all stock funds because they are invested differently than anyone index. That is the reason you diversify, to avoid having all your eggs in one basket.

Remember, if you were to simply buy up a total stock market index and leave it for 50 years, you would almost definitely see massive growth, more than any other asset allocation. However, what if you need income or principal within the next six months, three years, or ten years? It is an altogether different story. Same story for managed funds vs. index funds. You will wish you had all index funds when the market is rising, but you will be glad you had defensively managed funds on the way down.

So, it is not about timing the market; if it is, then do it yourself, and buy individual stocks! Better yet, borrow more money and leverage the heck out of your position! If you are right, you will make much more than any appropriately allocated retirement portfolio will make. However, if you are wrong, you could magnify your losses and lose much more than disappointment.

When you leverage your position by borrowing money, you must remember that you are on the hook for that borrowed money. If you have a $10,000 position, and you borrow another $10,000 to double your potential for gains, and the security falls 50 percent, you will still need to pay back $10,000; this would require you to sell your remaining position just to cover the debt, taking you down to *zero dollars in capital!* Still interested? **Any loss or gain is magnified both ways!**

After the financial-planning process is completed and a new portfolio has been constructed, ongoing research on various investment options, portfolio allocations, and investor-profile monitoring is required. See the list of portfolio monitoring activities below.

Please, take this process seriously. Things can change in your life, requiring different styles in portfolio allocations, liquidity preparation, or philosophical investment. You or your adviser should be aware of these monitoring categories and have a process to address them over time.

Ongoing timetable for monitoring investments, portfolio, and estate-planning:

- **Daily**

    —Monitor financial and political news to determine changes in expected interest rates, monetary easing or tightening, tax-law changes, and regulatory issues.

    - o With this updated information, your investments and portfolios are assessed to determine whether changes are necessary.

- **Weekly**

    —Monitor Morningstar and other independent research services' fund alerts.

    - o These are announcements of changes in funds that investors might currently hold; changes such as a fund's internal expenses, fund managers, investment styles, performances, fund ratings, regulatory issues, etc.

- **Monthly**

—Research and shop for new funds offered to investors, ones that have lower expenses, or provide unique structures and management of internal investments that might be beneficial to investors.

  o   Most of this research will be to locate lower-cost ETFs, in hopes of replacing old high-fee managed funds.

- **Quarterly**

—Review and monitor existing funds you hold for accumulated performance, expenses, ranking, and manager tenure, as well as changes in holdings.

  o   You should sell any fund that fails to meet all your required parameters.

- **Bi-annually**

—Monitor your portfolio for funds with a substantial increase in value, and possibly sell off a portion of excess value if gains seem short-lived.

  o   This is to prevent a future loss from a correction of share price due to changes in market conditions. This is relevant for specialty funds such as sector funds. Total market index funds would be exempt, although a total portfolio reallocation might be needed.

- **Annually**

—If working with an adviser, meet over the telephone, video chat, or in person. Update any changes to needed income, investment objective, risk tolerance, estate documents, beneficiary provisions, etc.

o   With this information, a portfolio diagnostic can be performed to assure the funds held and the allocations of the portfolio are in line with your current needs. This is a form of performance report. Our desire is for you to perform well relative to the diversification and risk levels, and to perform rebalancing, if needed, based on your updated risk tolerance, liquidity and income needs, tax situation, and previous fund performances. Remember to invest regularly and rebalance occasionally.

You'll also review your current tax status as it relates to your investment accounts (i.e. Roth conversions, tax-free bond funds, tax-efficient investing, deferred capital gains on real estate sales, family gifts, etc.).

Family changes will be reviewed, and updates to your accounts will be made. Also review such details as joint owners, beneficiaries, and changes to trustees and trust documents.

Finally, your adviser should occasionally inquire about your punch list items and encourage you to complete any projects left incomplete.

Post Planning Administrative Activities:
Whether you do your planning and investing or hire an adviser to assist you, you need to know the behind-the-scenes tasks that will need attention. Investors are frequently totally unaware of the administrative support and services they receive when having those done for them. You can't afford to miss any of these. One big concern would be future tax penalties for missing your retirement plan's required mandatory distributions (RMD's). You or your estate might end up paying a 50-percent penalty on your missed RMD's and cause the family to miss out on inheritance.

Let's take a serious look at areas you must watch very closely:

Monitor and manage your account security—Once you have set up your investment accounts and portfolios, you or your adviser must learn everything and do everything within their capability to secure your account from fraud and cybersecurity concerns. Because bad people can steal your information somewhere down the road, it's important to have someone looking out for you.

For example, if you have an account at a bank, brokerage firm, or with an adviser, they need to be very vigilant in protecting the access to your accounts. If the adviser receives an email from you to liquidate money and send it somewhere, here are just a few steps and questions he or she must investigate:

- The adviser should recognize your original email address
- The adviser should call you to confirm you originated the email
- The adviser should recognize your voice over the telephone
- The adviser should converse with you to make sure you don't sound like you are under duress or confused
- The adviser needs to inquire as to the reason you are taking money out of the account
- The adviser needs to do a tax calculation to determine potential tax liability, penalties or surrender charges if assets must be sold
- The adviser needs to help you determine which account to pull the money from--for example, IRA or non-IRA, Roth IRA, etc.
- The adviser needs to help you choose the appropriate internal asset to liquidate if you don't have enough cash
- The adviser needs to then reallocate the remaining funds.
- The adviser needs to confirm you have a signed instruction form on file for authorization of how and where to send the funds
- The adviser needs to confirm all transactions are completed and documented

The reason for all this effort is to protect your accounts from fraudulent transfers, computer hacking, and elder abuse, which can occur with strangers as well as family members. The Government requires your adviser to be aware of and make every effort to protect you and your accounts. Believe it or not, if your adviser ignored these concerns and you were violated, they could face fines, penalties, and even jail time!

Bill has a standing joke with his clients. He reminds them not to call his office and ask for money after having had one too many cocktails! Ha-ha, we might be mandated to contact the authorized "trusted contact" person listed on their account. This is one of the most important procedures we practice ensuring that you are not compromised or in danger.

Mandatory required distributions from retirement plans—Here, your adviser will remind you of your mandatory distribution dates. Your adviser will also assist in the calculation and disbursement of the yearly required distributions. He or she will fill out the forms, seek your signature, then guarantee your signature. Next, he or she will document where you wish the funds to be sent to, plan whether you wish taxes to be withheld or not and determine how often you desire the distribution be withdrawn. With this information, the adviser can then process your request, document his or her actions, and create a computer task to follow up on any required tasks in the future.

Manage reallocation of funds to be used for RMD liquidations—As the years go by and more annual distributions are necessary, you'll need to plan which funds will be repositioned in preparation for liquidation to satisfy your need for funds.

Process any regular or occasional cash distributions needed—As explained above, examples might be additional income beyond your required minimum distribution or unforeseen lump-sum needs. Your adviser will take your request, calculate which funds should be liquidated, and determine where you need the funds to be sent and whether to withhold taxes--not to mention which securities to sell to produce the cash and how to reallocate the account.

Updating registration of non-retirement accounts to a new trust— You may need to change the designated title of your investments. If you have established a new trust, we like to check in frequently to make sure the appropriate investments are in the name of the trust. Don't let your adviser miss this one.

Examples of other account registrations:
- Individual
- Transfer upon death
- Joint tenancy with right of survivorship

- Joint tenancy with right of survivorship with per stirpes
- Community property
- Tenants in common
- Special Needs trust

As indicated previously, you must update these registrations if any changes occur to your designated registrations, such as the death of a partner, beneficiary, or trustee.

Confirm and update your desired beneficiaries—Every year, your adviser should review your designated beneficiaries on all accounts. Check on whether they are all living and are still your choices.

Assist in the distribution of beneficiary accounts—When an account holder dies, necessary forms and applications are required to either cash out inherited accounts or, if desired, re-register the account in the beneficiary's name. You must ask yourself who will take on this task after your death. Is your new trustee knowledgeable and prepared? Unfortunately, many advisers are not very experienced in account-transitioning and follow-up.

Set up education-funding investment accounts, 529 plan, student loans, etc.— You will need to research the most appropriate state-sponsored plans, process all paperwork & applications, and recommend which funds in the plan to invest.

Research tax information—You should research your cost basis of stocks or mutual funds to assist your tax preparer in determining how much of the profit is taxable. For managed accounts where you determine when and what to sell, you should research the tax liability *before* you act. (If you have an adviser, he/she should be doing this research.)

Setting up new accounts—This process can require substantial paperwork, regardless of whether you are setting up a brokerage account, buying directly from the fund company or buying through an adviser. Government rules require information regarding not only your identity and where the funds came from but also your investor suitability and risk tolerance while investing. When using an adviser, you will be required to answer several questions on your applications; these questions pertain to appropriate mixtures of investments and levels of risk. If working with an adviser, only a senior adviser should help you determine your risk tolerance and asset allocations.

Rolling over outside investments—Whether rolling over a retirement plan from your old employer or an investment company, there are extensive applications and questionnaires required. Confirming your identification, proper ownership of the plan's assets (a spousal release may be required), the tax treatment of the rollover, beneficiary designations, and appropriateness of doing the rollover in the first place, regarding whether this rollover is in the best interests of the owner, which is you.

You should avoid combining a rollover IRA where the funds come from a large company retirement plan with a smaller individual IRA. Tax complications and loss of asset-protection features may occur. For older Americans, certain investments like annuities being cashed out could cause not only income taxes to rise but the cost of Medicare supplements to go up.

Documenting Fiduciary Standards

When assisting you in setting up new investment accounts, your adviser is required not only to do what's right for you; he or she is required to verify where your investment money came from and attempt to verify that you are not a criminal or terrorist. If you are advised to liquidate an old investment, your adviser must check on the potential capital gains taxes and early withdrawal penalties that might be due. A mistake here could result in an increase in taxable income in any one year. This could raise your tax bracket to very undesirable levels.

An adviser must document and justify all advice given to the client, especially when making changes to your investments. He or she must document and justify why certain investments were sold and why others were purchased. Even after the portfolio is fully allocated and established, a documented process is required. Every year, your adviser must show why he or she needs to reallocate the funds or leave the funds unchanged. This rule is designed to avoid what is known as "reverse churning," a behavior in which fees are charged and no services are rendered. Advisers are required to be fully accountable to regulators for any fees charged for services provided.

As we learned previously, it is our belief the adviser should:

Daily—Watch interest rates and politics

Weekly—Follow fund alerts

Monthly—Screen new mutual, index, and ETF funds

Quarterly—Screen existing funds held in your portfolio

Biannually—Screen and sell specialty funds considered overpriced

Annually—confirm the client's needs, goals, & objectives, risk tolerances, and personal-health changes. Assess the overall level of satisfaction the client has for the quality of his or her life, as well as for the services the adviser provides.

Other research and assistance an adviser should provide include:

Social Security Income planning

Charitable Gifting

Health Saving Account investing and distributions

Other important facts & resources
How Advisers are paid

Fee for Services:

Of course, planning and investing on your own will save on all the fees normally charged. You will, however, be required to become your adviser and stay current on all the disciplines that make up financial planning, not just investing. If you hire an adviser, you should expect the adviser to do much, if not all, of what has been outlined in this book; otherwise, you should question the adviser's value.

Unlike many advisers, we don't believe the firm or adviser should charge hundreds or thousands of dollars for financial reviews and diagnostics. We would prefer that the adviser be a positive impact on the client's process. The adviser should give you time to think about his or her recommendation before suggesting that you become a client.

Bill, his associates, and his staff respect the fact that in other firms, some advisers charge for analyzing your finances and creating a financial plan. Bill's firm, however, believes that the adviser should be willing to take on some speculative risk, investing time, and energy upfront in hopes that you will choose to become a client. In Bill's office, any workups, analyses, diagnostics, or reports are all performed at no cost to the prospective client.

These services are offered as Bill's way of committing time and resources in good faith. He hopes the investor will appreciate and trust what his firm has to offer you by allowing his firm to place investments in managed accounts where his firm is paid a very small fee (percentage of assets under management) to continue its asset management services. By charging an asset-under-management fee, the adviser has skin in the game. *The adviser benefits when you benefit.*

An example of fees that you might expect advisers to assess on managed accounts. (Each layer of investment receives a different rate; a large portfolio charges an average of these levels, not cumulative levels)

A portfolio of $1,000,000.00 would pay an average annual fee of 1.1%

1.2 percent per year/.10 percent monthly on accounts of less than $500,000
1.0 percent per year/.083 percent monthly on $500,000 to $750,000
.95 percent per year/.079 percent monthly on $750,000 to $1,000,000
.85 percent per year/.070 percent monthly on $1,000,000 to $2,000,000
.65 percent per year/.054 monthly on $2,000,000 to $4,000,000
.45 percent per year/.037 monthly on $4,000,000 to $6,000,000

All services and costs related to the managed account are combined inside this fee. Other advisers might add additional charges outside of the management service for things such as trading fees, platform fees, IRA fees, 12b-1 fees, etc., *so ask questions!*

The actual fee is determined based on the adviser's anticipated workload and activities planned for the client. Also, the type of portfolio may affect the fee. An all-bond portfolio will require less monitoring and management and thus a reduced fee.

As clients consolidate outside accounts, the combined assets may bring the fee down. Lastly, clients that attend one of Bill's lengthy investment classes may qualify for a slight discount.

Other Ways Financial Advisors Are Paid

Hourly—Financial advisers who charge by the hour generally do not sell or manage investments; however, some do.

Retainer Fee—An adviser may charge a flat fee every year for ongoing management, or a quoted fee for a one-time financial plan.

Commission—Financial advisers may be paid a commission on the sale of mutual funds, annuity products, limited partnerships, REITs, individual stocks, bonds, options, etc. The commission is generally a percentage of the investment amount. Your investment professional is required to provide disclosure of all costs related to the purchase and sale of investments. You should always receive or be shown how to gain access to a current investment prospectus which will document all fees, surrender penalties, and legal details. This way of paying an adviser, in our opinion, will be eliminated in future years.

Avoid these Common Mutual Fund Commission Structures:

Although we recommend only "no-load" mutual funds, you may still hold some of these fund shares listed from past investments.

Class A Shares—An up-front commission is deducted from your initial dollars invested. This type of sales charge is often referred to as a "load." The commissions on Class A shares contain breakpoints, which reduce the load percentage for larger investments. Front-end loads can range from about 1 percent to 5.75 percent. Class A shares also charge 12b-1 fees, which can be as high as a quarter of one percent every year.

Class B Shares—Rather than a front-end load charged at the time of the initial investment, B-share commissions are charged when you sell shares of the fund. There is a much higher ongoing management fee, compared to A-shares, and a declining surrender charge based on the number of years the investment has been held. These shares are being phased out for mutual funds, yet they still exist within variable annuities.

Class C Shares—There are no up-front loads or commissions on C-shares. There is typically a 1 percent early withdrawal penalty if funds are withdrawn within 12 months. C shares, therefore, lend themselves to investors who anticipate repositioning or liquidating their investments after one year or so. C-share funds will often have a higher expense ratio than A-shares, to pay the adviser, and the extra fee does not decrease over time. However, mutual-fund companies are beginning to place a 10-year limitation on the extra expense used to pay the adviser.

Should you pay commissions, asset-management fees, hourly rates, or just do it yourself?

The important thing to remember, if you use an adviser, is that you need to be aware of all commissions, management fees, and expenses associated with a proposed investment; also be aware of whether the charges are front-end loaded, back-end loaded, or ongoing. Generally, however, we seriously encourage you to invest only using "no-load", low expense ratio funds, and ETF's. If using an adviser they should be fee-based or fee-only practitioners.

When investing on your own, we recommend that you do business with well-known fund companies and research potential investments. Start conservatively, and do not be rushed to invest. Unless you are responding to a tax deadline or a pressing personal situation that requires immediate action, your strategy should be to never act under pressure or deadlines when investing.

Be aware that not everything you read or hear regarding investing is valid, appropriate, or relevant to your situation. There is so much information easily available, especially on the Internet, that research can seem overwhelming at times. Our advice to investors is to create your goals and investment strategies first, based on your needs, then use your plan as a road map in navigating the mountains of information. Let common sense direct you and listen to your internal voice of reason when it tells you, "This sounds too good to be true."

Do not be in a hurry to invest. There is a saying in this business:

Investing is like a train, there is always another one coming. There are always areas of the market that might seem like a good buy. Whether that ends up being true or not, we cannot know for a while, but you will always have options and opportunities.

Don't rush the process.

Whether you do it yourself or hire an adviser, do not ignore the need to plan. Start today. Regardless of whether you are currently retired, are soon to retire, or are years from retirement, now is the time to be in action. In the realm of financial planning, it is rarely too late and *never* too early.

Whether you are a novice or an experienced investor, there are several questions you need to consider before setting your investment goals:

- What are your priorities?
- Are you a short- or long-term investor?
- Do you plan to use your investments for tax savings or current income?
- How much risk are you willing to accept? How much of your money can you afford to lose?

If investing on your own, read every publication you can get your hands on. Learn everything you can about insurance, estate planning, taxes, investing, and investment logistics.

Selecting someone to manage Your money

The most important factor is the reputation of the adviser and how comfortable you feel with this individual. You should never be pressured to purchase any service or investment product. People who are paid for investment advice are required to be a Registered Investment Adviser (RIA) through the SEC and/or the state in which they provide advice.

Fee-based asset managers and hourly-only financial planners act in your best interests as a fiduciary and are either an RIA themselves or an associate of an RIA. Thus, you should feel comfortable not being pressured.

Many advisers sell their services under the umbrella of a hybrid broker-dealer/Registered Investment adviser. The broker-dealer is licensed with the SEC in each state in which they do business, and with the Financial Industry Regulatory Authority (FINRA). FINRA can be contacted at (800) 289-9999 or www.finra.org. The broker-dealer is responsible for supervising his or her registered representatives and associate advisers.

Never work with an adviser you haven't done a background check on. Review their background for customer complaints, industry violations, and believe it or not "criminal convictions".

For questions regarding a member's disciplinary history, the SEC, which regulates Registered Investment advisers, can be contacted at 800-SEC-0303 or www.sec.gov

To check on your adviser's background you can go to www.brokercheck.org

Hunter William (Bill) Bailey, is a registered adviser associate with Securities America Advisors, Inc. and is a registered representative with Securities America, Inc. a registered Broker/Dealer, Member of FINRA/SIPC, Securities offered through Securities America, Inc. Member FINRA/SIPC. Advisory services offered through Securities America Advisors Inc., California Insurance License #0589198

You should avoid:

Unlicensed Activity—All brokerage firms or securities representatives who conduct business must generally be registered with the FINRA or another regulatory organization such as the NYSE. Investment advisers must generally be registered with the SEC or with the states they conduct business in.

Unregistered Securities—Securities offered to you *should* be registered with the SEC, unless exempt.

Unauthorized Trading—Brokers must not trade on your account without consulting you personally unless you have provided *written* authorization for them to do so.

Unsuitable Recommendations—Brokers and advisers are required to make suitable recommendations based on your personal financial goals, which include investment needs. It is unethical and *illegal* for them to make recommendations that purely benefit themselves.

Tax-deferred redundancy—Avoid placing tax-deferred annuities inside a tax-deferred IRA. You are losing out on low-cost investment options, and the insurance agent is advising you incorrectly--and possibly for his or her benefit to make a commission.

Account Churning—Excessive trading of a customer's account is an illegal practice if it is done solely for generating sales commissions. You should be given a disclosure if changing positions will cause you to lose money to fees.

Reverse Churning—This is a situation in which an adviser charges you a fee to manage your assets, but once the original portfolio is constructed, little or no attention to monitoring or reallocating your investments is done. You are simply paying a fee to hold your money in an account that gets no personal attention. Some advisers circumvent this rule by employing computers to do automatic rebalancing, giving no consideration to your situation. If you are in a group "bucket" portfolio plan, your specific needs are forgotten, and the computerized generic-reallocation model takes over.

Untimely Trades— Brokers and advisers are required to promptly execute customer orders at or near the same price that was quoted at the time you, the client, authorized the trade. As soon as possible, the brokers must make every effort to execute a trade that you have requested. An exception is the discretionary managed account.

Unauthorized Transfers of Assets—No funds may be transferred to different accounts or be withdrawn without your written consent. Trades and reallocations within an account can take place if the adviser has a limited power of attorney to trade, in your best interests; but no funds or money should ever be moved from account to account without your approval.

If in doubt, do not invest!

Before you take advice from a professional, look at the experience of the adviser and the adviser's connection to the local community. The adviser should already have many satisfied clients and referrals. The adviser should be respected as an understanding and non-pushy professional.

Look for any conflict of interest. Ask yourself questions like: Is your tax preparer trying to sell you an annuity? Is your insurance agent trying to sell you investments? Is your bank teller trying to do your financial planning? These professionals should stay within their respective fields of expertise. The reason this is a conflict of interest is that they already have your personal information. They are representing their employer, not you, the client.

Most professionals are paid for what they do. Find out how and from where the compensation comes. Make sure you are okay with the compensation package for the adviser.

Avoid FOMO (fear of missing out) and investing too soon. Don't take the advice you find suspicious. If you are not comfortable with an adviser's advice, don't take it! The suggestion might be great for the adviser's risk tolerance but may be off the mark for yours.

That's not to say all financial advisers out there are self-serving. Most advisers are looking out for their clients' best interests. However, you need to keep your financial goals and risk tolerance requirements in mind.

This section may seem like a sales pitch to hire an adviser, but it is not. It is just a reminder of what you will need to take on yourself, which is extremely exciting if you have the interest and time. If not, you will be better prepared to know what you deserve to get as a client. Let's see how much you've learned about the process from reading to this point. Answer the following questions and assess whether you are prepared to take the process on yourself, or whether you should turn the process over to an adviser.

Congratulations! You made it!

Do you know enough about the investment and financial planning process to do it yourself or to determine if your adviser is serving your best interests?

Test your knowledge about the subjects you have learned in this workbook. *(The answers to the self-test are located after the Readiness List.)*

Self-Test

1) What is the responsibility of a Fiduciary?
   a) To sell you the most popular investment
   b) To invite you to a complimentary steak dinner and seminar
   c) To put your needs and best interests first

2) What does "beta" mean?
   a) The historical return of a fund
   b) The fund's and portfolio's market-risk level
   c) Price indicator

3) What is the standard deviation?
   a) Average bond rating
   b) Historical market trends
   c) Historical fund volatility measurement

4) What is a step-up in basis?
   a) Indicates the investment's cost-basis increase upon the death of an owner, resulting in the elimination of taxable capital gains tax.
   b) An increase of the death benefit provided in an annuity contract upon the death of the annuity's owner.
   c) A home exercise using stairs

5) What is an index fund?
   a) A low-cost fund simulating the same holdings of the desired market index
   b) A fund that invests in a specific sector of the market
   c) A fund that guarantees the original investment

6) What is a tracking error?
   a) Lost performance data
   b) Risk of underperformance compared with the desired index
   c) Incorrect buy/sell order input

7) What is the elimination period?
   a) The waiting period before long-term care insurance benefits begin
   b) Declining investment life span
   c) The date that the income of a portfolio runs out

8) What is a Roth IRA conversion?
   a) The mandatory date in which you must withdraw funds
   b) The process of transferring a Roth account to beneficiaries
   c) The process of transferring money from an old taxable IRA to a nontaxable Roth IRA

9) What is a Fiduciary Standard?
   a) Required income calculations at age 72
   b) Legal standards for financial advisers to follow
   c) Level of risk for retiree

10) What does the term "rebalancing" mean?
   a) Bouncing from one investment to another
   b) Correcting an original trade-request mistake
   c) Reallocating back to original portfolio balances

11) What is a durable power of attorney?
    a) Legal document giving a trusted person legal authority over medical, financial, or legal decisions in the case of your medical incapacity.
    b) Long-lasting medical equipment
    c) Giving your trustee full freedom to change your trust

12) What is a 1031 Exchange?
    a) 1031 tax-free trades
    b) Tax-free exchange of stocks for bonds
    c) Tax-deferred real estate exchange

13) What is a Stretch IRA?
    a) IRA payout over 10 years to non-spouse beneficiaries
    b) Lifetime income investment in bonds
    c) Rising and falling dividends over time

14) What does the term "bond duration" mean?
    a) The lifespan of a bond
    b) A measure of calculating risk to a bond when interest rates rise. For every 1 percent interest-rate rise, the bond will fall in value by its duration parameter.
    c) Bond credit rating over many years

15) What does lateral integration mean?
    a) Staging out investment from short-term, intermediate-term, and long-term holding patterns
    b) Portfolio-construction method
    c) Weaving cash, bonds, and stocks into a portfolio

16) What does the term "multifactor ETF" mean?
    a) A fund with multiple investments inside it
    b) A portfolio full of multiple ETFs
    c) Exchange-traded fund targeting specific factors of indexes

17) What does the term "smart beta ETF" mean?
    a) An ETF that attempts to reduce market risk
    b) An ETF that smart people invest in
    c) An ETF that is not available to the public

18) What does the term "Sharpe ratio" refer to?
   a) Sharp-looking allocations
   b) Risk/reward ratio
   c) Efficient share pricing

19) What does the term "time-series momentum" mean?
   a) Momentum accumulation in value and market trends
   b) Investing regularly over time
   c) The trend of an asset with its past performance

20) What does "SEC yield" refer to?
   a) Sector fund's yield
   b) The yield based on the most recent 30 days fund price, then calculated as an annualized yield.
   c) Total return based on yield and share-price appreciation

21) What is the meaning of a negative correlation?
   a) A negative rate of return resulting in losses
   b) Historical volatility calculations
   c) Positions in a fund or portfolio which are opposite the index or market they are being compared with

22) What is Modern Portfolio Theory?
   a) Modern investment style
   b) Study of risk, return, correlation and diversification, the basics of the "efficient frontier" concept
   c) A belief that diversification is a good method of investing

23) What are leveraged ETFs?
   a) Multiple securities inside an ETF
   b) Low-cost ETFs
   c) A fund that borrows additional money to magnify your investment, increasing the potential for gain or loss

24) What does the term "vertical integration" refer to?
   a) Constant increasing in share price
   b) A fund-allocation method of combining total market, index, and managed funds within a portfolio
   c) The calculation to average the total fund's portfolio expenses

Get your answers after you also complete a "Readiness Exercise"

Readiness Check List

Now that we have checked your knowledge about the process, let's check your readiness. Check off each item listed, indicating whether you have completed that item, are planning to complete it, or don't need to address it.

Trusted Contact(s): People you want to be contacted if you become confused, incapacitated or die
__yes__no__n/a

Emergency contact(s): Trustee/trusted family member or friend available to step in and help in an emergency or death
__yes__no__n/a

Adequate cash reserves that are immediately accessible to you and a family member
__yes__no__n/a

Safe-deposit box and home safe for holding legal documents
__yes__no__n/a

Home survival supplies for power outages or other emergencies, such as food, water, medical supplies, etc.
__yes__no__n/a

Home-safety inspection: Inspect electrical, gas, water, fireplace, trip hazards, crime prevention, and emergency-contact measures
__yes__no__n/a

Proper Medical insurance, deductibles, co-pays and supplements
__yes__no__n/a

Long-term care insurance, waiting periods, coverages if needed (disability insurance for younger employed investors)
__yes__na__n/a

Supplemental Liability insurance coverages (umbrella, professional liability, E&O, rental property insurance coverage, etc.)
__yes__no__n/a

Life insurance, if needed, planning to cash in or convert to long-term care insurance
__yes__no__n/a

Plan to purchase travel insurance when traveling
__yes__no__n/a

Current will(s)
__yes__no__n/a

A current durable power of attorney for medical (end of life)
__yes__no__n/a

A current durable power of attorney for legal and financial
_yes__no__n/a

A current living trust(s)
__yes__no__n/a

Online and physical emergency document storage
__yes__no__n/a

Planned and implemented a "lateral integration" investment plan
_yes__no__n/a

Planned and implemented portfolio "vertical integration" plan
_yes__no__n/a

Re-evaluated tax strategies and investment positions
_yes__no__n/a

Do you plan to pay off the home mortgage and use that monthly mortgage payment to invest in the market for future inflation protection?
__yes__no__n/a

Have you paid off your home mortgage and used those previously allocated monthly mortgage payments to invest, instead, into the market for future inflation protection?
__yes__no__n/a

Financial Monitoring (are you or an adviser doing the following?):

Daily, monitoring of interest rates, taxes & politics
__yes__no__n/a

Weekly, evaluation of investment-fund news and alerts
__yes__no__n/a

Monthly, research new investment funds opportunities
__yes__no__n/a

Quarterly, monitor performance of existing investments
__yes__no__n/a

Biannually, evaluate high-performing funds to harvest gains
__yes__no__n/a

Annually, re-evaluate each item listed below:

present & future income sources
__yes__no__n/a

insurance coverages
__yes__no__n/a

estate-planning documents
__yes__no__n/a

present and future tax status
__yes__no__n/a

investment and portfolio update & risk rebalancing.
__yes__no__n/a

re-evaluate DIY plans, current adviser, or seek help.
__yes__no__n/a

"Now see here, you had better do your homework or all hell will break loose. Doing the investment process, yourself is not so easy, is it? You could also do your own brain surgery, but it gets really hard, even with a mirror."

See how you did by comparing your test answers to the correct ones listed in the table below?

Correct test answers:

1) c	13) a
2) b	14) b
3) c	15) a
4) a	16) c
5) a	17) a
6) b	18) b
7) a	19) c
8) c	20) b
9) b	21) c
10) c	22) b
11) a	23) c
12) c	24) b

How did you do? Ready to take it on yourself? Or are you appreciating your adviser more? Remember, if you need advice or assistance, feel free to contact us. It is what we do.

You already know the answers to the "readiness questions," so get to work!

"Cliff Notes"

The Process
(A brief description for classes & meetings)

Introduction

What Happens When You First Begin the Process?

If you work with an adviser, a welcome letter will be sent to you detailing the process, explaining what you can expect, along with a biography of your adviser(s), their organization, the staff, and their qualifications. You will also be asked to fill out an extensive questionnaire detailing your present financial situation and future needs. If, however, you are managing your finances, you will need to pay close attention to the following diagnostic analysis since no one will be watching out for you. We call this "the discovery stage."

Developing Goals-Based Planning

Analyses must be performed; these are referred to as the "diagnostic reviews." These diagnostic reviews will be performed with you in person at your first visit or, if necessary, after your appointment, and then followed up with a written list of recommendations.

Phase I—Financial-planning process--questions to ask:

Personal cash-flow diagnostic: Do you know how much you will receive from all retirement sources when needed?

Insurance diagnostic: Are you fully insured for all risks relating to your life, assets, and activities?

Estate-planning diagnostics: Have you established all the necessary legal documents needed?

Tax diagnostic: Are you paying avoidable or unnecessary taxes?

Existing investments & portfolio diagnostic: Before deciding to keep or change existing investments, you first must know whether the investment fits your needs and whether it's of good quality. The

208

various investment parameters you should consider are listed below, as well as how they stack up inside your old portfolio.

(The following parameters relate to the individual funds and, in some cases, the overall portfolio):

- Internal-asset allocations
- Structure-index funds, managed funds, or ETFs
- Comparative ranking
- Turnover ratio
- Total assets held
- Expense ratio compared with its category
- Performance compared with its index
- Bond duration
- Bond credit ratings
- Fund SEC yield

Existing portfolio's diagnostic
- Asset allocations, sector weightings, and cash balances
- Total securities
- Equity & fixed-income style-box ratios
- Historical 3-month, one-year, three-year, five-year, and ten-year performances
- Best- and worst-performing time frames for the most recent past three-month, one-year, and three-year time frames
- Total number of funds in the portfolio
- Risk/reward scatterplot
- Modern portfolio statistics of portfolio
- Historical standard deviation
- Historical beta (risk related to the overall market)
- Historical upside & downside capture ratio
- Sharpe ratio
- Sortino ratio
- Historical alpha
- R-squared
- Portfolio account registration
- Beneficiary designations
- Tracking of mandatory retirement plan distribution after age 72 (reserve assets for liquidation, etc.)

Post Diagnostics Punch List—Examples of items that may need your attention:
- ✓ Maximize all liability-insurance levels
- ✓ Purchase disability and/or long-term care insurance
- ✓ Purchase or cancel life insurance as needed
- ✓ Review or set up wills, durable power of attorney
- ✓ Re-register certain assets in the name of your trust
- ✓ Review or change beneficiaries to certain accounts
- ✓ Delete deceased trustee when needed
- ✓ Maximize existing retirement plan contributions, if working
- ✓ Reallocate existing retirement plans to appropriate levels
- ✓ Rollover existing plan to a self-directed IRA if appropriate
- ✓ Pay off or refinance residence
- ✓ Replace certain investments found to be flawed
- ✓ Reallocate retirement plans at your workplace, if needed
- ✓ Visit your accountant to perform a yearly tax estimate
- ✓ Assess whether a Roth IRA conversion would be wise

Post Punch List: It will take time, and this list will be helpful as you research and complete all the necessary items that need your attention both immediately and over time.

Phase II–Portfolio construction using rules-based investing

New Portfolio-Construction Process: Developing a new portfolio is a profoundly serious endeavor. You will need to manage and allocate your portfolio carefully but only based on strict criteria relating to your liquidity needs, income, philosophies, and risk tolerance.

Managing Your Old Appreciated Funds: For non-retirement portfolios, deferred capital gains can cause significant pain if positions are sold. Determining the cost basis of funds sold or exchanged is critical.

The "New Portfolio concepts" will contain no-load funds from well-known investment companies and lesser-known companies that have been vetted and monitored.

- **Lateral Integration**—Here, the concept of time and need for liquidity (cash availability) is imperative when constructing an investment portfolio. Three stages of different funds are layered to provide less volatility at the time of liquidation.

- o **Stage 1–** (short term needs such as unforeseen emergencies): Money Market funds, short-term government funds, short-term bond funds, etc.

- o **Stage 2—** (Intermediate-term such as when additional income or opportunity cash is needed): short-term investment-grade funds, intermediate-term bond funds (taxable and tax-free), balanced funds, total return funds, asset-allocation funds, etc.

- o **Stage 3—** (long-term needs intended to accumulate for the long-term appreciation to supplement things like late retirement or long-term care needs in the distant future): Stock funds, international stock funds, Sector funds, Real estate funds, etc.

Next is the determination of which types of funds to use and where to place them.

Vertical Integration—There are three levels of a portfolio utilizing three distinctly different types of no-load investment funds. Imagine a pyramid in three equal horizontal levels

Pyramid levels:

- o **Level One, the base of the pyramid—**Here, the largest portion of the pyramid is a variety of low-cost total market index funds that are chosen from many different well-known investment fund companies.

- o **Level Two, the midsection of the pyramid—**This middle section is reserved for more specific categories of low-cost index funds and various exchange-traded funds.

- o **Level Three, top of the pyramid—**The smallest part of the portfolio is a handful of well-managed funds chosen based on their historical performance, or history of lower volatility, history of superior management, etc.

211

New Portfolio Design: Using the lateral and vertical Integration concept, you will use ten to twenty different funds from the areas discussed. You will have screened and selected the funds that meet your objectives, the parameters we mentioned, and the various companies you are comfortable with. You can start with a generic allocation plan. We usually do this by simply dividing the number of funds into the amount of money you want to invest. Next comes listing the selected funds and their starting allocation in a computerized-analysis program. We use Morningstar. With the portfolio allocation started, you can quickly go to the results page of the software and look at what your beginning parameters are. For example:

Overall starting Portfolio Parameters:

- Standard Deviation for different time frames
- The yield of the portfolio
- Average combined fund expense ratio
- Beta or the compared risk of the portfolio to its index
- Alpha or performance of the portfolio compared with others
- Sharpe ratio or risk-return ranking
- Average bond credit ratings

These are just a few of the overall parameters to get you started. Now you can start to "shuffle the deck" or reallocate among the funds to meet your desired parameter levels.

It may take several allocations to meet your objectives, so do not be discouraged. You will find the ultimate portfolio takes effort. Don't forget, past results are no guarantee of future performance.

Phase III–Investment, portfolio & monitoring process

Investment & Portfolio Monitoring: After the financial-planning process is completed and a new portfolio has been constructed, various ongoing research, portfolio allocations, and investor-profile monitoring are required.

Ongoing planning and investment service timetable:

- **Daily**—Monitor financial and political news

- **Weekly**—Monitor independent research service alerts, such as Morningstar, etc.

- **Monthly**—research and shop for new funds

- **Quarterly**—Review and monitor existing funds held

- **Biannually**—Monitor portfolios for a substantial increase in value

- **Annually**—Update any changes to needed income paid out by the portfolio, investment objectives, risk tolerance, tax changes, etc. With this information, perform a detailed portfolio diagnostic.

Financial-planning follow-up

Ongoing administrative activities:

- Mandatory required distributions from retirement plans
  - ✓ Manage reallocation of funds to be used for RMD liquidations
  - ✓ Process any regular or occasional cash distributions needed
  - ✓ Update registration of non-retirement accounts to a new trust
  - ✓ Confirm and update your desired beneficiaries' planning
  - ✓ Assist in the distribution of beneficiary accounts
  - ✓ Set up education-funding investment accounts, 529 plans, etc.
  - ✓ Research tax information for cost basis
  - ✓ Set up new accounts
  - ✓ Additional capital gains planning
  - ✓ Roth IRA conversion planning
  - ✓ Charitable giving
  - ✓ Social Security planning
  - ✓ Intergenerational asset transfer and planning
  - ✓ College funds and liquidation planning for college expenses
  - ✓ Student-loan analysis
  - ✓ Estate-planning and asset-protection planning
  - ✓ Questions regarding existing 401k allocations
  - ✓ Health Savings Account planning, funding, and distributions
  - ✓ Rollover outside investments

- ✓ Update investments and registrations as laws change
- ✓ Review tax situations as tax laws change
- ✓ Re-evaluate portfolios, assets, and cash positions
- ✓ Re-evaluate income-distribution methods

Fee for Services:

If using the services of a fee-based asset manager/adviser, a detailed list of possible fees, disclosures, conflicts of interests, and services should be reviewed and examined. You will receive a disclosure document called the ADV document, which details all the governmental required information regarding how the adviser runs his or her practice.

To check on your existing/proposed adviser please go to BrokerCheck.org. This valuable site will provide you details about your adviser, such as background, education, licenses, length of service. It will also tell you whether he/she has ever been reprimanded, fined, sued, suspended, or barred from the profession.

Adviser websites are required to list a link to this Government site, so it should be very accessible. Good luck!

Portfolio diagnostic

This report will replicate the Morningstar portfolio-analysis information gleaned from inputting all the various investment funds you hold in your portfolio. The report will provide data analysis and consolidate the average figures among all your funds.

Mutual fund and exchange-traded fund research checklist

This list of fund questions provides various data points and elements necessary for you to complete your fund research and selection. ETFs require additional questions regarding intra-day trading concerns.

Glossary of Investments

Commonly Used Investments

Stocks and bonds—A stock represents partial ownership (*equity*) in a corporation. Usually, a corporation has a maximum number of shares it can issue, as authorized by its corporate charter. While the common stock is the basic ownership element, a corporation may be authorized to issue more than one class of stock.

Preferred stock, for example, allows those shareholders to receive special privileges, such as the payment of dividends. It also includes preference over common stockholders in the distribution of assets during corporate bankruptcy. Corporate bonds constitute a company's debt, borrowed at a certain interest rate, to be repaid over a specific period. When a company is liquidated due to bankruptcy, bondholders receive the distribution of corporate assets after creditors but ahead of stockholders. There are several different types of bonds available.

Municipal bonds—Municipal bonds support general state or local government needs or special projects. Issuance must be approved by referendum or by an electoral body. Before the Tax Reform Act of 1986, the terms "municipal" and "tax-exempt" were synonymous because most municipal debts were exempt from federal income tax as well as from most state and local income taxes. The Tax Reform Act of 1986 divided municipal bonds into two broad groups: public-purpose bonds, which remain tax-exempt and can be issued without limitation, and private-purpose bonds, which are taxable unless specifically exempted.

Savings bonds—US government instruments are issued in denominations ranging from $50 to $10,000. They are purchased at a discount and redeemed at face value at maturity.

Treasury bonds—Negotiable US government long-term debt instruments are secured by the full faith and credit of the US Treasury. They have 10- to 30-year maturities and are issued with a $1,000 minimum denomination (par value). Treasury bond income is exempt from state and local taxes but not federal taxes.

Zero-coupon bonds—Unlike other bonds, these earn no periodic interest payments. Zero-coupon bonds are purchased at a fraction of their face value (discount), and the investor is paid the full or par value ($1,000) at maturity. These securities might not mature for 25 years, so as we have already learned, a commitment like this can cause a substantial level of short-term volatility. Also, even though the interest is not paid out until maturity, the annual interest earned is taxable each year.

Mutual funds—These are professionally managed pools of investment money for investors who have similar objectives. Investors are buying shares of the fund, each of which represents proportional ownership in all the fund's assets.

A fund's manager will buy a wide range of stocks, bonds, or money market instruments. The benefit of mutual funds is that they allow an investor to access a wider range of securities than he or she might not be able to afford otherwise if purchased individually. Earnings are distributed to shareholders in the form of dividends and capital gains. There are two types of mutual funds: "open-end" and "closed-end." An open-end mutual fund is considered a typical mutual fund. The open-end mutual fund continuously creates new shares as investors buy into the fund. You can redeem your open-end fund shares at any time without a specific buyer. Open-end mutual funds are sold at net asset value (NAV), which is calculated by taking the net assets (market value of the securities, less any liabilities) of the fund and dividing by the number of outstanding shares. This means the shares in an open-end mutual fund may be worth more or less than the original investment, depending on the market value of the securities inside the mutual fund.

Unlike open-end mutual funds, closed-end mutual funds have a limited number of shares available to be bought and sold. Closed-end mutual fund shares are traded on the open market, so there must be a specific buyer of the fund's shares when sold. This means that the market price for a closed-end mutual fund share could be valued at more or less than its net asset value (NAV), depending on market demand for the fund's shares.

A fund with a sales load should be avoided. No-load mutual funds do not assess a sales charge on the purchase or sale of shares.

Exchange Traded Funds (ETFs)—For the knowledgeable and experienced investor, costs may be kept to a minimum with the use of a brokerage account and the ability to purchase exchange-traded funds (ETFs). Traded like stocks but diversified like mutual funds, these securities are for the more experienced do-it-yourself trader. These securities are usually designed to reflect various indexes, sectors, and strategies of the markets.

Other Investment Options

Cash or currency
While a bank is a convenient source for holding cash, you need to be fully aware of the scope of a bank's options when it comes to managing your money. When you deposit money in the bank, the bank will negotiate to lend your money to borrowers who pay much higher interest to the bank than you get on your savings account.

Certificate of deposit (CD)
Certificates of deposit (CDs) are another form of currency but with some restrictions. Depositors are required to commit to leaving their funds with the bank for a period, typically one month to five years.

US Treasury bills (T-bills)
Treasury bills (T-bills) are a form of a CD with a maturity range of one year or less, issued by the United States Government.

US Treasury notes
This asset is like T-bills, but with longer maturities, generally lasting up to 10 years.

US Treasury bonds
These bonds are designed for long-term investors who want a stable income. The time frame for this asset can be as long as 30 years. If investors want to redeem the bonds, they can sell the asset in the open

market. However, the US government does not guarantee the resale. The bond's face value can only be guaranteed if held until maturity, so unless you purchase a Treasury bond that is maturing soon, you will have to brave the market.

A bond's market volatility is related to interest-rate risk. If interest rates drop and your bond is earning a higher interest rate than a new investor could obtain, your bond will become more desirable, allowing you to sell it at a premium. The opposite is true when interest rates rise.

Commercial paper
This asset is like a CD and is offered by both profit and nonprofit corporations and municipalities. The time frame is usually less than one year, so this asset works well as a short-term liquid asset. The investor has the option to wait for maturity or sell in the market. The issuer backs the security against default, not the Government.

Money market mutual funds
This investment is designed to provide the investor with convenience and stability. This type of fund is composed of several short-term money market instruments ranging from US Treasury securities and CDs to tax-free municipal securities. Money funds provide the investor with a large degree of diversification of assets within the fund. The fund is constantly reinvesting ("rolling over") maturing securities, thus creating liquidity and providing the investor with the ability to write checks on the account.

A money market fund offers:

- Price stability (although not guaranteed)
- Current interest rates
- Liquidity
- Check-writing privileges
- Transferability among other mutual funds within a family of funds, without a sales charge.

There are a few variations of money market funds:

Money fund–one that holds CDs

Government money fund—holds short-term US Treasury securities

Tax-Free money fund—holds short-term municipal securities

History has shown that short-term liquid investments have not produced high levels of income and capital gains. They do, however, work great for cash reserves.

An investment in a money market fund is not insured by any government agency. Although the fund seeks to preserve the value of your investment at $1 per share, it is possible to lose money by investing in the fund.

A CLOSER LOOK AT DIFFERENT FORMS OF MUTUAL FUNDS:

Mutual funds, index funds, & exchange-traded funds

Mutual funds ('40 Act funds, i.e., the Investment Company Act of 1940)
Mutual funds were designed to give the small investor the opportunities of stock market investing without requiring large sums of capital or a great deal of knowledge. The investor can participate with small capital contributions into the fund.

The fund company's portfolio manager is responsible for choosing which securities are held within the fund, as well as when those securities are bought and sold. The manager typically diversifies the investments among a large number of securities within each fund. Studies show that diversification among different types of investments may produce less volatility, compared with investing in one class of investment.

US government bond funds, tax-free municipal bond funds, balanced funds, and income funds were designed as an alternative to stock-oriented mutual funds. Investors turned to these funds for high levels of current income and, in the case of municipal funds, tax-free income. Bond mutual funds may be a source of income with less default risk than one individual bond. The large variety of funds provides many options for diversifying risk and gives the investor the ability to pick among funds that best suit their investment objectives.

Another benefit of mutual funds, aside from the ability to reduce relative risks, is that they are regulated by authorities such as the SEC. The SEC regulates the mutual fund company's management, sales practices, and the practices of its sales representatives. While the SEC regulates the industry, it makes no guarantees or assurances to the investor.

Having discussed mutual funds in general, let's explore some of the many different funds available today. We will begin with the more conservative funds (money market funds) and work up to the most aggressive funds (aggressive growth funds).

These same types of funds will be replicated by the new Exchange-traded funds market. Originally the ETFs mirrored popular indexes like the S&P 500, Total Stock Market index, and even Total bond market indexes. Since investors are migrating away from the higher expense cost in managed mutual funds, many of those same fund companies are creating similar yet passively managed ETFs. They are simply doing the same thing as an ETF as they did as a managed mutual fund, just cheaper and more appealing to the investor. The fund categories to follow can be purchased either as a mutual fund with a higher fee, or the same fund can be purchased as an ETF with a lower fee.

Popular managed mutual fund & ETF categories:

Short-term US Government Securities Fund—This type of fund holds short-term US Treasury notes and US Treasury bills. As a result of their short-term maturities, the fund's share price usually remains more stable than other long-term bond funds. The internal maturities are usually less than four years. The interest income may be lower than other funds, but the stability of the share price makes this fund attractive to many investors. Additionally, the knowledge that the US Treasury directly backs the securities in the fund (though not the fund itself) in case of default is reassuring. Although these funds seldom provide growth through capital gains, they do, however, generally pay a higher income than a regular money market fund. This investment works well as a savings vehicle.

Short-term income fund—Similar to the US government securities fund, this fund holds corporate securities such as short-term corporate bonds and commercial paper. This type of mutual fund is liquid at net asset value; therefore, money is available whenever it is needed. The interest income is generally slightly higher than the short-term US government fund.

Short-term tax-free income fund—This fund is like the other two in that it holds short-term securities. However, these securities contain municipal issues that earn tax-free interest. Additionally, interest income may be higher than the tax-free money market fund. Internal bond maturities usually range from one to four years.

Short-intermediate US Government Securities Fund—Made up of short-term and intermediate government securities, primarily intermediate-term US Treasuries and other government issues, with maturities of one to ten years. Longer maturities usually mean higher yields.

Short-intermediate income fund—Similar to the short-intermediate US Government Securities Fund, this fund holds bonds with longer maturity dates, which increases market volatility and produces higher yields as well. This fund is made up of corporate issues with bond maturities of up to ten years. A portfolio may contain a variety of securities that mature in one, three, five, and ten years. As with layering CD maturities, this method reduces the risk of fluctuating interest rates.

Short-intermediate tax-free income fund—These funds are remarkably like the US government and income funds, the primary difference being that the fund is made up of intermediate-term municipal bonds. If you recall, this means the investor can receive income federally tax-free. Investors can sometimes avoid state income taxes if they reside in the same state as the issuing state of the bonds in the fund. Again, the longer the internal maturities, the greater the resale volatility.

Adjustable-rate securities fund—This fund holds variable-interest-rate corporate securities. Although not immune from market volatility, they are less vulnerable to interest-rate risk because these securities tend to keep up with rising interest rates.

Adjustable-rate US Government Securities Fund—This type of fund invests in adjustable-rate US government mortgages. These funds are very similar to adjustable-rate securities funds and are made up of US government-backed securities: GNMA, FNMA, and FHLMC.

Senior floating-rate fund—These short-term senior corporate loans are like corporate CDs. However, they are not guaranteed by the government and usually hold middle- to low-rated corporate loans that are not securitized with assets. If all goes well, meaning the company maintains its ability to repay its debts, the yield is generally higher than regular CDs and the market volatility is relatively low.

Government bond fund—Although the name would seem to indicate that this type of fund holds only government securities, it may hold a variety of corporate securities and other positions as well. Read the prospectus to determine exactly what securities a fund holds.

The Government National Mortgage Association (GNMA) bonds are extremely popular mortgage-backed securities. If purchased inside a mutual fund, you can eliminate the risk of spending down your principal as you receive principal-and-interest payments. This is because, inside this type of mutual fund, the fund manager reinvests the principal received from the mortgage payments into new GNMA mortgages and pays out the interest portion to the investor for income or reinvestment.

The traditional US Treasury funds can be a wonderful source of market appreciation if purchased when interest rates are high and rates decline after the fund is acquired. This makes them popular among investors, enabling the owner to sell shares and demand a premium since buyers will get higher interest income than they could get by buying newer lower-yielding bonds. Be aware that the reverse is true when the US Treasury fund you purchased produces lower yields than what newer buyers receive, which makes your shares less desirable and likely, if sold, to sell at a discount.

For income, these funds are desirable. Yields are not guaranteed, however, as they will rise, and fall based on the sale of bonds within the fund and new money entering the fund.

Disclaimer: Generally, bond values will decline as interest rates rise. Conversely, bond values can rise if interest rates fall. Changes in credit rating will also affect bond prices.

If we have thoroughly confused you, you are beginning to understand the complexity of proper investment planning. Hang in there; there are plenty more details to come.

Municipal bond fund—Usually known as tax-free or income funds, these funds offer a variety of portfolios. Some funds hold long-term municipal bonds from around the country, which provides federally tax-exempt income. Other funds hold insured bonds, which are municipal bonds that have the principal and interest guaranteed by an insurance policy in case of default. This generally costs the investor about ½ of 1 percent. Then there are the state tax-exempt bond funds. For example, if you live in California and invest in a California tax-free income fund, you will receive interest income that is exempt from both state and federal taxes. These funds help the state as well as the investor because the money stays local.

Because tax-free funds often hold long-term bonds, just like the long-term US Treasury bond funds, the market value can decline with rising interest rates.

Corporate bond fund—As with all bond funds, a corporate bond fund value can fluctuate with interest-rate changes. Since these funds are designed to compete with US government bond funds, the internal maturities of the bonds are usually long-term. These long-term maturities usually provide higher yields. One big difference between corporate and US government bond funds is the credit rating of bonds inside the fund. There is no default risk with US government bonds and usually little risk with municipal bonds (although one should be aware of the municipal bond ratings). Corporate bonds have a wide range of creditworthiness.

High-yield income fund—These are like corporate bond funds. However, nearly all the bonds in the fund will have lower credit ratings. These bonds became known as junk bonds in the late 1980s and early '90s. With low credit ratings, the yields are usually 2 percent to 3 percent higher, when compared with safer higher credit-rated bonds. This higher yield can sometimes make all the difference to an investor who needs income.

Multisector bond fund—Comprising of different types of bonds, these funds provide the investor with many diverse positions (for example, government and corporate bonds, both foreign and the US) that, in theory, present greater stability against changing markets. These funds are also diversified regarding credit ratings. The fund could have holdings ranging from low-yield, high-grade corporate bonds to high-yield, low-grade corporate bonds.

World bond fund—Unlike the multisector bond fund, which tries to diversify among bond classes, this fund focuses on bonds from many countries. A global government bond fund's goal might be to diversify among government issues world-wide. The biggest concern with this fund is currency risk and political unrest.

Convertible bond fund—With income as the primary goal and growth secondary, this fund holds a variety of convertible corporate bonds that pay interest. These bonds can be converted to common stock if the portfolio manager so chooses. This is an attractive feature because, while in the form of bonds, the investor enjoys a moderately high-interest income. If the underlying stock value rises significantly, the bonds can be converted to stock at a lower predetermined price, which means a profit to the investor. If the market doesn't rise, the investor continues to receive income.

Balanced fund—The balanced fund provides a little of everything for passive investors. The fund is invested in stocks, bonds, and cash, so the investor can simply own one fund and be satisfactorily diversified. Of course, we always recommend additional diversification because no portfolio manager or single fund can provide everything to every investor.

Asset-allocation fund—This type of fund usually invests in cash, bonds, and stocks. The asset-allocation fund seems like the balanced fund with one primary difference: asset-allocation fund managers have the authority to position the portfolio among the different classes as they see fit without having to conform to predetermined asset class percentages. This is the closest to a true asset management portfolio.

Lifestyle fund—The allocation model for this fund will change and rebalance, starting with an aggressive approach and becoming more conservative over time.

Equity income fund—This fund usually pursues current income by investing at least 65 percent of its funds in stocks of companies that produce above-average dividends such as large-cap value bricks-and-mortar, blue-chip stocks.

Growth and income fund—Here, the mutual fund invests everything in stocks except for its cash reserves. The stocks purchased are income-producing (for example, blue-chip stocks). With the portfolio's stocks producing dividends, the fund may pass them along to the fund's shareholders annually in the form of a mutual fund dividend. Not all growth and income mutual funds distribute the income they receive; others choose, instead, to reinvest dividends internally.

Domestic stock fund—This fund invests only in US stocks. These domestic companies, however, do business overseas, so you will want to become familiar with their practices and determine whether they meet your investment criteria. Few domestic companies do business strictly in the US, so we recommend you do your homework.

Growth fund—This fund invests primarily in stocks of growing corporations that reinvest earnings back into the company rather than producing dividends. It may buy stocks in companies that use some form of financing to expand, which is called *leveraging*. This debt can help a company expand, and successful expansion will boost the earnings of the stock and the stock price will rise. On the other hand, if the company takes on debt and is not successful, its market value can plummet. Here, "the trend is your friend", the stocks in the growth fund tend to be on a trend upward and are very popular during their run in the market. Trends don't last forever!

World stock fund—This fund invests primarily in equity securities of issuers located throughout the world. It also maintains a percentage of the fund's assets in the United States. Most investors don't have the time or the resources to be knowledgeable about stocks half a world away. The world stock fund provides the investor with another layer of assets, management, and diversification in their portfolio.

European stock fund—This fund limits its stock purchases to European countries and/or their affiliated companies.

Small company fund (small-cap)—If you are a long-term investor, small company (small-cap) funds may be for you.

These funds buy stock in small corporations, determined as those with less than $1 billion in assets. The companies are less established in their markets and track record and are therefore less appealing to conservative investors but more so too optimistic, long-term buyers. These funds may have fewer up days and years in the stock market than others, but when they are up, they are up. The converse is also true, as these volatile funds can drop significantly in value.

International/foreign stock fund—This fund invests primarily in the stocks of companies located outside the United States. They also offer tremendous latitude, allowing the investor access to foreign markets in the familiar form of a mutual fund. The fund manager will create a portfolio of stocks issued by foreign countries and/or US companies doing business in foreign countries.

Multi-asset global fund—This fund is a global asset allocation fund that provides the portfolio manager an unlimited discretion in choosing which countries and what kinds of assets will be placed in the fund.

Pacific Stock Fund—This fund invests primarily in issuers located in the Pacific Basin (Japan, Hong Kong, Malaysia, Singapore, and Australia).

Sector fund—This type of mutual fund is the closest thing to buying individual stocks. The fund invests only in one segment (*sector*) of the economy. This is great for the investor who believes a specific area of the economy is going to rise. The benefit to the investor lies in the diversification within the chosen sector. The risk of a total loss, which would face the buyer of an individual company's stock if that company went bankrupt, is lessened.

Emerging markets fund—Here, the fund's manager travels the world looking for stocks in "emerging" countries that have great growth potential. Examples of emerging countries are Vietnam, Russia, and China. Remember that this fund has one of the highest risk levels among funds, but it also has the potential to produce higher returns.

Aggressive growth fund—A mutual fund that seeks rapid growth of capital by accepting higher risks in its portfolio, generally through the purchase of smaller-company stocks. The fund manager will also practice frequent trading (borrowing to buy stocks and selling off stocks) within short periods. This is referred to as "selling short" or "short selling."

Index Mutual Funds

This type of mutual fund's objective is to mirror a stock market index or bond market index. It will purchase and hold the securities listed on the desired index. The fund provides diversification and performance exactly like that of the target index. An index fund is not managed; the fund seldom sells or repositions security; thus it can charge low management expenses. Many "experts" swear by index funds, arguing that they offer the needed diversification for investors without a fund manager buying and selling. Still, others point out that with an index fund, you are unable to take advantage of market opportunities.

Where there is an index, there is an index fund. Index funds come in categories that vary from fixed income (bonds) to equities (stocks), so here are a few categories:

- Short-term bond index
- Intermediate-term bond index
- Long-term bond index
- International bond index
- Global bond index
- High-yield bond index
- Total bond market index
- Total stock market index
- International total stock market index
- Global index
- Sector index funds (utilities, energy, real estate, gold, etc.)
- Small-cap value index
- Small-cap growth index
- Mid-cap value index
- Mid-cap growth index
- Balanced index
- Balanced tax-managed index
- Etc.

For the passive investor, the index fund allows the investor to allocate as desired while substantially reducing fund expenses.

You will notice that we like to use index funds as the base (core) for our client portfolios to provide a vast level of diversification of internal securities and an exceptionally low fund expense ratio.

Exchange-Traded Funds

ETFs are similar, yet different, than the managed funds and index mutual funds. Except for many features. ETFs come in all the categories already reviewed. The mutual fund, however, is created by the fund company; they take the investors' money, and in exchange, give them shares of the in-house managed fund. When the shareholder wants to sell the shares back to the issuing company, they can only do so at the end of the trading day. This issuing company tallies up the assets in the fund, determines a share price, and buys back the shares from you at that value.

The exchange-traded fund is bought and sold throughout the day at a fluctuating value based on the internal asset value, which will, of course, fluctuate daily. The investor buys and sells shares from other investors through a broker/dealer or, if in large amounts, from an intermediary who, in turn, buys the securities that will be put into the ETF. If the investor wants to sell shares, he or she sells to other investors through a broker/dealer or market maker such as Schwab, TD Ameritrade, or Fidelity.

For large transactions, the ETF gives the internal securities back to the intermediary, who sells them and gives the cashback to the investor. Here, the investor, not the other shareholders of the fund, is the one who pays any capital gains taxes due. Therefore, we hear the term "tax-efficient" when discussing the ETF.

This point is important because the index fund and managed fund must sell securities "across the board" if they lack the cash for liquidations. For fund investors who plan to hold on to their shares, they might be impacted by internal sales that could cause them to owe taxes even if they never sold any shares but were forced to take taxable gains. The ETF fund's shares are sold by the exiting investor; they are not sold by the fund itself.

When using the ETF, the investor can choose to sell shares at any time during the day for good or bad. Be advised, however, that if the investor chooses to sell shares at the bottom of the market, he or she may find that the shares could recover in value by day's end. More control of when to sell is the primary reason people buy ETFs. We do not encourage frequent trading during the day since price spreads severely eat into any profit. It is best to purchase for long-term holding patterns and to only sell when reallocations or liquidations are necessary. ETF funds usually (but not always) provide much lower fund expense ratios.

Unlike the managed mutual fund that is only required to disclose its holdings every quarter, the ETF remains fully transparent, allowing the investor to know what they hold throughout the trading day. Shares of an ETF provide an investor the ability to add similar features they might with a single stock--features like using a stop-loss limit order, selling short, call options, and others. In summary, for the aggressive investor, ETFs are a particularly good fit. The rest of us need to be careful with these features; they could be dangerous for the novice investor.

Exchange-traded products—There are investments out there under the exchange-traded theme. Be careful, however; an "exchange-traded note," might sound good, but it may lack liquidity or trading volume. Watch out for the "too good to be true" investment.

Exchange-traded notes—As we indicated, the liquidity and protection of the ETN are suspect. Like annuities, these products are designed to get you to invest for the long term and to accept a minimal return with promises of high long-term profits with no risk. How do they do this? Like an index annuity, banks and brokerage houses construct the ETN for the investor solely to focus on the guarantees, not disclosing the reality of what the note is invested in. It is usually better to invest, accepting the reality in risk and volatility inherent in your portfolio's long-term investment.

Annuities—Insurance companies offer this investment but do not be misled by the institutional name. Annuities are constructed in a variety of forms. Historically, they were offered as a fixed interest-bearing, tax-deferred vehicle. As competition with mutual fund companies increased, the insurance companies created an alliance with mutual fund companies and began offering some interesting products.

There are two basic types of annuities, fixed and variable, and a newer equity-indexed annuity. All offer the investor a tax deferral on the capital accrual and/or appreciation. This is significant because the insurance company can offer investment returns that are competitive with banks and mutual funds without the investor having to pay current income tax on the earnings if earnings are held inside the annuity. Once withdrawn, they will pay "ordinary income tax rates."

Fixed annuity—This investment is simply a savings account with an insurance company. You receive a tax-deferred accumulation of earnings. There is a large variety of terms to choose from. These annuities promise a guaranteed, fixed investment return of from one to ten years.

A fixed annuity is remarkably like a bank CD, but the annuity's terms are usually longer, and the early withdrawal penalty is greater. Although the fixed annuity is great as a long-term asset, it is important to understand that there are strings attached: fixed returns, early withdrawal penalties, risk of the insurance company going out of business, and ordinary income taxes on gains when withdrawn.

Variable annuity—The term "variable" indicates that this investment will vary in value. Constructed of subaccounts, which act like mutual funds, the variable annuity offers growth opportunities not found with fixed annuities. The subaccounts in the variable annuity offer all the different types of investment options that mutual fund companies offer. This is no surprise because many of the top mutual fund companies provide the management of variable annuity subaccounts. One must remember that this variable annuity comes with no guarantee of principal from market fluctuations, only if you die.

The value of the subaccounts will fluctuate with the market and thus will rise and fall in value with no guarantee. As with all annuities, all gains are taxed as ordinary income when withdrawn. Also, remember that not only does the variable annuity charge extremely high mortality and expense fees, administrative fees, and policy fees; they also mark up the expense ratio of the underlying funds in the contract.

Registered index-linked annuity-a new version of an index-linked annuity that provides more participation of the index than the traditional index annuity but limits the upside performance while limiting the downside risk.

Equity-indexed annuity—This is a hybrid of both the fixed and variable annuity. It offers all the safety and guarantees of the fixed annuity, but it also offers the potential for enhanced value through participation in equity market performance. This is usually accomplished by linking (indexing) the credited performance rate to an equity index. The most popular index used is Standard & Poor's 500, which can be manipulated in favor of the insurance company.

Let us look at the many benefits and features annuities offer:

For fixed annuities, the insurance company guarantees the entire principal invested. So, if the stock or bond market is down, you don't have to be concerned, because you will continue to receive the stated amount of interest on the contract. These guarantees are only as good as the insurance company itself, so make sure you go with highly rated companies.

The principal guarantee attached to the variable annuity is only for the annuity owner's beneficiaries. For a fee, the insurance company will not only guarantee the original principal (minus any withdrawals) for the beneficiary but increase the amount of coverage to a variety of different calculations, all designed to interest the prospective buyer.

The index annuity provides guarantees and participation in the upside of the market by holding your money and promising you a low-interest rate. The insurance company invests your money in its portfolio with high-yielding preferred stocks, utility stocks, intermediate-term bonds, government bonds, and high-yield bonds as well as real estate investments. The hope is that the insurance company will honor the promised low yield payable to you. The insurance company will then take the excess to pay itself back the agent's commission that they advanced. Next, with a small portion of your money, it buys "call options" each year. If the market is up and the insurance company cashes in, you will receive only part of its profits; the rest is kept for itself.

Let's see how the insurance company does this…

The insurance company will invest, say, 80 percent of your money in high-yield securities. If the company can earn 3 to 4 percent, it can pay you the promised minimum of 2 percent and keep another 1 to 2 percent for themselves.

Next, the insurance company will use the other 20 percent to purchase call options on the stock market, using 2 percent each year, in hopes of profiting, and then sharing the profit with you.

If the insurance company claims that the investment is guaranteed by the Government, they simply buy government zero-coupon bonds, bonds that are purchased at a discount, and will mature at full value in ten years; hence the guarantee to get your original investment back. The other 20 to 30 percent of your deposit is used to buy stock market options and pay the company back for the up-front commission paid to the agent and the parent company.

You get half the profits from what the insurance company invested, and it gets the rest. No wonder insurance companies are so rich!

Also, your gains do not enjoy special tax breaks, such as low capital gains tax rates or a step-up in basis upon the death of the owner. The investor can, however, transfer among internal fixed or variable subaccounts without concern for capital gains tax implications. All transactions within the annuity are still tax-deferred; nothing is taxable until the funds are withdrawn. At that time, all earnings are taxed as ordinary income.

Limited Partnerships
Here's an investment that will raise the eyebrows of experienced investors who are familiar with the devastation that limited partnerships suffered during the 1980s. Limited partnerships experienced some of the most disappointing investment results that an investor could have. Most lost everything. Due to sweeping tax changes that eliminated the tax advantages of limited partnerships as tax planning tools, many partnerships failed.

Different types of limited partnerships that you may come across include but are not limited to, include the following:

Real estate
Mortgages
Leasing assets
Technology
Research and development
Cattle
Wind Energy
Cannabis
Wineries
Movie Productions

The partnership allows the limited partner to limit their exposure to losses and legal liability to the amount invested. The managing general partner assumes all responsibility and risk beyond your investment capital. When considering the use of a limited partnership, we recommend allocating no more than 10 or 15 percent of your investments to limited partnerships. Do your homework, and always thoroughly review the prospectus.

Although it is more profitable to get closer to the origin of the investment rather than waiting for publicly traded diluted shares, the risk rises exponentially. Be careful, however, and heed the warning of this saying, *"Going into the partnership the general partner (promoter) has all the experience, and you (the limited partner) have all the money. Coming out of the partnership, the general partner has all the money, and you have all the experience."*

So, be careful, and trust no one. Do background checks on everyone running the partnership. Start with www.brokercheck.org. Then at least go online and search for everyone you can.

Real Estate Investment Trust (REIT)
Like limited partnerships, the REIT purchases real estate and/or real estate mortgages. There is a general partner in charge of the trust. The big difference with the REIT is that the investor doesn't have to be tied

into an investment that can go on for decades. There is usually a ready market in which to sell the REIT shares.

Stay away from non-publicly traded anything! What this means is that the up-front cost can be extremely large, and the real net resale value could be alarmingly low--if there are buyers at all. Non-publicly traded REITs and partnership tout that they have less market risk. Think about it: The stock market just dropped 50 percent, and you look at your partnership statement, and the value listed is still the same.

As the author speaking here, wow, I want that investment. The reality, however, is that because it is not publicly traded, there is no current comparative price. Just like when your home dropped in value, if no one in your neighborhood could list and sell their home, you would never have any idea of what a buyer might pay you. The real resale value of your home could be half, but you would never know it. So no, stay away from non-publicly traded anything.

A safer way of owning this asset would be to purchase a mutual fund, index fund, or ETF that holds 100 or more REIT stocks inside of it. This investment would give you liquidity, provide up-to-date resale values, and little or no up-front cost.

Glossary of Terms

Numerals

12b-1 fee—A fee for the promotion, sale, or other activity connected with the distribution of a company's mutual fund shares, determined annually as a flat dollar amount or as a percentage of the company's average total net asset value during the year.

30-day distribution rate—A figure that indicates what the 12-month yield would be, considering the most recent distribution and the month-end offer price. While yield calculations use the actual distributions over the most recent 12 months, the 30-day distribution rate is calculated by annualizing the last distribution and dividing by its recent offer price.

30-day wash rule—IRS rule stipulating that losses incurred from selling securities may not be used to offset gains if equivalent security is bought within 30 days before or after the date of sale. Selling one S&P 500 fund from one company and buying the same fund, but through a different provider, is not allowed.

A

The asking price—The price at which a dealer is willing to sell a security.

AUV (accumulation unit value)—A unit of measurement to determine the value of a cash subaccount unit, determined by the same process as the net asset value (NAV) of mutual fund shares. The AUV is calculated by taking the NAV and adjusting it for insurance expenses (mortality and expense [M&E] rate and administration expenses).

Average annual total returns—The annualized return for the security, averaged over the specified time.

Average annual turnover ratio—A measure of the amount of buying and selling activity of security. Turnover is defined as the lesser of securities sold or purchased during a year divided by the average monthly net assets. A turnover of 100 percent, for example, implies that positions are held, on average, for about a year.

Average bond quality–The average quality value of all bonds held by the security. Bond quality indicates the likelihood of default by the bond issuer. The default probability is rated from AAA (highly unlikely) to D (in default).

Average duration–The average duration in years for all securities held by the fund or subaccount relative to the risk of rising interest rates. A five-year duration calculation would assume a 5 percent loss if interest rates went up one full percent, or conversely, a 5 percent gain if they fell by 1 percent. Investor emotions, however, would be the final factor in determining the price of the assets.

Average P/B (price/book ratio)—The market price divided by stock equity for all equities held by the fund or subaccount. The ratio shows how much investors are willing to pay for each dollar of company equity.

Average P/E (price/earnings) ratio—The share price of the stock divided by earnings per share (EPS) for all equities held by the fund or subaccount. The ratio shows how much investors are willing to pay for each dollar of the company's earnings.

B

Basis point—A basis point is equal to .01 percent of bond yield. An increase of 100 basis points is a 1 percent increase in yield.

Beta—A measure of a security's volatility with the equity market as measured by the market index relative to each security's investment category. This statistic reflects only the market-related portion of an investment's risk, and thus it is a narrower measure than the standard deviation, which reflects total risk (market-related and unique). In general, the volatility of the relative market index is 1.00, so a beta of 1.50 would indicate a volatility level 50 percent greater than that of the market. Since this statistic is relative to the market, betas for securities with little or no correlation to the market are less significant. Consider the R-squared as a measure of more significance. Also, see "Squared."

Bid—the price a mutual fund will pay you to redeem shares, also referred to as NAV (net asset value), or the price a dealer is willing to pay to buy a security.

Bond-rating—A rating method based on the range from AAA (highly unlikely) to D (in default) measures the likelihood of default by the bond issuer.

Book value—The book value is normally considered as the company's assets minus its liabilities. Intangibles, like goodwill, are usually excluded from assets.

Bottom-up—investing strategy that focuses on good firms or securities first, then the industry and economic trends. The theory supposes that a portfolio of well-chosen securities will have long-term success in any environment.

Breakpoint—A volume-based percentage discount in the commission charged by an investment. Larger investment amounts qualify for increasingly generous discounts.

C

Callable—A bond option that allows the issuing company to redeem (buy back) the security before its scheduled maturity. Bonds are usually called when interest rates drop, allowing companies to issue new bonds at lower rates.

Capital gains—The profit derived from selling a security at a higher price than that paid to acquire it. A mutual fund may distribute all or some of its accumulated capital gains to its shareholders annually.

Closed fund—A mutual fund that no longer issues shares. Normally, a fund will close because the fund's manager feels there are a limited number of good investments left, or the fund needs to keep net assets low enough to enter and exit holdings quickly.

Clean shares—A fund that does not charge a load (commission) or maintain 12b-1 service fees

Convertibles—Corporate securities such as preferred stock or bonds that can be exchanged at a pre-stated price for a set number of shares of another security, like common stock.

D

Death benefit–If the annuity contract owner dies before annuitization (structured income payout), the insurance company will pay the annuity beneficiary the contract's accumulated value less any withdrawals, or the number of premiums paid less any withdrawals, whichever is greater. Variable-annuity contracts never pay beneficiaries less than 100 percent of the investment minus previous withdrawals. The death benefit for annuities and life insurance is paid out in full and is tax-free.

Dividends—Distributions resulting from the income and dividends from the mutual funds, index funds, ETFs, and other securities.

Dollar-cost averaging (DCA)—A strategy that diversifies the prices of security by buying a specific amount over set intervals.

E

The exchange-traded fund (ETF)—An investment vehicle through which shares can be bought and sold during trading hours. Assets in this type of fund originally mirrored an index; however, new versions come out every day.

Expense ratio—A mutual fund's annual expenses (management fees, 12b-1 fees, and other operating expenses) expressed as a percentage of its average net assets. The total return data provided reflects performance after operating expenses are deducted.

F

Future value—The calculated value of a specified current investment compounded at a fixed rate over a set number of years.

Factor investing—A numerical characteristic common across a broad set of securities

Global fund—A mutual fund that invests in both foreign and domestic securities. These funds differ from traditional international mutual funds because they can keep a significant portion of their assets in US stocks and bonds.

Health savings account (HSA)—A tax-deductible savings account for employees and employers, designed to provide funding for medical-plan deductibles. Contributions to the plan are tax-deductible, and withdrawals for qualified medical expenses are tax-free.

Inception date—The date an investment commenced operation.

Income distribution—A distribution to a security's shareholders of the accumulated net income from investments.

Index—A hypothetical, unmanaged, often weighted portfolio of securities, the performance of which is used as a benchmark in measuring the performance of actual securities. Common examples are the Dow Jones Industrial Average (DJIA) and the Standard & Poor's (S&P) 500.

Index fund—A fund designed to match the performance of a particular index. For example, an S&P 500 index fund would buy the same companies with the same weightings that are found in the S&P 500. This is more of a passive management style, which should convey lower management fees to investors.

Initial public offering (IPO)—A corporation's first offering of stock to the public.

Internal rate of return (IRR)—The interest **rate** at which the net present value of all the cash flows (both positive and negative) from a project or investment equals zero. **The internal rate of return** is used to evaluate the attractiveness of a project or investment.

Investment category—the stated purpose or goal of a security's operations. This term often determines the types of investments the security makes, the results expected, and the level of risk with which it is associated.

Investment-grade bonds—Bonds with ratings of BBB or above.

Individual retirement account (IRA)—Originally, IRAs were individual pension accounts available to anyone not covered at work by a qualified pension plan. Effective January 1, 1982, all wage earners, including those already in company pension plans, can make tax-deferred contributions to IRAs, with income limits, however.

J--K

Junk bonds–Bonds with ratings of BB and below.

L

Lateral integration–A mental picture of a horizontal line broken into three stages. One represents investments with noticeably short horizons, like certificates of deposits and money market funds. The second stage is designed to hold investments with moderate risks, like bonds and balanced funds held for an intermediate time frame. And finally, the third stage is made up of long-term investments like stock, real estate, etc.

Leveraged buyout (LBO)–The practice of buying a company by using borrowed funds or replacing existing equity with debt.

M

Management fee–the amount paid by a mutual fund, index fund, or exchange-traded fund to the investment fund manager. The industry-wide average annual fee is about .002 of 1 percent of fund assets.

Market timing–Buying and selling funds (or any security) based on economic indicators or market forecasts, the intent being to outsmart other investors.

Market value–The current share price of a security.

Maximum front-end load–The utmost sales charge that can be assessed upfront to invest in a security. The front-end load fee is assessed at the time of purchase, with the charge amount often dependent on the dollar amount of the purchase.

Moving averages–An average of a security's prices over a specific period, used with many commodity prices to show trends.

N

Net asset value (NAV)–A mutual, index, or exchange-traded fund's share price, computed by subtracting total liabilities from total assets and dividing by the number of shares outstanding.

Net assets–The mutual fund's or variable annuity's total assets after liabilities.

No-load fund–A Fund without an up-front or back-end sales fee. Also, see "load."

Negative correlation–Indicates the opposing similarities of an investment fund compared with the general market.

O

Option–The right to buy or sell a security at a certain price within a specified period. The option itself is a contract and entitles the holder to buy or sell if exercised. "Call" options allow the holder to buy a security at a predetermined price whereas "put" options allow the holder to sell a security at a predetermined price.

Other insurance expenses–All insurance-related charges other than the mortality and expense (M&E) charges. The fee also includes administrative charges.

P--Q

Policy fee–an expense charged by a variable-annuity contract to cover the maintenance of annuity records.

Portfolio composition–A percentage breakdown of securities holdings in several specified categories.

Preferred stock–Class of stock that pays dividends at a specified rate and that has preference over common stock in the payment of dividends and the liquidation of assets.

Present value–The current value of a future payment or stream of payments, adjusted for fixed-rate compounding.

Prospectus–A document mutual funds are required to send to investors before they can enter the fund. Prospectuses include information regarding fees and expenses, objectives and strategies, buying and selling shares, risk factors, distributions, management and organization history, and other services. (Now available online)

R

Rebalancing–The act of setting a portfolio of securities back to its original target percentages for each asset class.

Redemption fee–A fee charged at the time of redemption; some reduce over time. Mostly assessed to insurance products.

Risk:

Market risk–The risk of change in the general level of market prices for investments, caused by political, social, or economic changes; systematic risk represented by the fund's beta.

Inflationary risk–The risk that investments will not keep pace with inflation and purchasing power will be reduced.

Currency risk–The risk that currency fluctuations may affect the value of foreign investments or profits when converting them into the investor's local currency.

Event risk–The risk that a company may become the subject of a takeover bid or leveraged buyout involving additional debt so that its existing bonds are downgraded.

FOMO–Fear of missing out; investors tend to follow trends simply because they want to follow the crowd.

Interest-rate risk–The risk that interest rates may rise and decrease the value of an investment.

Credit risk—The risk that a company, agency, or municipality may have trouble paying its debts.

R-squared– (R2) is a statistical measurement used for investment analysis and research that investors can use to determine an investment's correlation with (similarity to) a given benchmark. ... R-squared reflects the percentage of a fund's movements that can be explained by movements in its benchmark index. A portfolio with a well-diversified and conservative allocation might have an R-square of 80+, in which case it is hoped it would hold up well if the overall stock market declines.

S

Sales charge–The cost to buy individual securities, mutual funds, annuities, partnerships, etc. It is charged at the time of purchase.

Secondary market–The trading in existing or outstanding shares of securities as opposed to new issues or initial public offerings. Transactions in the secondary market occur either on an exchange or in the OTC market.

Sector fund–A mutual fund that invests in the stocks of industry, such as the airline industry, utilities, technology, gold, etc.

Securities and Exchange Commission (SEC)–A federal agency created in 1934 to regulate the securities industry. The SEC is made up of five commissioners, each appointed by the President for a five-year term. No more than three commissioners from the same political party may serve at any one time.

Self-directed IRA–An IRA that is managed by an account holder or adviser who appoints a custodian to carry out instructions. This kind of IRA is subject to the same types of restrictions and limitations as a regular IRA.

Selling short–The sale of a security that the investor does not own to take advantage of an anticipated decline in the price of the security. To sell short, the investor must borrow the security from the broker to make delivery to the buyer. The short seller will eventually have to buy the security back, or "buy to cover," to return it to the broker. Selling short is regulated by Regulation T of the Federal Reserve Board (FRB).

Sell stop order–An order to sell a security at the market price once the security trades through a specified price, called the "stop price."

Senior securities—Securities that have prior claim to a corporation's assets in the event of bankruptcy. Debt securities and preferred stocks are senior to common stock.

Settlement date–The date when the buyer and seller of security are expected to settle a transaction, as evidenced by the seller delivering the security and the buyer paying for it. Most securities, but not all, settle in three business days.

Shares –A measurement of the amount of ownership in a corporation.

Small-cap–companies with a market capitalization less than $1 billion.

Spread–The difference between the price you pay for an investment and the markup the seller made.

Standard deviation–A statistical measure of the month-to-month ups and downs of a security's returns. Money-market securities, which have stable asset values, have standard deviations of zero. Volatile, aggressive-growth portfolios can have standard deviations of 25 percent or more.

Stock ownership-of a corporation represented by shares.

Style drift–Divergence of investment object from its original design

Subsequent investment–An investment of additional money into an existing account.

Surrender charge period–The time frame in which an insurance company can charge investors or policyholders for early withdrawal.

Surrender value–The amount that the insurer will return to the policyholder upon cancellation of a policy.

Symbol– A five-letter identifier for mutual funds, usually an abbreviation of the fund name; exchange-traded fund may be different.

T

Tax-deferred–investments whose accumulated earnings are not taxed until the investor takes possession of them. In IRAs, for example, all dividends, interest, and appreciation accumulate until the account owner starts withdrawing funds from the account, usually at age 59½ or later.

Tax-exempt money market fund–A mutual fund that invests in short-term municipal securities that are tax-exempt. The fund distributes the income-tax-free to shareholders.

Tax-exempt security–A debt obligation in which interest is exempt from federal, state, and local taxes--commonly called a "municipal bond" or "municipals." All tax-exempt bonds are federally tax-exempt, as well as exempt by the state in which the investor resides.

Tax selling–Securities sold to realize a loss that can be used to offset any capital gains of the other positions sold. This is usually done at the end of the year.

Tender–To submit a bid to buy a security, as in a US T-bill auction, or to surrender ownership in a corporation's securities in response to an offer to buy them at a set price. See "tender offer."

Tender offer–An offer to buy shares from the target company's shareholders by another company or organization. The offer may be for cash, securities, or both. Often, the goal is to take control of the target company. The suitor may be hostile or friendly. During a specified time, shareholders are asked to tender (surrender) their shares for a stated value, usually at a premium, subject to the tendering of a minimum and the maximum number of shares.

Testamentary trust–A trust that is established within a person's will.

Thin market–Market for a security that has too few buy and sell transactions occurring. Large trades can have a marked effect on securities prices, making the security much more volatile. Institutional investors usually avoid buying stocks that have a thin market for this reason--that is, it is hard for them to get in or out of a position without substantially affecting the security's price.

Ticker symbol–Letters used in trading to identify a corporation's securities on the ticker tape.

Time deposit (TD)–Certificates of deposit (CDs) or savings accounts that are held in a financial institution for a set amount of time.

Time horizon–The period one can stay invested (e.g., number of years to retirement). Longer time horizons can reduce volatility risk.

Time value–The amount of an option premium that exceeds the intrinsic value. A call option with a strike price of 30, for example, has a premium of 3.

If the underlying stock is at 32, the call has an intrinsic value of 2, and the time value is 1.

Top-down–An investment strategy that looks at the economic outlook and overall industries first, then which companies will benefit the most from a favorable forecast.

Total returns–The annual return on an investment that includes income, capital gains, and interest.

Tracking error–A divergence between the price behavior of a portfolio and the price behavior of a benchmark.

Treasury bill (T-bill)–A short-term debt obligation of the US Government that is purchased at a discounted price and matures to face value. They are sold in denominations of $10,000 to $1 million and have maturities of either 13, 26, or 52 weeks.

Treasury bond (T-bond)–A long-term debt obligation of the US government that has a maturity of more than 10 years. They are issued in $1,000 denominations and pay interest semiannually.

U--V--W--X

Undervalued–A security that is selling beneath its liquidation value or whose price is below what analysts believe it merits. Among other reasons, a stock may be undervalued because the corporation has an inconsistent earnings history or because the corporation is not well-known.

Vertical integration–A mental image of a pyramid structure designed with three equally staged horizontal compartments. The largest compartment at the bottom of the pyramid holds total market index funds; the middle stage holds factor index exchange-traded funds, and the smallest portion at the top is made up of a few managed mutual funds.

Y--Z

Yearly Total Returns–The sum of a security's return for 12 months corresponding to calendar years.

Special credit and thanks to:

Greg Phelps, author of "Portfolio Architect "a very advanced and complete technical investment manual type book

Andrew Ang, author of "Asset Management, A Systematic Approach to Factor Investing"

ETF University at ETF.com for your extensive news and educational material regarding the latest news and trends of ETFs.

Scott Hansen & Pat McClain, successful local advisers setting new standards in the financial advisory industry, improving the care and fiduciary standard for their clients while setting a new standard for other advisers to attempt to replicate.

Rick Edelman, Chairman, and Co-founder of Edelman Financial Engines, author of several financial books and host of a very successful national radio show.

Investopedia.com, a polished resource for investment information

Roxanne Hardenburgh, a wonderful resource for financial and tax advice

For additional assistance from Bill's office and resources simply go to:

www.hunterwilliambailey.com

or call 1800-603-1393

For:

Free newsletter

Free forty-page Investment workbook download

Future investment classes schedule and locations

Request for Public Speaking arrangements by the author(s)

Schedule an in-person, telephone or online appointment

Assistance with planning and portfolio management services

Hunter William (Bill) Bailey, is a registered adviser associate with Securities America Advisors, Inc. and is a registered representative with Securities America, Inc. a registered Broker/Dealer, Member of FINRA/SIPC. Securities offered through Securities America, Inc. Member FINRA/SIPC. Advisory services offered through Securities America Advisers Inc., California Insurance License #0589198

Thank you so much for taking the time to read this book!

If you enjoyed or found any of the information contained inside helpful, please consider leaving an honest review.

We appreciate your feedback!

Made in the USA
Monee, IL
23 September 2020